Milton's Theatrical Epic

Milton's Theatrical Epic

The Invention and
Design of *Paradise Lost*

JOHN G. DEMARAY

HARVARD UNIVERSITY PRESS
Cambridge, Massachusetts, and London, England   1980

Copyright © 1980 by the President and Fellows of Harvard College
Printed in the United States of America

Library of Congress Cataloging in Publication Data

Demaray, John G
    Milton's theatrical epic.

    Includes index.
    1. Milton, John, 1608–1674.   Paradise lost.
2.   Theater—History—16th century.   3.   Theater—History—
17th century.   I.   Title.
PR3562.D44   821'.4   79-23139
ISBN 0-674-57615-2

183188

For Hannah

Acknowledgments

ESSAYS printed elsewhere have been revised and incorporated into the text by permission of the original publishers. "Love's Epic Revel in *Paradise Lost:* A Theatrical Vision of Marriage" appeared in the *Modern Language Quarterly* 38 (1978): 3–20; and "The Thrones of Satan and God: Background to Divine Opposition in *Paradise Lost*" in the *Huntington Library Quarterly* 31 (1967): 21–33. The University of Illinois Press has granted permission to quote from Harris Francis Fletcher's edition *John Milton's Complete Poetical Works Reproduced in Photographic Facsimile,* and Odyssey Press to quote from Merritt Y. Hughes's edition *John Milton: Complete Poetry and Selected Prose.*

I am grateful to the Research Councils of Rutgers University and the University of Kentucky for grants in support of this study. Special thanks are due representatives of the New York Public Library for use of the Frederic Lewis Allen Room and for ready access to excellent collections. Appreciated too is the assistance of staff members of the British Museum, Courtauld Institute of Art, Bibliothèque Nationale, Cini Foundation, Vatican Library, University of Kentucky Library, Pierpont Morgan Library, and Hunter College Library.

Many unnamed debts are owed to students, colleagues, and friends for advice and assistance. I wish to acknowledge individually my obligation to the late Merritt Y. Hughes for early suggestions on my reading of *Paradise Lost,* and my obligation to John M. Steadman, Irene Samuel, and C. A. Patrides for encouragement and good counsel. Thanks are due Barbara Lewalski for her very helpful critical observations. My many literary associates in the Allen Room of the New York Public Library—particularly Waldemar Hansen, Robert Caro,

Acknowledgments

Lawrence Lader, and Ferdinand Lundberg—provided spirited support together with incisive comments on diverse literary vast designs. But for constant encouragement, scholarly aid, and perceptive criticism, I am most indebted to and once again thank Hannah Disinger Demaray.

Contents

Illustrations

(following page 44)

The figure Fame in Jonson's *Chloridia* (Devonshire Collection, Chatsworth; reproduced by permission of the Trustees of the Chatsworth Settlement)

The drawing of Charles I in *Eikon Basilike* (Reproduced by permission of the British Library)

A Dutch print showing the execution of Charles I (Reproduced by permission of the Ashmolean Museum, Oxford)

A Hell's mouth probably used in Davenant's *Britannia Triumphans* (Devonshire Collection, Chatsworth; by permission of the Trustees)

An inferno scene by Alfonso Parigi for *Le nozze degli dei favola* (Collection of the Istituto per le Lettere, la Musica, e il Teatro Veneto, Fondazione Giorgio Cini, Venice; from an etching by Stefano della Bella after Alfonso Parigi)

Vulcan's cave designed by Alfonso Parigi for *Le nozze degli dei favola* (Collection of the Istituto per le Lettere, la Musica, e il Teatro Veneto, Fondazione Giorgio Cini, Venice; from an etching by Stefano della Bella after Alfonso Parigi)

A satanic figure with monsters in Giulio Parigi's setting for *La liberazione di Tirreno* (Gabinetto Disegni e Stampe degli Uffizi, Florence; from an engraving by Jacques Callot)

Preface

JOHN MILTON'S declarations of poetic originality in the invocations of *Paradise Lost*, though by now very familiar to modern readers, retain their power to startle. For the statements when freshly encountered are indeed audacious, and they have a distinctive force because delivered in tones of singular sincerity and conviction. They announce the invention of a new kind of epic poetry.

Milton through the persona of a narrator proclaims that he will "assert Eternal Providence" (I.25) in a manner previously untried by any other writer. The voice of the narrator insists that his subject is "more Heroic" than central episodes in Virgil's *Aeneid* and Homer's *Iliad* and *Odyssey* (IX.14–19); that his argument is "higher" than any adopted by authors—Tasso and Ariosto doubtless among them—who wrote of "fabl'd Knights / In Battles" (IX.30–31); and that his "advent'rous Song" (I.13), in soaring to the loftiest poetic heights under the inspiration of the Heavenly Muse of Mount Sinai or Mount Sion, will present through a great Argument "things unattempted yet in Prose and Rhyme" (I.14–16).

Although the tone of Milton's epic voice is distinctive, the claims themselves are by no means extraordinary given the general aims of Renaissance epic poets. Milton and his fellow Christian writers of heroic verse were engaged in the grand Renaissance enterprise of reforming native and foreign literary structures, subjects, and styles in accord with supposed classical regulations and patterns but with a new, transcendent Hebraic and Christian prophetic illumination. The ultimate goal of the enterprise was to create national or Christian heroic works having a power and universality equal or superior to those of classical pagan tradition.

The products of this Renaissance literary endeavor—which include Dante's *Commedia*, Ariosto's *Orlando furioso*, Boiardo's *Orlando innamorato*, Tasso's *Gerusalemme liberata*, and Spenser's *The Faerie Queene*—can be defined with ease or with some slight straining as epics. But I think that it will be conceded that each has individualizing literary qualities that are novel and perhaps even peculiar.

Paradise Lost is no exception. The poem was invented and disposed by Milton in the belief that the views of Aristotle and the literary models of the Ancients should be followed. But the poet believed as well that biblical texts together with "heroic" Renaissance Christian shows, stage spectacles, and writings, all thought to contain superior divine truths, should also necessarily be emulated. Yet there was strong and sometimes strident disagreement on the Continent among writers, academicians, musicians, stage designers, and artists—and in England among Ben Jonson, Inigo Jones, William Davenant, Thomas Hobbes, John Dryden, and to some extent Milton—about exactly how this pagan-Christian merger of heroic literary and theatrical forms might be accomplished. The academic wrangling over the pagan-Christian form and content of Tasso's *Gerusalemme liberata* and its revision, for example, may well have helped to drive the poem's ill and suffering author to distraction. On the subject of heroic pagan-Christian poetry, Milton proved himself a Christian "classicist" of the special Renaissance variety. In *The Reason of Church Government* and in the preface to *Samson Agonistes* he acceded to the "grave authority" of the now relatively unknown biblical exegete David Pareus with all the respect accorded the poetic statements of Aristotle. Pareus clearly viewed Revelation and other supposedly heroic biblical texts as depicting prophetical shows or representations divided into acts.

The new Christian epics of the Renaissance frequently grew from works written in divers modes and genres by the same or by different authors. Some of the central themes of the *Commedia* developed from passages of Dante's *Vita nuova; The Faerie Queene* may well have derived in part from Spenser's *Cantos of Mutabilitie. Paradise Lost* unmistakably emerged from Milton's early theatrical outlines of a projected sacred representation of the Fall and from lines of his *A Mask Presented at Ludlow Castle*, the work popularly known as *Comus*. Milton's epic was published in its final twelve-book form, in the second edition of 1674, just as Dryden finished a competing five-act theatrical adaptation of the epic entitled *The State of Innocence*.

The final version of *Paradise Lost* in fact embodies a series of thematically interrelated prophetic shows and theatrical triumphs, both sacred and profane, of a sort derived with alterations from Renaissance court masques, outdoor processional pageants, *sacre rappresentazioni*, the Italian *tragedie di lieto fine*, and grand Continental staged spectacles, the last often performed against designs of the universe with "infinite" perspectives. Writing on a Christian topos "higher" than "War, hitherto the only Argument / Heroic deem'd" (IX.28-29), Milton focused his work centrally upon the Fall and promised future Triumph of man. He recorded in the epic as well the pseudo-Triumphs of Satan and the divine Triumphs of God. In these various representations and Triumphs, "disguised" and "revealed" heroic character-types, in harmony or in antithetical opposition, ritualistically act and declaim their roles in disparate parts of a universe where time and space are infinite. Events take place throughout creation and sometimes unfold simultaneously as past, present, and future tend to blur and unite. The restrictions of classical form seem to dissolve into a Christian eternity.

Yet the overall action of *Paradise Lost* is viewed and ordered through the human perspective of the illumined epic narrator. Because this human view necessarily predominates, the finite restraints of classical literary structure and convention are indeed imposed upon resistant materials. The prophetic Christian representations or shows emerge modified by and yet contained within a traditional twelve-book epic form.

Although Watson Kirkconnell, John Arthos, Gretchen Finney, and others have made important contributions relating Milton's writings to certain *drammi per musica* and *sacre rappresentazioni*, the full "vast design" of *Paradise Lost* still needs to be examined with an awareness of the varied pageants, masques, and staged spectacles of Renaissance Italy and England. For the horizons of Milton commentators, though very wide, have not sufficiently extended to the theatrical world of Renaissance Europe; and critical theatrical vocabulary remains limited and awkward.

"A reader coming to *Paradise Lost* for the first time, and going rapidly through it to the end of Book X," writes Merritt Y. Hughes, introducing his excellent notes to the epic, "is likely to get the impression that he is reading a drama." Hughes refers to nine important "dramatic" episodes and adds that "*Paradise Lost* is an epic built out of dramas." But he next observes that the work contains "a heightened kind of drama which is too big for the stage and too rich for it." Then, turning to another theatrical genre, he calls Satan's transformation in the palace Pandemonium "a grand opera scene." John Dryden labeled his eighteenth-century theatrical adaptation of *Paradise Lost* an opera but defended his adaptation's particular sort of imaginative imitation by citing Ben Jonson's *Masque of Queenes* and Shakespeare's *A Midsummer Night's Dream*. In the previous century Milton's nephew Edward Phillips called his uncle's now lost fifth draft of a developing sacred representation of the Fall a tragedy. In 1698 John Toland remarked in *The Life of Milton* that Milton had written of spiritual love "in his inimitable Poem of *Paradise Lost;* and before this time in his *Comus* or Mask presented at Ludlow Castle, like which Piece in the peculiar disposition of the Story, the sweetness of the Numbers, the justness of the Expression, and the Moral it teaches, there is nothing extant in any Language." Late in the eighteenth century Dr. Samuel Johnson boldly asserted in *The Lives of the Poets* that the masque *Comus* was a "drama in the epic style" and claimed that poetically "what is shown with greater extent in *Paradise Lost* may be found in *Comus.*" In an enigmatic statement, which in two hundred years has yet to be fully explored, this lively neoclassical formalist noted that in *"the Masque of Comus . . .* may very plainly be discovered the dawn or twilight of *Paradise Lost."*

The traditional classical and Renaissance epic structures and conventions of *Paradise Lost* have been examined at length by, among others, C. M. Bowra, John M. Steadman, and Davis Harding; but the emphasis of my work has been upon the poem's special theatrical qualities and upon Milton's success in portraying within the epic prophetical shows of a distinctive variety, shows that cannot be adequately embraced by a single term such as "masque," "dramma per musica," "tragedy," "comedy," "drama," or "opera."

Paradise Lost is a theatrical epic constructed from a series of scenes that, when considered in themselves, have a recognizable structural unity of their own and compose an exceptional visionary *sacra rappresentazione*. Grand but unholy enacted spectacles, arguments, and anti-Triumphs in the eternity of Hell are counterpoised, following principles adopted from seventeenth-century antimasque and main masque structures, against opposing but holy spectacles, arguments, and Triumphs in the eternity of Heaven. In the middle books set in Eden, Adam and Eve, like main performers in a central space between antithetical demonic and virtuous seats of power, enact a "revel" of love and a subsequent fall. In the last books, Adam beholds visions of the future that reflect elements derived from sixteenth-century *sacre rappresentazioni* and processional masques and pageants. Then the First Parents, before their theatrical banishment from the Garden, joyfully learn of God's future intercession and the future Triumph of man.

But *Paradise Lost* is a theatrical epic of a unique kind that interweaves and fuses divine prophetic shows in eternity with a multitude of classical allusions, conventions, and patterned episodes, a work that partially transforms and yet remains daringly contained within a classical epic structure. The enacted prophetic shows, when examined in isolation, sweep the reader imaginatively into infinity to observe events alternately from the perspectives of Satan, God, and prelapsarian and fallen man. Yet within the context of Milton's epic, figures and shows are merged with restraining classical elements and encountered through the mediation of a prophetic but human epic narrator. This narrator sings of matters eternal with a human awareness of mortal time, place, and action. The epic voice, after calling attention to a single action, "Man's first disobedience," begins the narrative in *medias res* with an account of Satan's fall and punishment, next introduces with sad confessions of physical blindness a scene in Heaven, and then exhibits a deep compassion for man in explaining that "Meanwhile" the Archfiend is journeying to the seat of the human race. This human voice pervades the epic and supplies in context a limiting and balanced human view of eternal enacted scenes which in themselves strain against the containing classical structure. It is through the illumined human experience of the narrator, with his deep sympathy for man, that the reader views episodes arranged and revealed according to the dictates of heroic convention and form.

In this study *Paradise Lost* is critically interpreted with a consciousness of its origins and development. Attention is given to Milton's linguistic-poetic theories and techniques; to Italian, English, classical, and Continental literary and theatrical influences; and to Renaissance disputes in which the poet engaged on the nature of epic and theatrical composition. An analysis is made of how *Paradise Lost* evolved from the poet's diverse early writings and theatrical outlines into a ten-book heroic poem in 1667 and finally in 1674 into a Christian-classical work with a conventional twelve-book epic form; and of how Milton's progressive invention, disposition, and imagistic "veiling" of an expanding great Argument were directed toward the intellectual grasp and disclosure of what the poet believed to be an immaterial, inmost spiritual and historical reality. In the course of these varied investigations, textual readings are offered of the Hell, Heaven, and Eden of *Paradise Lost*.

About two centuries ago Dr. Samuel Johnson, pausing as he reviewed Milton's prophetical outlines, remarked with earthy wit: "It is pleasant to see great works in their seminal state pregnant with latent possibilities of excellence. Nor could there be any more delightful entertainment," Dr. Johnson continued, "than to trace their gradual growth and expansion, and to observe how they are sometimes suddenly advanced by accidental hints, and sometimes slowly improved by steady meditation."

It is my hope that this study, written with Dr. Johnson's ruminations in mind, will afford readers some measure of new insight into the rich theatrical-literary forms, meanings, and textures in the vast design of *Paradise Lost*.

When I beheld the Poet blind, yet bold,
In slender Book, his vast Design unfold,
Messiah Crown'd, God's Reconcil'd Decree,
Rebelling Angels, the Forbidden Tree
Heav'n, Hell, Earth, Chaos, All; the Argument
Held me a while misdoubting his Intent,
That he would ruin (for I saw him strong)
The sacred Truths to Fable and old Song
(So *Sampson* grop'd the Temple's Posts in spite)
The World o'erwhelming to revenge his sight.

    Yet as I read, soon growing less severe,
I lik'd his Project, the success did fear;
Through that wide Field how he his way should find
O'er which lame Faith leads Understanding blind;
Lest he perplex'd the things he would explain,
And what was easy he should render vain.

    Or if a Work so infinite he spann'd,
Jealous I was that some less skilful hand
(Such as disquiet always what is well,
And by ill imitating would excel)
Might hence presume the whole Creation's day
To change in Scenes, and shew it in a Play.

    Pardon me, Mighty Poet, nor despise
My causeless, yet not impious, surmise.
But I am now convinc'd, and none will dare
Within thy Labours to pretend a share.
. . . . .

    Where couldst thou words of such a compass find?
Whence furnish such a vast expense of mind?

From Andrew Marvell's dedicatory poem
to the 1674 edition of *Paradise Lost*

I

The Inward Vision

WHEN a youthful John Milton at the age of nineteen first explicitly illustrated the poetic and linguistic techniques later used in the composition of *Paradise Lost*, he did so as the featured participant in a vacation romp of schoolboys held at handsomely appointed Christ's College Hall, Cambridge, in July 1628. The main attraction of the evening was the performance of a brief play by Milton, a satire on Aristotelian metaphysics.

There was much outrageous tomfoolery. As part of a ceremonial "orgy," the boys passed through or near "flames," "fires," and "whirling clouds of smoke" from out of which peered the college's chief porter and his attendants. Then with a rhetorical flourish Milton, in the unlikely role of Father of the festivities, directed the bacchanalian revelers to refreshments. With spirited exaggeration, he spoke of the "tables spread with quite Persian luxury, and loaded with the most exquisite dainties, such as would delight and appease the most Apician taste."[1]

A few among the schoolboys, it appears, had come to the "orgy" after having recently indulged in a not very humorous prank: the destruction of the town of Cambridge's water supply system. Milton confesses surprise that he rather than the youthful leader of this escapade was chosen Father. The other student, Milton notes, "some little time ago laboriously led about fifty Sophisters armed with short bludgeons through the Barnwellian field, and . . . did in proper military fashion throw down the aqueduct, that he might force the townsmen to surrender by thirst." Though the poet does "mightily grieve that the gentleman has gone off," one wonders if the master of Christ's College, less grieved than the speaker, did not hasten the departure of this "veteran soldier" and thus ensure that Milton, nicknamed the Lady by his fellows, replaced him as dictator of the vacation activities.[2]

However he gained his position, Milton ruled over a colorful and rather shaggy lot. Cambridge students of this period were renowned for their "long frizzled hair," "new fashioned gowns of any colour whatsoever ... without uniformity," "feminine cuffs at the wrist," "stockings of diverse colours reversed one upon the other," and "boots with spurs" or, for the more temperate, shoes adorned with "fair roses."[3] Father Milton and his student "Sons" were probably the most extravagantly dressed of all, for they were the comic entertainers in the poet's short farce *At a Vacation Exercise in the College.*

In the play, words are identified with the gaudy or somber costumes that the actors wear, and the immaterial ideas or substantial forms "dressed up" by the words are by implication identified with the actors. The personified figure Language is addressed as a kind of theatrical property master who rummages through wardrobe "coffers" selecting decorous disguises for the performers, that is, for the ideas and substantial forms.[4]

After apologizing to Language for two years of "dumb silence" followed by "childish trips" of "imperfect words ... / Half unpronounc't" (3-5), Father Milton, representing the Aristotelian principle of *Ens* or "Being," announces that he has some "naked thoughts" that will "rove about" until Language has "deckt them in thy best array." But these naked thoughts are not of a serious or stately kind. The poet rejects having Language clothe them in "new fangled toys, and trimming slight / Which takes our late fantastics with delight." Rather, pleasure will be produced, the speaker insists, only if Language brings the "chiefest treasure" from its wardrobe. "Cull those richest Robes, and gay'st attire," Milton commands, "Which deepest Spirits, and choicest Wits desire" (18-26).

Even these "chiefest" coverings are found indequate for certain profound conceptions. Quite unexpectedly, Milton changes his tone and shifts the locus of his thoughts. In one long passage he gives up his attempt to amuse his schoolboy audience and intrudes into the otherwise rollicking skit a personal confession of having sublime thoughts of a sort that, when properly clothed in a garment of verbal imagery, will one day result in the creation of his visionary epic poem. Again addressing Language, Milton says, "Yet I had rather, if I were to choose, / Thy service in some graver subject use." The speaker now desires his "transported mind" to soar "above the wheeling poles," to fly upward through the "misty Regions of wide air," and, after arriving at

"Heav'n's door," to "Look in, and see each blissful Deity." He admits his desire to sing "of secret things that came to pass / When Beldam Nature in her cradle was" and to relate tales of *"Heroes* old" in the manner of the bard Demodocus in Homer's *Odyssey*. Still, the speaker realizes that it is most difficult to clothe the transported mind's grave ideas in words having suitable sounds and conveying appropriate visual images; Language is, accordingly, told that it will be necessary to "search thy coffers round" to discover the right verbal garments (29–47).

The performance concludes with an exchange of remarks between Father Milton and his ten student followers representing Aristotelian predicaments. Milton urges the Predicaments to dress up the figure Substance and then, addressing the boy playing the part, mockingly asserts that a sibyl once predicted that Substance would be "subject to many an Accident" (75). Milton further exhibits his adolescent wit when he comments upon Substance's paradoxical metaphysical-theatrical position:

> Yet being above them, he shall be below them;
> From others he shall stand in need of nothing,
> Yet on his Brothers shall depend for Clothing.   (80–82)

This superficially ludicrous but essentially serious work suggests, as does the body of his writings from youth through old age, that Milton held a very definite view on the relationship of poetry to external reality.

For Milton the artistic imitation of reality consisted, first, in having the logical and intuitive powers of the mind conform to and so comprehend the supposed intelligible but immaterial substantial forms or essences to be rendered; and then in using words to garb these comprehended substantial forms or essences in a decorous veil of sensuous imagery.[5]

This traditional Renaissance practice of mimesis, promulgated in books of rhetoric and adopted by various Continental theorists, was aptly suited to a poet who wrote in his major works not only of the fallen material world but also of the perfect earthly world before the Fall and of the eternal, immaterial realms of heaven and hell. "But what sort of things shall we say subsist? Are they the intelligible or the visible?" asked J. C. Scaliger in a sixteenth-century discussion of poetical-philosophical matters in his *Discorsi*. "Certainly," came his own, rather extreme reply, "they are the intelligible."[6]

Milton in a quite traditional fashion assumed the creative obligation

[3]

of apprehending the supposed intelligible inner core of reality, the forms and essences invisible to mortal sight, through the natural and sometimes prophetic illumination of what he believed to be his largely logical but partially intuitive rational mind.[7] He next sought to invent the best possible ornamental sensuous covering, which he sometimes acknowledged to be inappropriate for completely spiritual heavenly beings, by interweaving images derived from the physical world and from such human arts as poetry, music, dance, painting, theater, and architecture.

A number of modern studies have considerably advanced critical understanding of how Milton and his contemporaries garbed their defined abstractions in a sensuous veil of imagery, how these writers ornamented and disposed their poems, and how the criteria of decorum, appropriateness, and proportion were observed in the creation of imagistic veils.[8] Yet, as commentators have become ever more absorbed in detailed investigations of Elizabethan rhetorical processes—the ways in which a poem is constructed as an artifact—they have been distracted from a counterbalancing awareness of early neo-Aristotelian metaphysical-epistemological views on the relation of poetic abstraction and imagery to reality, that is, the intellectually and emotionally experienced grasp of the poem upon the supposed inmost core of being. The concentration upon Elizabethan rhetoric at the expense of seventeenth-century philosophical attitudes has resulted in the sometimes unconscious emergence of a modern aesthetic and positivistic bias in studies purporting to have their foundation in the Elizabethan world view. The seventeenth-century poem tends to be increasingly regarded as a somewhat isolated mythic artifact of didactic associations cloaked imaginatively in images rather than, as was the case in the earlier view, a metaphysical-artistic object having an allegedly inner correspondence with the essences, forms, predicaments, and qualities of the existent universe.[9]

Although Milton's seventeenth-century poetic and philosophical outlook is, admittedly, archaic, an understanding of the earlier view, it seems to me, leads to subtle critical assessments of what happens in the poet's verse. One can then gaze imaginatively for a brief time with the inward eye of the seventeenth-century poet-seer rather than with the external, functional eye of the modern empiricist.

In the comprehensive, two-volume study that Milton published late in life, *A Fuller Institution of the Art of Logic* (1672), he reasserts the central epistemological ideas that he first advanced in his youthful schoolboy satire. The *Art of Logic* is hardly his most popular book; for in this work Milton, despite his disciplined development of ideological formulations, becomes engrossed in the redundancies, circular "proofs," and self-evident propositions of a highly abstract, seventeenth-century inductive logic. He writes that "to know the internal form of anything, because it is usually very remote from the senses, is especially difficult."[10] Nevertheless, the *Art of Logic* supplies a logical pathway to such presumed metaphysical knowledge.

Milton defines *"Form"* as the *"cause through which a thing is what it is."* By means of form *"a thing may be distinguished from all other things"* (I.7.59–61). But Milton immediately points out the difference between "common forms," which he believes to be inherent in beings of the same kind, and "forms single and proper," which he thinks are inherent in individual beings. Stating that individuation is an attribute of both the single and proper forms and the essences of beings, Milton thus claims that beings separate in number are separate in their single and proper forms and in their essences. Following the views of Scaliger, Milton adopts a nontraditional metaphysical stance by employing the terms "forms single and proper" and "essences" interchangeably to denote the individualized nature of beings.[11] Common forms denote for the poet the generic nature of beings:

> Single things, or what are commonly called individuals, have form single and proper to themselves; certainly they differ in number among themselves, as no one denies. But what is differing in number among themselves except differing in single forms? For number, as Scaliger rightly says, is an affection following an essence. Therefore things which differ in number also differ in essence; and never do they differ in number if not in essence.—*Here let the Theologians awake.*—Because if whatever things differ in number differ also in essence, but not in matter, necessarily they differ among themselves in forms, but not in common forms, therefore in proper ones. Thus the rational soul is the form of man generically; the soul of Socrates is the proper form of Socrates. (I.7.59)

When Milton subsequently uses the terms "essence" and "form," he becomes rather imprecise and fails to explain whether he is referring to individualized single and proper forms or to common forms. Still, granting the vagaries of seventeenth-century metaphysical speculation, his general position is reasonably clear. Milton again insists that man can attain rational knowledge by the correspondence of the mind with the inner nature of things.

Referring apparently to individualized being, Milton observes that the "cause which especially constitutes the essence, if it is noted, above

[5]

all brings knowledge." This metaphysical knowledge comes from a "definition *when it is explained what a thing is.* It is called a definition in that it defines the essence of a thing, and circumscribes it as though by its boundaries." The poet quotes Boetheus with approval: "Every definition is equalled to the thing which it defines." Such a definition, Milton believes, can be tested by "conversion" when "what is defined ... *can be argued from the thing defined*" (I.30.261). Yet, without further defining of his own terms, he concludes that "a perfect definition is nothing else than a universal symbol [*universale symbolum*] of the causes constituting the essence and nature of a thing" (I.30.265).

Alluding apparently to the common form of being, Milton maintains that the "cause in common, ... the fount of all knowledge, is understood especially to apply to form." He adds that *"when the form is given, the thing itself is given"*; for example, "the rational soul is the form of man"; "the form of geometric figures appears in their being triangles or quadrangles"; and the "form of physical things" resides in the innate and different natures of beings such as "earth, trees, and fishes" (I.7.61). He observes, however, that "perfect definitions of forms are difficult to come by," and so he claims that *"Description* has been devised to supply their scarcity" (I.31.267).

Milton argues that description depends upon "adjuncts" or "accidents" of being that are "added to the subject over and above the essence." The "essence of the subject is not changed by the accession or removal" of the adjuncts, "nor is the subject made something different, but merely exists in another mode" (I.11.85). Among the adjuncts or accidents that can be defined and used in descriptions are "qualities that can be experienced," natural powers, and relations. Including sounds, colors, proportions, and capacities in these categories, Milton next illustrates his points by quoting passages on the figure Fame from Book IV of Virgil's *Aeneid* (I.31.275-279).

In *Paradise Lost* lines about the nature of beings and the power of man's reason confirm and, in some instances, amplify the views outlined in the *Art of Logic.* The angel Raphael, explaining to Adam how the hierarchy of being is imbued with matter and form, states that God

> ... created all
> Such to perfection, one first matter all,
> Indu'd with various forms, various degrees
> Of substance, and in things that live, of life;
> But more refined, more spiritous, and pure,
> As nearer to him plac't or nearer tending
> Each in thir several active Spheres assign'd,

> Till body up to spirit work, in bounds
> Proportion'd to each kind.   (V.471-479)

Raphael also tells Adam that the "being" of the soul is "reason" and that in mortal man the "logical" or "discursive" power is joined with the "intuitive." The angel declares:

> . . . the Soul
> Reason receives, and reason is her being,
> Discursive, or Intuitive; discourse
> Is oftest yours, the latter most is ours,
> Differing but in degree, of kind the same.   (V.486-490)

Earlier, Adam himself observes that man's reason acquires rational knowledge through abstractions based upon "external things / Which the five watchful Senses, represent" (V.103-104) to the soul's faculties. But soon after his own creation, Adam, without yet having attained a logical knowledge of causes, effortlessly and immediately intuits the nature of the beings around him and so is able to name them. Adam says to Raphael:

> But who I was, or where, or from what cause,
> Knew not; to speak I tri'd, and forthwith spake,
> My Tongue obey'd and readily could name
> Whate'er I saw. Thou Sun, said I, fair Light,
> And thou enlight'n'd Earth, so fresh and gay,
> Ye Hills and Dales, ye Rivers, Woods, and Plains
> And ye that live and move, fair Creatures, tell,
> Tell, if ye saw, how came I thus, how here?   (VIII.270-277)

Through the intervention of Heaven, moreover, the directly illumined reason of both Adam and the epic narrator receives powers of prophetic vision. The narrator "sees" spiritually with inward "eyes" even though his mortal sight has been "quencht" with a "drop serene" or "veil'd" with a "dim suffusion" (III.25-26). In the presence of Michael, Adam is "forc't to close his eyes" when "three drops instill'd," penetrating "Ev'n to the inmost seat of mental sight," give the First Parent spiritual vision into reality (XI.415-418). In these episodes Adam has already fallen, but Milton was obviously convinced that with heaven's aid virtuous postlapsarian man also could "see" into the nature of things.

Milton held throughout his artistic life that the inmost nature of angels, devils, prelapsarian creatures, trees, flowers, men, and other beings could be captured and poetically rendered through some degree of identification of the mind's immaterial conceptions with the immate-

[7]

rial forms and essences of these beings. Qualities, capacities, proportions, and other adjuncts or accidents of being, he believed, also could be intellectually grasped and depicted in verse, though such adjuncts were considered ancillary "modes" of being dependent for their existence upon substantial forms and essences. These views provided Milton with a metaphysical basis for the representation of divers moral, physical, psychological, and religious manifestations of experience. States of being were often intellectually distinguished and given a stylistic "garment" of verbal images through the personification of death, envy, sickness, chastity, or faith. Time and change came poetically alive in such figures as Day, Night, the Hours, Seasons, and Years. Man as a microcosm or "little world" embodying elements of all created being; the state as a body politic having the nature of a monolithic, living person; the universe as a macrocosm harmoniously corresponding in its makeup to the smaller parts of creation—all these could be represented, with their deepest interrelationships or differences disclosed, through the decorous presentation of personified figures of virtue or through the outward distortion of personified figures of vice.

Although Milton unquestionably conceived of poetry as having an interior correspondence with the concealed "truths" of being, he also clearly believed that his poetry grasped within the central nature of things not only immaterial, logical content but also intuited meanings that extend beyond the formulations of the discursive intellect. As a result, Milton's evaluative analogies, metaphors, conceits, and figural references intermesh with didacticism to produce a poetry that is richly symbolic. The tonalities and complexities of this verse disallow a consistent and simplistic reading of it as an "allegory of the poets," an airy fable concealing one or more traditional categories of fixed ideas. On occasion, conventional allegorical meanings may suffice to explicate allusions to beings, events, actions, and places; but usually, allegorical elements within unfolding poetic contexts delicately deepen into symbols that, like prisms casting multicolored light, radiate varying shadings of value. Milton's poetry in its metaphysical dimension is an attempted symbolic representation of reality.[12]

The play *At a Vacation Exercise in the College* reveals the rudiments of Milton's linguistic practices. The Latin academic exercise *On the Fifth of November* (1626) shows how at the age of seventeen Milton somewhat awkwardly applied these practices to certain basic themes, to divine and human character-types, and to vast panoramic backgrounds suggestive of those in *Paradise Lost*. A Cambridge tutor presumably asked Milton to write on Roman Catholic Guy Fawkes's gunpowder plot, a topos which in its historical detail Milton studiously avoided. After five short attempts, only two containing direct allusions to Fawkes, Milton at last found his "graver subject." He tried to objectify poetically an experience of satanic evil that lurked in the universe and appeared in strange guises to trouble and destroy man.

On the Fifth of November, with its far-ranging narrative action and heroic character-types, has been somewhat loosely called an "epic in little," for the work is indebted to Virgil's *Aeneid* and other heroic compositions.[13] Yet what limited epic qualities Milton's exercises have are infused with the patterned conventions of Renaissance spectacle. One discerns in the poem the introductory descent of an evil figure to earth; the donning of a disguise by the evil figure; the processional entry of figures of vice; the descent of the figure Fame to restore order; and the final triumphant dances by figures of virtue.

Milton's opening description of Satan surveying the earth is couched in inflated Latin rhetoric, but the description has a rudimentary power. Satan circles the world stirring up tempests, hatred, and war; stares down upon and curses the British Isles; soars over the "frosty" Alps; and comes to rest in the papal city, Rome. Thereafter, the work is generally forced and episodic.

The theatrical structure of the exercise is modeled after a stylized "representation" with "antic" and "virtuous" intermezzi, which in Milton's work are given insufficient cohesion by the gunpowder plot topos. After Satan's flight to this world, the main antic action unfolds. Evil kings and mendicant brothers, chanting in orgiastic disharmony, march into grossly large temples. The "hollow domes" and "void spaces" of the temples fill with sounds resembling "the shrieks of Bacchus and the followers of Bacchus when they chant their orgies" (64–67). The analogy is strained, but it reveals the evil figures as precursors of the antimasquers in *Comus,* who enter and then, with "sound / Of Riot and ill-manag'd Merriment" (171–172), engage by night in orgiastic worship of Cotytto.

A further antic note is struck when Satan puts on a theatrical disguise and urges the Pope to destroy the English parliament. The Archfiend then flees as the Pontiff summons from the underworld a typical antic crew: Murder, Treason, Discord, Gile, Calumny, and Fury.

Virtuous actions by heavenly figures resolve the work. God orders the brash but good Lady Fame to spread news of the plot on earth. Dressing in accord with her inner nature and flying to this world, Fame is featured in a modest concluding "scenic spectacle" resembling those that highlighted the descent of glittering main masquers from stage

[9]

heaven just before a revel of dancing. Fame "assumes strident wings and covers her slender body with parti-colored feathers, and in her right hand she takes a trumpet of Temesan brass." She "makes no delay, but on her wings goes oaring through the yielding air," her speed outstripping the clouds and winds (206–210). Fame's descent is similar to that of the masquelike figure Peace, whom Milton was later to portray moving down past "amorous clouds dividing" (50) in *On the Morning of Christ's Nativity* (1629).

With Fame's descent complete, the exercise ends with a disquietingly abrupt summation that includes a reference to jubilant dances: God "thwarts the outrages the Papists have dared . . . In throngs youth goes dancing. Throughout the whole year there shall be no day more celebrated than the fifth of November" (220–226).

In attempting to capture poetically the inner nature of evil, Milton in this work plays somewhat crudely upon his artistic sense of the division of appearance from reality in evil figures. The more evil the inward spiritual nature of a figure, the more virtuous its outer disguise is likely to be. In his mature verse the breach between inner and outer identities assumes rich aesthetic and spiritual dimensions. In *On the Fifth of November*, however, the evil Tempter does not suffer from such dissociations but simply dresses up discordantly in the outward flounces of virtue.

A false beard and tonsured wig are evident. Satan's temples "shone under the disguise of grey hairs; a long beard covered his breast." The Deceiver also wears an "ash-colored robe . . . with a long train on the ground; a hood dangled from his shaven crown; and—to make his wiles complete—his lustful loins are bound with hempen rope and his slow feet are thrust into laced sandals." Milton states that this guise, though adopted by the "impious" Saint Francis, has the appearance of holiness because Saint Francis "bore the pious word of salvation" (80–106). The poet was in fact well acquainted with performers whose disguises were at variance with their ostensible social and spiritual position. In *An Apology for Smectymnuus* (1642) Milton writes of his scornful reaction to those divinity students in "periwig, or a vizard" whom he saw playing roles in Latin plays at Cambridge: "They made sport, and I laughed; they mispronounced, and I misliked, and, to make up the atticism, they were out, and I hissed."[14]

Although it is helpful to note Milton's bifurcation of satanic evil into false image and underlying nature, it is also instructive to observe the poet struggling in his early letters and verse to find harmonious images for his intellectual and emotional experience of the supposed inner truths of reality—for instance, his attempt to capture in "speaking pictures" the sharp pang of youthful love.

With some excitement Milton at the age of twenty writes in Latin to his tutor, the younger Alexander Gill, and tells of passing some attractive girls on the street. "I let my *eyes* meet their eyes," confesses the emboldened student; he dares to glance at one girl "pre-eminent over the rest." But in what images does the student-lover addressing his pedagogue deck out this fleeting experience of youthful passion? Milton falls back upon the traditional image of Cupid, who is said to appear with "painted wings," "quiver," and "sweetly threatening eyes." The poet relates how Cupid "wounds my heart, alas! in a thousand places. Immediately unaccustomed pains were felt in my heart. Being in love, I inly burn: I am all one flame."[15]

One can at least accept that Milton was unaccustomed to this "pain." Nevertheless, the imagistic veil is so conventionalized and so formally remote that one is inclined to have some doubts about the completeness of the poet's amorous "incineration."

In his first antiprelatic pamphlet *Of Reformation in England* (1641), Milton does better when he creates the imagery he thinks appropriate for his experience and concept of England's spiritual deprivation. The island-nation in this and in a second reformation tract, *The Reason of Church Government* (1642), is regarded by the poet as a unified, living body politic with an individualized identity. "O Sir," writes Milton to the reader in the first tract, "if we could but see the shape of our dear Mother England . . . how would she appear, think ye, but in a mourning weed, with ashes upon her head, and tears abundantly flowing from her eyes?"[16] Again the imagery is formal and artificial, but it does effectively clothe Milton's idea of and feeling about an England suffering from spiritual loss.

In the same tract Milton contends that poets can give a "personal form," that is, a personified representation through imagery, to "what they please."[17] He probably had in mind as subjects both the allegedy objective, substantial forms of existing beings and the subjective fancies and dreams of authors. Milton, one remembers, mentions in *L'Allegro* the "Wood-notes wild" of "fancy's child" (133–134), Shakespeare, who had peopled *A Midsummer Night's Dream* with fairies and other imaginary figures. And in *L'Allegro* Milton gives to fancies names and visual shapes through references to dreamlike "Faery Mab" and the "drudging Goblin" Puck (102–105). But the poet personifies the subjective products of dreaming fancy only rarely in his verse. He prefers to disclose external reality employing illumined reason as a primary faculty in defining poetically the existent universe.

Milton's verse contains an unforgettable progression of figures that seize upon and seem to objectify some predicament, quality, essence, or form of reality. Every reader of Milton can no doubt supply innumerable examples: relentless Death overcoming his victim in the first of the two poems entitled *On the University Carrier* (1631); Nature and the lusty Sun growing subdued in the opening stanzas of *On the Morning of Christ's Nativity* (1629); Night acting as a patroness in *The Passion* (1630); "heart-easing Mirth" in *L'Allegro* (1631?) dancing forward with Laughter, Jollity, Quips, Cranks, Wiles, Nods, Becks, Wreathed Smiles, Sport, Laughter, and, most significantly, "The Mountain Nymph, sweet Liberty" (13, 36); somber Melancholy in *Il Penseroso* (1631?) passing by with "musing gait" (38) and joining with Leisure and Contemplation. Even the most superficial list quickly grows longer: the Milkmaid, the Plowman, and Tragedy in *Il Penseroso;* Hymen, "the God that sits at marriage feast" (18) in *An Epitaph on the Marchioness of Winchester* (1631); Fame, Envy, and Necessity in *Arcades* (1632?); Faith, Hope, Chastity, Cupid, and Psyche in *Comus* (1634); and the procession in *Lycidas* (1637) of the Herald of the Sea, the river Camus, and the Pilot of the Galilean lake. With this list far more exclusive than inclusive, one can turn to *Paradise Lost* (1667) and find Sin, Death, Chaos, Night, Spring, Summer, Nature, and Heavenly Love as well as many other human and divine actors.

With his loss of sight about the year 1652, there came to Milton a deepening and intensifying of his long-acknowledged experience, first enunciated in his academic exercises, of the nature of being. He repeatedly proclaims his conviction that a great poet-seer, even though blind as Homer and Tiresias were, possesses an inner vision of the mind that pierces the outer shell of the world's mortal being.

In Sonnet XXI, *To Cyriack* (1655?), Milton draws a contrast between outward, worldly "care," which is said to be only a "show," and inner, "deep thoughts," which afford occasions for "mirth" and lead to "solid good." True learning proves, the sightless poet writes, that man should not refrain from the good provided when "God sends a cheerful hour"; but "mild Heav'n" is said to disapprove of "that care, though wise in show, / That with superfluous burden leads the day" (5–14).

In Sonnet XXII, *To Mr. Cyriack Skinner upon His Blindness* (1655), Milton in a concluding couplet, after trenchantly stating that his eyesight has been lost in "liberty's defense" (11), adds in a quieter tone:

> This thought might lead me through the world's vain mask,
> Content though blind, had I no better guide.   (13-14)

It is God, the "better guide," who now enables the blind poet to see spiritually beneath physical disguises. The entire world has become a "vain mask," a great performance in which men, animals, and things act their parts beneath a garish sensuous fabric that hides true, immaterial forms. This sweeping theatrical metaphor hints again at Milton's consciousness of many partial dissociations between underlying reality and its vainly disfiguring external appearances.

Surveying the body of Milton's verse, one can distinguish in manifold passages poetic dissociations of images from underlying forms. These dissociations arise, not from any failure of visual imagination before or after Milton became blind, but from the self-conscious intention of an artist concerned with carefully planned aesthetic effects.

The depiction of incorporeal beings in heaven and hell obviously presented Milton with difficulties so great that a dissociation of image from form was inevitable. In *Paradise Lost* the angel Raphael outlines the analogical technique that Milton himself used in attempting to unfold in images "The secrets of another World" (V.569). But the angel, asking a rhetorical question, casts understandable doubt upon the efficacy of the technique. Raphael says that he will delineate

> ... what surmounts the reach
> Of human sense ...
> By lik'ning spiritual to corporal forms,
> As may express them best, though what if Earth
> Be but the shadow of Heav'n, and things therein
> Each to other like, more than on Earth is thought? (571-576)

Because spiritual forms "surmount" the reach of human sense, the images depicting them will be inadequate. The images will be like insubstantial shadows, which point to a higher, and perhaps quite different, reality. Although veiling the spiritual forms of Heaven, the images will, nevertheless, have a transparent luminosity that will be in general harmony with the holiness of the beings depicted; the images cloaking evil will be opaque distortions that are radically dissociated from malignant underlying essences and forms.

The imagistic representation of prelapsarian nature in *Paradise Lost* came somewhat more within the range of Milton's illumined intellectual and poetic power. Ideal prelapsarian nature in its appearances was to Milton similar to the fallen but redeemed nature sensuously experienced by corrupt man. The artistic problem was simply that prelapsarian reality was a "Heaven on Earth" (IV.208) and so escaped appropriate analogies. Milton could rationally and intuitively grasp, presumably with some degree of objectivity, the nature of Adam, Eve, the Serpent, the Garden, and the prelapsarian animals. He could also comprehend the supposed historic truth of the ideal existence of the First Parents, their Temptation, and their Fall. Yet the prelapsarian imagery with which Milton enshrouded these grasped "truths" is an analogically unbalanced and unreliable fiction that contains only disparate "likenesses." The reader is not asked to believe that Adam and Eve really spoke the words attributed to them, that they actually held hands while walking in the Garden, or that they dined on the fruits and dulcet creams introduced through the learning and inventive intelligence of the Puritan poet. Again a dissociation partially divorces concepts of a prelapsarian reality from the encompassing dialogue and imagery.

Only when Milton writes of this world after the Fall do dissociations between imagery and immaterial concepts diminish, for Milton considered himself subject to Original Sin and a part of postlapsarian nature. To create epic poetry about flawed humanity in a flawed world, he could rely in large measure upon his immediate experience and apprehension of fallen reality. Milton in his poetry frequently creates distorted images of this reality, thus suggesting this imperfect world's vanity. But the criteria of decorum, appropriateness, and proportion can now be more properly observed. The images, though artifacts, can more suitably clothe the essences and substantial forms poetically rendered.

In *Paradise Lost* Milton plumbs new depths of emotion when, unable to see either natural light or "Nature's works" (III.49), he writes of his sightless isolation:

> ... Thus with the Year
> Seasons return, but not to me returns
> Day, or the sweet approach of Ev'n or Morn,
> Or sight of vernal bloom, or Summer's Rose,
> Or flocks, or herds, or human face divine;
> But cloud instead, and ever-during dark
> Surrounds me, from the cheerful ways of men
> Cut off. (40–47)

It is difficult to read these and other lines written after 1652 without some sense of pathos. Not that there is self-pity in Milton's expression of separation from the visual world. It is simply that suffused emotions arise when a great artist hails the "holy light" of the sun and then records that his own eyes "roll in vain / To find thy piercing ray, and find no dawn" (23-24). A stark finality permeates the restrained words: "Nature's works to me expung'd and ras'd, / And wisdom at one entrance quite shut out" (49-50).

Unable to see Nature's work physically, Milton calls upon his muse for spiritual illumination:

> So much the rather thou Celestial Light
> Shine inward, and the mind through all her powers
> Irradiate, there plant eyes, all mist from thence
> Purge and disperse, that I may see and tell
> Of things invisible to mortal sight. (51-55)

From youth through old age Milton created his major work, including *Paradise Lost, Paradise Regained,* and *Samson Agonistes,* with an ever-growing awareness of this "inward vision."

II

Inconstant Theatrical Designs

MILTON'S friend Andrew Marvell, in composing his dedicatory poem for the planned 1674 twelve-book edition of *Paradise Lost,* had special reason to fear that "some less skilful hand" in "ill imitating" the earlier ten-book version "Might hence presume the whole Creation's day / To change in Scenes and shew it in a Play."[1] In late 1673 and early 1674 there existed the possibility that John Dryden might publish or produce his theatrical adaptation of *Paradise Lost* before Milton published the epic in twelve books.

Dryden registered "a booke or coppy" of *The Fall of Angells and man in innocence, An heroick opera* with the Stationer on 17 April 1674. He had, apparently, begun work on his opera in July or September of 1673 and, in the preface, claims to have finished the piece within a month.[2] If the sometimes unreliable notes of John Aubrey, forwarded in 1681 to Milton's biographer Anthony Wood, can be credited, Dryden had obtained Milton's consent for the adaptation during a memorable visit to the epic poet's household:

> Jo: Dryden Esq. Poet Laureate, who very much admires him, & went to him to have leave to putt his Paradise-lost into a Drama in Rhyme: Mr. Milton received him civilly, & told him he would give him leave to tagge his Verses.[3]

Irony tinges Milton's supposed remarks in the only other reference to this meeting, a third-hand account published in *The Monitor* of 1713:

> We shall here beg the Reader's pardon for mentioning a passage told a Gentleman of our Society almost Forty years since by Mr. Dryden, who went with Mr. Waller in Company to make a Visit to Mr. Milton and desire his Leave for putting Paradise Lost into

Rhime for the stage. Well, Mr. Dryden, says Milton, it seems you have a mind to Tagg my points, and you have my Leave to Tagg 'em, but some of 'em are so Awkward and Old Fashion'd that I think you had as good leave 'em as you found 'em.[4]

Dryden was seemingly well prepared for his task. He had created, in collaboration with former masque writer William Davenant, a rhymed musical version of Shakespeare's lyrical last play *The Tempest*, which was produced at the Duke of York's Theatre in London on Thursday, 7 November 1667. *The Tempest* was presented with songs, dances, and large-scale scenic effects depicting a storm, a ship sinking, a shower of fire, an idyllic island, several figures flying simultaneously, and a rising sun.[5]

Although Dryden in his adaptation of *Paradise Lost* again included flying figures, a rising sun, and pastoral scenes, the poet laureate's opera, commissioned for the pending Roman Catholic marriage of James, Duke of York, and Mary of Modena, was never staged. Publication was delayed until 1677, when the work finally appeared in rhymed heroic verse under the title *The State of Innocence and the Fall of Man*. By that time Milton's twelve-book version of *Paradise Lost*, printed in June 1674 with an author's preface defending blank heroic verse, had been available to the public for three years.[6]

Preoccupied though they were with the question of rhyme in heroic poetry, Milton and Dryden shared a related but far more elusive artistic problem in writing of the First Parents' Fall. Each sought a structure capable of embracing a confused diversity of literary-theatrical modes and genres then in transition.

Milton, beginning work in the 1640s on the outlines of "Adam Unparadiz'd," wavered in his approach before he struck upon a relatively unconventional theatrical structure as the means for integrating other theatrical elements within the broader context of a growing, twelve-book epic design. Through this original literary maneuver, he successfully fused within his epic the themes and figures of *sacre rappresentazioni*, the cosmic scenic effects and symbolic "hieroglyphs" of Italian and English court spectacles, the episodic "speaking pictures" of processional "triumphs," the grand choral ensembles of *drammi per musica*, and the cloud descents, dances, and "presentations" of Renaissance court masques.

Dryden, rewriting the epic in the 1670s after the demise of the Stuart theater of the 1640s, tried to constrict his epic opera within the formalized five-act structure of a Restoration stage play. He was thus forced either to exclude magnificent theatrical effects or to reduce them to the demands of a refined neoclassical verisimilitude. But even after making some radical excisions and rendering other material with stylized "realism," he could not decorously contain the remaining grand characters, actions, declamations, choreography, music, and scenic splendor of *Paradise Lost* within the bounds of his limiting neoclassical form.

In the 1670s Dryden was hampered by new and restrictive theatrical conventions and staging practices. Allegorical sacred representations, elaborate *drammi per musica,* and outdoor processional triumphs had given way in Restoration England to light, rhymed musical dramas. Although even Shakespeare had surrendered in his last plays to the spell of the masque and produced works filled with magic, spectacle, and music, the masque itself, as a genre exalting the victories of kings and aristocrats, had become archaic after the fall of the monarchy in the 1640s.[7] Dryden's collaborator, William Davenant, had written the last great masque *Salmacida Spolia* in 1640 before turning to the production of an "opera" *The Siege of Rhodes* (1656, 1663), stylized dramas, and "sophisticated" adaptations of Shakespeare's plays.[8]

As the political, social, and artistic climate radically and permanently altered, so did the design of playhouses. By the 1670s the open-air Elizabethan theaters with their thrust stages, minimal scenery, and audiences of standing "groundlings" and seated spectators had disappeared. Gone too were the aristocrats' indoor masquing halls with a framed stage at one narrow end, steps leading from the stage to a carpeted dancing space in the hall proper, a chair of state facing the stage at the far end of the dancing space, and tiers or "degrees"—modern bleachers—against three walls of the hall to accommodate the aristocrats who attended.

In the new indoor public theaters of the 1660s and 1670s, parallel rows of seats fronting the stage replaced the dancing space, the chair of state, and the ground-floor tiers. Visored aristocratic performers could no longer "pace" down from the stage, dance in symbolic formations, unmask before the state, and establish an electric social and emotional bond with the surrounding noble spectators. And no more could there be a final revel of dancing, an emotional release in which both aristocratic performers and aristocratic spectators participated. After the revolution, when King Charles II appeared for the first time on 28 June 1661 at a public show and sat as a spectator in a box at the Duke of York's Theatre, the masque conceived of as a triumph of kings suffered its official deathblow. The king no longer ruled the theatrical and social world under Jove from a chair of state. He had become a member of an audience of mixed social classes that sat separated from actors performing within a proscenium arch. The theater of Dryden's detached and stylized heroic dramas had been born.[9]

Dryden began his transposition of an epic into a drama by changing narrative statements into "refined" rhymed dialogue, compressing all events into a five-act structure with an assortment of scenes, and limiting all action to a single, imagined framed stage space decorated with various props and scenic devices. He was obviously guided by the theories of Davenant, who, in the preface to his unfinished epic *Gondibert* (1650) dedicated to Thomas Hobbes, purported to demonstrate how epic and drama might be "interchanged." Davenant wrote that it was from "drama, and by that regular species, narratively and not in dialogue, I have drawn the body of an heroic poem." The "symmetry" of his epic, he claimed, grew from "proportioning five books to five acts, and cantos to scenes, and scenes having their number ever governed by occasion."[10]

In his friendly *Answer to Sir William Davenant's preface before "Gondibert,"* Hobbes with his usual crisp clarity, using the word "figure" to mean structure, confidently affirmed that the two genres ought to have the same form:

> the heroic poem narrative (such as is yours) is called an epic poem; the heroic poem dramatic is tragedy ... The Figure therefore of an epic poem and of a tragedy ought to be the same, for they differ no more but in that they are pronounced by one or many persons. Which I insert to justify the figure of yours, consisting of five books divided into songs or cantos, as five acts divided into scenes has ever been the approved figure of tragedy.[11]

Such lucid and rather unfortunate speculations doubtless inspired Dryden, who muted the emphasis upon tragedy, to prescribe in his essay *Of Heroic Plays* that "an heroic play ought to be an imitation, in little, of an heroic poem; and, consequently, that Love and Valour ought to be the subject of it."[12]

To reduce Milton's ten-book epic of 1667 to a five-act theatrical epic "in little," Dryden began by eliminating all scenes set in Heaven and the figures God the Father and God the Son. Although in his preface the poet laureate cites Jonson's *Masque of Queenes* to defend his introduction of angels and supernatural effects into the opera,[13] the neoclassical convictions of Dryden prevented him from exploiting the symbolic significance of the effects and figures he was imitating. He eliminated "disguising" as a means of suggesting bifurcations or complementary identities in personality and so produced one-dimensional character-types. He eliminated masque structure and the main masque ballet. He eliminated grand-scale symbolic hieroglyphs in masque scenery and costume. And he eliminated all verses specifically designated as songs or choral ensembles.

What remains is a formal, sometimes charming and occasionally didactic "set piece" of moral seriousness that nevertheless fails decisively in both its poetic and its theatrical quality. The First Parents express their mutual love in several delightful passages in Act III, scene i, but too often Adam speaks in jingles, using crabbed didactic arguments gleaned from the writings of René Descartes, Thomas Hobbes, and Bishop Bramhall. In his conversation with the angels Gabriel and Raphael in Act IV, scene i, Adam first listens to Gabriel's instruction:

> *Gab.* The Eternal, when he did the world create,
> All other agents did necessitate:
> So what he ordered, they by nature do;
> Thus light things mount, and heavy downward go.
> Man only boasts an arbitrary state.
>
> *Adam.* Yet causes their effects necessitate
> In willing agents: Where is freedom then?
> Or who can break the chain which limits men
> To act what is unchangeably forecast,
> Since the first cause gives motion to the last?
>
> *Raph.* Heaven by fore-knowing what will surely be,
> Does only, first, effects in causes see,
> And finds, but does not make, necessity.
> Creation is of power and will the effect,
> Foreknowledge only of his intellect.
> His prescience makes not, but supposes things;
> Infers necessity to be, not brings.
> Thus thou are not constrained to good or ill
> Causes, which work the effect force not the will.   (P. 145)

With God the Father and Son removed from the play, Satan assumes a most prominent role as a "flat" figure of melodrama. Even when appearing disguised for the first time in Act IV, the character of the Archfiend assumes no significant dimension. Satan, without speaking, simply enters as a serpent and in the presence of Eve "makes directly to the Tree of Knowledge, on which winding himself, he plucks an Apple; then descends, and carries it away" (p. 150). Dryden's only subtlety in this interlude is the reappearance of Satan. Disguised in human form and speaking with assumed spiritual authority, Satan succeeds in convincing Eve of the apple's supposed transforming power. She falls and in the last act seduces Adam. But before the First Parents are expelled from the Garden, their grief is lessened when Raphael descends and announces that the human race will

> ... revive
> How happy they in deathless pleasures live;
> Far more than I can show, or you can see,
> Shall crown the blest with immortality. (P. 165)

The stage directions for Dryden's curious opera give greater prominence to scenic effects and "discoveries" than to suggested musical interludes, for which scores were never composed. Yet the scenic descriptions encompass, not vast panoramas of the universe, but only "realistic" settings for one realm of the cosmos at a time. In Act I, scene i, the fallen angels tumble down through Chaos,

> wheeling in Air, and seeming transfixed with Thunderbolts; The bottom of the Stage being opened, receives the Angels, who fall out of sight. Tunes of Victory are played, and an Hymn sung; Angels discovered above, brandishing their Swords; The Music ceasing, and the Heavens being closed, the Scene shifts, and on a sudden represents Hell: Part of the Scene is a Lake of Brimstone or rolling fire. (P. 115)

The infinite perspectives of the "new" astronomy and of baroque art have been excised from this literal, mechanistic account. Sir Walter Scott in the nineteenth century can be excused his outburst against what he termed this "burlesque" angelic Fall into an "opera hell" composed of "pasteboard and burning rosin."[14] If this first neoclassical setting seems oddly literal, so too does the last: man's sinful actions after the Fall are represented to Adam by painted flats showing a "Battle at Land" and a "Naval Fight" (p. 146). Back flats and wing flats of a similar scene, however, had appeared on stage at the Duke of York's Theatre during Part I, scene ii, and Part II, scene i, of Davenant's *The Siege of Rhodes*. And settings for the Davenant-Dryden version of *The Tempest* resemble those of the other scenes that the poet laureate now included in his opera: a "Champain Country" (p. 126), "a Sun gloriously rising and moving" (p. 129), an earthly "Paradise" (p. 132), the First Parents' "Bower" (p. 134), and a place in Eden where "four Rivers meet" (p. 149). But in these scene-by-scene representations, as in the action, Miltonic grandeur and power are absent from Dryden's somewhat abstract, scrupulously detailed work. Created as an epic opera "in little," *The State of Innocence* was reduced to an unfortunate

miniature form when adapted in 1712 as a puppet show for performance in Covent Garden at Martin Powell's Punch Theatre.[15]

Practical problems in staging did not forestall the production of *The
State of Innocence*. Theatrical flats, cloud machines, and stage traps of
a kind available at the Duke's Theatre, if imaginatively used, could
have readily accommodated the planned effects. And on one point, no
credence can be given to the fallen Victorian taste of Walter Scott who,
echoing an earlier comment by Samuel Johnson, remarked fatuously
that "the *costume* of our first parents, had there been no other objec-
tion, must have excluded 'The State of Innocence' from the stage."[16]
Scott overlooked the centuries-old conventions of emblematic dress in
medieval mystery plays and Renaissance *sacre rappresentazioni* featuring the First Parents; and he neglected to observe that a clothed
woman said to be "habited like Eve" (139) enters in Act III, scene i, a
statement suggesting that a suitable prelapsarian costume satisfying
even the demands of neoclassical verisimilitude had been imagined for
the Mother of mankind.

The cancellation of the public marriage ceremony and related public
festivities for James and Mary, for whom the work had been written,
appears best to explain why *The State of Innocence* was not immediately staged.[17] The unpopular Roman Catholic marriage was held in
private, with the bride represented by proxy. Following this rather se-
cretive event, Dryden seems to have been deterred from producing or
publishing his opera by a real concern that it would be judged inferior
to *Paradise Lost*. "And truly I would be sorry, for my own sake, that
any one should take the pain to compare them together," wrote Dryden
in his 1677 preface to the opera dedicated to Mary, "the original being
undoubtedly one of the greatest, most noble, and most sublime poems
which either this age or nation has produced" (p. 136).

Critics, who have sometimes unknowingly accepted Restoration theatrical assumptions, have admonished Dryden for being overly bold in
his theatrical and scenic effects. But his deepest difficulty was that in
his total theatrical conception he simply was not bold enough. It is
largely through the diminished vision of Dryden with his flat character-types and limiting realm-by-realm scenes that modern criticism,
divorced from Renaissance notions of disguisings and the unity of the
theatrical arts, chooses to view the theatrical elements in *Paradise Lost*.

MILTON'S VIEW of biblical drama was in fact quite different from that
of eighteenth-century neoclassical formalists. In *The Reason of
Church Government Urged Against Prelaty* (1642), the poet writes:

The scripture also affords us a divine pastoral drama in the Song of Solomon, consisting of two persons and a double chorus, as Origen rightly judges. And the Apocalypse of St. John is the majestic image of a high and stately tragedy, shutting up and intermingling her solemn scenes and acts with a sevenfold chorus of hallelujahs and harping symphonies; and this my opinion the grave authority of Pareus, commenting that book, is sufficient to confirm.[18]

Pareus in his *Commentary on the Revelation,* to which Milton refers, calls Revelation a *"Propheticall Drama,* show or representation" in which "diverse Chores also or Companies of Musitians and Harpers do distinguish the diversity of the *Acts,* and while the *Actors* hold up, do with musicall accord sweeten the wearinesse of the Spectators, and keepe them in attention; so verily the thing it selfe speaketh that in this Heavenly Interlude, by diverse *shewes* and *apparitions* are represented diverse, or rather . . . the same things touching the Church." Revelation, Pareus believes, is divided into *"Acts, Scenes,* and *Chores,"* with the "diverse *Chores* or Companies beginning, or comming in between, or ending the Propheticall Action with musicall accord."[19]

The type of *"Propheticall Drama,* show or representation" described by Pareus is associated by Cambridge Platonist John Smith with the masque:

We must remember what hath been often suggested, *That the Prophetical scene or Stage upon which all apparitions were made to the Prophet,* was his imagination; and that there all those things which God would have revealed unto him were acted over Symbolicallie, as in a *Masque,* in which divers persons are brought in, amongst which the Prophet himself bears a part: And therefore he, according to the exigencie of this Drammatical *apparatus,* must, as the other Actors, perform his part, sometimes by speaking and reciting things done, propounding questions, sometimes by acting that part which in the *Drama* he was appointed to act by some others; and so not only Speaking, but by Gestures and Actions come in his due place among the rest."[20]

As early as 1629 in the unfinished poem *The Passion,* Milton had also associated the prophetical drama with the masque. He had metaphorically compared the incarnate Christ, the "Perfect Hero" of the imagined action, to a masquer in a star-sequined costume. Milton began the poem by recalling how on a previous occasion his muse had sung of the Savior's birth while music through "the stage of Air and Earth did ring" (2). But the poet's song then turned to the sorrowful subject of the Lord's Passion:

> Most Perfect *Hero*, tried in heaviest plight
> Of labors huge and hard, too hard for human wight.
>
> He sovereign Priest stooping his regal head
> That dropt with odorous oil down his fair eyes,
> Poor fleshly Tabernacle entered,
> His starry front low-rooft beneath the skies:
> O what a Mask was there, what a disguise! (13–19)

In the remaining thirty-seven completed lines, the narrator with "roving verse" (22) digresses from his theme and finally abandons the poem with the notation that the "Subject" was "above the years" of its author. But it seems evident too that Milton at the age of twenty-one was unable poetically to visualize Christ as the central figure in a prophetical show about the Crucifixion.

Milton again conceived of the Passion in theatrical terms when, outlining in the Trinity College manuscript plans for possible prophetical dramas, he included a two-line summary of the projected sacred representation *Christus patiens;* "his agony *make*," wrote Milton, "may receav noble expressions."[21] This theatrical work was never written.

In his middle years Milton, reflecting upon both epic and dramatic forms in *The Reason of Church Government* (1642), states that he is seeking a new "pattern of a Christian hero" for a new kind of literary work. The poet had written earlier in the Latin verse *Mansus* (1630) that he would someday sing in a heroic vein about his native land and about King Arthur (80–88); and in another Latin poem, *Epitaphium Damonis* (1639–41), Milton, through the persona of Thrysis, hints that he has begun such a work and that it will concern the history of the Britains from Brutus to Arthur (155–195). But the poet, doubtless more anxious to write on biblical themes than on what he regarded as the divinely directed trials and battles of the British, never again mentions Brutus or Arthur as the subject of his own heroic song.

The Reason of Church Government suggests that in 1642 Milton was still undecided about the exact nature of his future hero and the exact mode of his projected heroic work. Interweaving classical, Italian, and biblical sources, he expresses the wish that "what the greatest and choisest wits of Athens, Rome, or modern Italy, and those Hebrews of old did for their country, I, in my proportion, with this ever and above being a Christian, might do for mine." The poet is uncertain whether to attempt a work in "that epic form whereof the two poems of Homer and those other two of Virgil and Tasso are a diffuse, and the book of Job a brief model." He shows flexibility concerning the supposed "rules" of Aristotle and wonders whether they are "strictly to be kept, or nature to be followed, which in them that know art and use judgment, is not transgression but an enriching of art." On the questions of tragedy and pastoral drama, he defers to the authority of Pareus who drew his examples from Scripture. Years later in 1671, when Milton published the preface to his tragedy *Samson Agonistes*, he alludes to Pareus as an authority and acknowledges that the Italians as well as the Ancients are being followed "in the modeling . . . of this Poem."[22]

THE OPENNESS of Milton to literary innovation had been strengthened by his experiences during his Italian journey of 1638–1639. The burning sulfur fields near a traditional Virgilian "mouth of hell" outside Naples; the stupendous size and magnificence of the papal basilica St. Peter's; the craggy and irregular landscapes viewed both in reality and on great canvases; the frescoed ceilings and domes with ranked heavenly figures that seem to recede into infinity; the new classical-Christian epic verse of Tasso and his fellow Italian poets—all fired the creative intuition and intellect of the Protestant poet from the north and were recaptured and transfigured in his own heroic writing.[23] From direct exposure to the music, dances, dialogue, songs, triumphs, and scenic splendor of the innovative Italian baroque theater, Milton had experience of new and astonishing theatrical effects at their foreign source, and he later rendered them poetically in scenes of grand spectacle and novel but hideous antic grotesquery. At the time of Milton's Italian journey, these effects had already been imitated in lesser magnitude on the English court stage. The Chief Surveyor and Architect of His English Majesty's Works, masque scenic designer Inigo Jones, had preceded Milton to Italy and returned to London with theatrical sketches, texts, and theories that he pressed upon a succession of occasionally resentful court masque writers.

In a letter of 30 March 1639 to Vatican librarian Lucas Holstein, Milton writes approvingly of a "musical entertainment with truly Roman magnificence" that he attended in the ornate, three-thousand-seat Casa Barberini theater at the Quattro Fontane, Rome. He recalls with pleasure that he was personally greeted at the door by Cardinal Francesco Barberini, who, with his brother Cardinal Antonio, acted as host.[24] Because only one known work of "magnificence" was staged at the theater during the poet's visits to Rome, it seems very likely that early in 1639 Milton saw, upon his return from Naples to the Eternal

City, the sumptuous five-hour performance of the musical spectacle *Chi soffre speri*, with libretto by Giulio Rospigliosi and music by Virgilio Mazzocchi.[25] The spectacle was embellished with unusually elaborate scenic backgrounds, numerous grand choral ensembles, and a memorable second act: a "Fair of Fara" crowded with peddlers, buyers, passersby, groups of gay young girls, men with carts pulled by oxen, aristocrats in horse-drawn carriages, and knots of loiterers dancing and fighting. In this same theater gigantic religious spectacles had been performed in the years before Milton's arrival, notably, Rospigliosi's works *L'erminia sul Giodano* in 1633, *Sant' Alessio* in 1634, and *Santa Teodora* in 1635.[26]

In his *Second Defense of the English People* (1654) Milton tells of being "a constant attendant . . . at literary parties" held by the private academies of Italy, parties at which he met scholars and artists who formulated the theories for such presentations and who then collaborated in the creation of the actual works.[27] It is worth noting that in 1643 Costanzo Ricci wrote and published the well-illustrated volume *La maschera trionfante*, containing an author's preface dedicated to Milton's former host, Cardinal Antonio Barberini.[28] Ricci, with dutiful thoroughness, described in ten-line stanzas the meaning of the figures on chariots drawn in triumph through the city. The chariots carried huge representations of allegorical figures and mythic birds, animals, and monsters. The year before Milton went to Italy the other Barberini cardinal, Francesco, had been honored by a similar volume, Giuliano Bezzi's *Il fvoco trionfante* (1637), whose dedicatory page had been imprinted with the bee emblem of the Barberini family and a cardinal's hat. The text was accompanied with drawings of a triumphant procession of floats and chariots bearing representations of Moses, Saint Elmo, various other saints and prophets, and the usual allegorical figures.[29]

In the cities that Milton visited, theaters designed with great originality, like the Casa Barberini in Rome, Bernardo Buontalenti's structure within the Uffizi in Florence, and the two playhouses financed by the Tron and Michiel families in Venice, featured framed playing areas, multilevel sets, surprising changeable scenery, and sometimes a dancing space in the hall proper before the stage.[30] Wondrous stage "tricks" were thus possible. In the final sky scene of Giovanni Coppola's *Le nozze degli dei favola* performed in Florence in 1637, the heavens opened on Jove and his minions stationed on four levels; circles of heavenly figures whirled round in colored light; and giant clouds descended with choruses of singing musicians. Dancers at stage level in the foreground performed in circular and triangular formations.[31] The fourth intermezzo of Giulio Parigi's setting for *Il giudizio di paride* (1608), also presented in Florence, was graced with massed figures suspended beside Jove on banks of crescent-shaped clouds.

The first intermezzo of Parigi's work, showing a giant "Palace of Fame," and the fifth, exposing hordes of martial and infernal figures poised in dance before Vulcan's flaming forge, obviously influenced Jones when he designed the Palace of Fame and the fiery Hell for Jonson's *Masque of Queenes*. Jones introduced the same two scenes, only slightly altered, into Davenant's *Britannia Triumphans* (1638). The designer's setting for a huge mouth of Hell opening upon a burning lake, apparently used in the second masque, also bore a strong resemblance to the one in Ottavio Rinuccini's *Balletto delle ingrate* (1608), a masque presented in Mantua with music by Monteverdi.[32] Hell was visible too, with a gigantic winged Satan dwarfing smaller devils, in the second intermezzo of Parigi's *La liberazione di Tirreno* performed in Florence in 1617. And various infernal creatures, including winged, flying devils, soared and cavorted before Pluto, enthroned in his evil chair of state at center stage, in Coppola's *Le nozze degli dei favola*.[33]

Such were the conventionalized scenic hieroglyphs of the "other world" that informed the designs of Inigo Jones and influenced the theatrical imagination of John Milton. It was an Italian Heaven and Hell that passed across the stages of Europe and eventually appeared, by way of the English court masque, in passages of *Paradise Lost*.

Garden scenes in the middle of the completed epic also owed much to English court presentations. But as originally devised by Milton in the outlines of "Adam Unparadiz'd," these scenes grew most directly from Continental theories and published *sacre rappresentazioni* that depicted the Fall as a paradoxical tragedy with a merciful Christian ending, a holy *tragedie di lieto fine* as distinguished from a pagan *tragedie miste*. Many Italian academicians tried to prove, and Italian artists to demonstrate, that the poetic principles of the masterful pagan Aristotle applied wholly in form but not in content to "heroes" acting within a Christian universe. In treatises and sacred dramas, the crushing force of inexorable Fate was seen to be mitigated by a beneficent Christian God who intervened to assist the flawed, fallen, but penitent hero. These exercises in omnipotent mercy dominated the *sacra rappresentazione* and were conflated in the sixteenth century into a blurred diversity of Christian presentations, whose theoretical classification has strained the wit and good sense of both early and modern commentators: the Italian masque, *favola in musica, dramma musicale, dramma per musica,* and *opera rappresentata in musica.*[34]

Milton could hardly have avoided speaking personally with one of the more important artists and theorists of the sacred drama, Girolamo Bartolommei, secretary of the Florentine Accademei degli Svogliati. At a meeting of the academy in 1638, the two men shared the reader's platform; the English visitor recited his Latin poems and Bartolommei his Tuscan verse. Milton may also have been present at another meeting held on 28 June 1638 that the Italian is known to have attended. A few years before the academic association of the two men, Bartolommei had maintained in the lengthy preface to *Tragedie de Girolamo Bartolommei* (1632) that the grace of God contravened the power of classical fate, that Christian heroes were usually men of middle estate, and that classical forms should be preserved in the presentation of Christian arguments. He categorized his musical plays as *dramme morali* and *dramme sacri* and wrote a number of works that he labeled *tragedie sacre.*[35]

IT HAS LONG been recognized that Milton, before or after visiting Hugo Grotius in Paris in 1638, may have read his host's prophetical Latin drama *Adamus Exul* (1601). Later in Italy the poet may also have become acquainted with Giambatissta Andreini's *L'Adamo* (1613). Both these representations with music are similar to most Italian musical prophetical dramas, but different from the masque, in that the action in five acts is confined to an envisaged area on stage and does not conclude with a courtly presentation to the state and a revel of dancing in a central hall.

Grotius's *Adamus Exul,* subtitled *Tragedeo,* exemplifies the more classically formal and literary type of Christian theatrical work in which stage spectacle is subordinated to action that focuses upon the Fall and its consequences. *Adamus Exul* contains extensive and rather discursive dialogue but a very limited number of character-types. Adam, Eve, Satan, an angel, a chorus, and a Voice of God perform or are heard before settings of an "eminence" overlooking Eden, and the Fall occurs in the second act. The tragic note is muted in the last act, however, when the Voice of God promises Adam and Eve that "HIMSELF shall come," "take on human flesh," and be "the Saviour of mankind."[36]

Andreini's *L'Adamo,* with its thirty-five scenes, five acts, twenty-five character-types, and two choruses, is far more digressive and depends heavily upon song, dance, and spectacle. This prophetic speaking picture, which in an apology the author rightly maintains is an outward hieroglyph of the First Parents' spiritual condition, has a marked allegorical cast and ends in a fashion that can best be characterized as happy. The angel Michael defeats Satan in battle and tells the First Parents that through repentance they can attain Heaven; then the angelic chorus sings a hymn of praise to God. Andreini in the apology refers to himself as a "speaking painter" who works through the media of "images and voices." Given the externalized nature of the work and the large cast, which includes the Eternal Father, numerous angels and devils, divers allegorical figures, and a chorus of hobgoblins, one can readily agree with John Arthos's assumption that this representation, when performed in 1613 at the Palazzo Ducale, Milan, was lavishly mounted on a stage replete with cloud machines, musicians stationed at different levels, and vast scenic perspectives.[37]

Whether or not Milton was immediately acquainted with either or both of these representations, it was from Christian prophetical works of their kind that he borrowed for "Adam Unparadiz'd" the theatrical character-types of Eve, Adam, Lucifer, and allegorical figures of evil and good. Milton also appropriated the conception of the Christian *tragedie di lieto fine* and freshly discovered the "pattern" of a paradoxical Christian hero and heroine in Adam and Eve.[38] He used the processions and movements of evil figures in intermezzi—more than twenty intermezzi appear in *L'Adamo*—by introducing into his fourth outline "a mask of all the evils of this life & world."[39] The same outline discloses that Milton, like Andreini, imagined action unfolding, probably in its entirety, on a multilevel stage having cloud machines and a station for the chorus. Milton seriously considered following the classical five-act form employed by the Italians, for he listed five acts in the third draft of his outlines for "Adam Unparadiz'd." But in revising his work he drew back, as will be seen, from adopting either the five-act form or the practice of limiting action entirely to an envisaged multilevel stage. He thus gained a theatrical perspective that greatly aided him in transforming his outlines into the epic *Paradise Lost*.

THE PRINCIPAL theme of "Adam Unparadiz'd" and *Paradise Lost*, man's Temptation and Fall by free, rational choice, was derived from the masque as well as from the Bible and such works as Edmund Spenser's *The Faerie Queene*. Milton had a knowledge of Aurelian Townshend's *Tempe Restored* (1632), a masque that had among its performers Henry Lawes, Milton's collaborator on *Comus*, and Lady

Alice Egerton, who had played the Lady in *Comus*.[40] *Tempe Restored* is about the power of virtuous figures to overcome the enchantments of Circe. At the beginning a "yong Gent" declares that he has attained his freedom from Circe because he wishes "to be a man againe, / Govern'd by Reason, and not ful'd by Sense."[41] The yong Gent then introduces a theme that echoes throughout Milton's works:

> Tis not her Rod, her Philter, nor her Herbes,
> (Though strong in Magicke) that can bound mens minds;
> And make them Prisoners, where there is no wall
> It is consent that makes a perfect Slave:
> And Sloth that binds us to Lusts easie Trades,
> Wherein we serve out our youths Prentiship,
> Thinking at last, love should enfranchize us,
> Whome we have never, either serv'd or knowne:
> "He finds no helpe, that uses not his owne." (P. 85)

Two years later in 1634 Milton wrote similar lines for Lady Alice Egerton who, in the role of the Lady, rejects the temptations to intemperance proposed by Comus, the son of Circe. "Thou canst not touch the freedom of my mind / With all thy charms," avows the Lady (663–664). Though she has wandered inadvertently into the physical darkness that Comus prefers, the light of her virtue and right reason remains unimpaired. As the Elder Brother explains,

> He that has light within his own clear breast
> May sit i'th' center, and enjoy bright day,
> But he that hides a dark soul and foul thoughts
> Benighted walks under the midday Sun;
> Himself is his own dungeon. (381–385)

Milton included all the lines quoted above, both the Lady's and the Elder Brother's, in the revised version of the masque published in 1637. Only a few years later, sometime early in the 1640s, a passage with a similar theme was read aloud by Milton to his nephew Edward Phillips. According to Phillips, the lines were written for the figure Satan as part of a tragedy upon which his uncle was then working.[42] The passage quoted by Phillips, like a comparable passage in *Comus*, reveals the hatred of an evil figure for the sun. Again, wrong choice dictated by pride and ambition causes the figure to fall victim to temptation. The implied darkness of evil within the figure awakens memories of a previous state:

> O thou that with surpassing glory crown'd!
> Look'st from thy sole dominion, like the god

Of this new world; at whose sight all the stars
Hide their diminish'd heads; to thee I call,
But with no friendly voice; and add they name,
O Sun! to tell thee how I hate thy beams
That bring to my remembrance, from what state
I fell, how glorious once above thy sphere;
Till pride and worse ambition threw me down,
Warring in Heaven, against Heavn's glorious King.[43]

These same lines appear, of course, as part of Satan's address to the sun in Book IV of *Paradise Lost* (32–41), but with the word "glorious" in the last line changed to "matchless." Allan H. Gilbert rightly suggests that the difference may be Phillips's error; "glorious" is used twice within several lines in Phillips's rendering, and the repetition could easily have been a mistake.[44]

IT WAS FROM English sources that Milton acquired the special theatrical structure that he employed in both *Comus* and *Paradise Lost.* He developed in the epic what Merritt Y. Hughes has been observed to call somewhat loosely "a new kind of drama—a drama of contrast between situations." "What happened in Hell," Hughes asserts, "is a parody of what happens in Heaven."[45] But after surveying hexameral and theatrical antecedents of the epic, Watson Kirkconnell also attests to the poet's unique but unexplained use of what he terms opposed correspondences and parallels as a structural principle within *Paradise Lost:* "These correspondences . . . are the very nerves and sinews by which the epic is made a living organism; yet they had been rarely used in hexameral literature. It is Milton's unique achievement to have used them as a major structural device, completely in harmony with his poetic material."[46]

This major structural device as used by Milton arose largely from Ben Jonson's balancing of patterned, parallel but antithetically opposed character-types, themes, actions, and scenes in antic and main segments of masques. This antimasque–main masque form was employed by Jonson in *Hymenaei* (1606) and then again in *The Haddington Masque* (1608), but it was first explained by him in the preface to *The Masque of Queenes* (1609). Jonson observes that the leading performer in the masque, Queen Anne, "had commaunded mee to think on some *Daunce,* or shew that might praecede hers, and haue the place of a foyle, or false-*Masque.*" Referring to *The Haddington Masque,* Jonson continues:

Last year, I had an *Anti-Masque* of Boyes; and therefore, now, deuis'd that twelue Women, in the habite of *Haggs*, or Witches, sustayning the persons of *Ignorance, Suspicion, Credulity*, &c. the opposites to good *Fame*, should fill that part; not as a *Masque*, but as a spectacle of strangeness, producing multiplicity of Gesture, and not unaptly sorting with the current, and whole fall of the Deuise."[47]

With this theatrical plan Jonson drew together the usual antic intermezzi into a single, discordant "false" masque of evil witches that did indeed effectively oppose the harmonious concluding main masque actions and dances by the featured character Fame and his heroic companions. The false masque of antic figures, movements, noises, speeches, and grotesque scenery—all contained on stage within a proscenium arch—began when the spectators suddenly saw

an ougly *Hell;* wch, flaming beneath, smoakd unto the top of the Roofe. And, in respect all *Euills* are (*morally*) sayd to come from *Hell* . . . These Witches, with a kind of hollow and infernall musique, came forth from thence. First one, then two, and three, and more; till theyr number encreased to Eleuen; all differently attir'd; some, with ratts on theyr heads; some, on theyr shoulders; others with oyntment-potts at theyr girdles; All with spindells, timbrells, rattles, or other *beneficall* instruments, making a confused noyse, with strange gestures. (24–36)

Jonson notes that these figures, "Vizarded and masqu'd" like supposed witches at meetings, fall into a wild dance before reciting their evil charms. They are joined by a monstrous Dame, who calls the witches "Opposites / To *Fame & Glory*" (132) and urges them to let "shrunke-up Chaos . . . rise, / Once more, his darke, and reeking head, / To strike the World" (312–314). The witches, the Dame fiercely states, should "blast the light; / Mixe Hell, with Heauen; and make *Nature* fight / Within her selfe" (146–147). Then the witches, after further speeches, engage in antic and "*magicall Daunce*, full of praeposterious change, and gesticulation" (346–347).

The abrupt transition from antic masque to main masque, made with stage effects copied by Jones from the Italian theater, takes place when

not only the *Hagges* themselues, but theyr *Hell*, into wch they ranne, quite vanishd; and the whole face of the *Scene* alterd; scarse suffring the memory of any such thing: But, in the place of it appear'd a glorious and magnificent Building, figuring the *House of Fame*, in the upper part of wch were discouerd the twelue *Mas-*

quers sitting upon a Throne triumphall, erected in forme of a *Pyramide* and circled with all store of light. (336–363)

After various figures and chariots descend from the heavens—including Fame, who holds "in her right hand . . . a trumpet, in her left an oliue-branch" (451–452)—the main masquers gracefully pace down from the stage into the hall, where they perform three dances before the chair of state. The "third *Daunce*," according to Jonson, has a *"numerous* composition . . . *graphically* dispos'd into *letters*, and honoring the Name of the most sweete, and ingenious *Prince, Charles, Duke of Yorke* Wherein, beside that principall grace of perpicuity, the motions were so euen, & apt, and theyr expression so iust; as if *Mathematicians* had lost *proportion*, they might there haue found it" (750–756). The performers then unmask, are presented to the state, and participate in the revels.

Dryden, writing in 1674 for the new Restoration theater, could not incorporate into *The State of Innocence* an antimasque–main masque form leading to a presentation and the revels. But Milton in 1634 superbly adopted the Jonsonian form for *Comus* and later reflected it in the theatrical structure of *Paradise Lost*.

Comus obviously was written to be performed, first, in a limited stage area where two instantaneous changes of scenery could be made in sequence. A "wild Wood" (p. 90) is replaced by a "stately Palace" (p. 105); the palace disappears and "Ludlow Town and the President's Castle" (p. 112) are seen. Next, the Lady and her two Brothers are led by the Attendant Spirit from the stage area to a place where the Spirit "presents them to their father and mother" (p. 112); that is, before the chairs of state in the rear center of the masquing hall. From this position the Earl of Bridgewater, that "noble Peer of mickle trust and power" (31) for whom the work was written, brings harmony to the masquing world by reigning under Jove from a chair of state in the hall. The iniquitous counterpart to the virtuous peer is Comus, who, through the power of "dark veil'd Cotytto" (129), instigates evil from his palace and chair on stage. Thus, Comus and the peer are the two figures of authority in direct opposition. And just as Comus reigns surrounded by his rabble from his palace located at the stage end of the performing space, so too the peer reigns, surrounded on three sides by aristocratic spectators "met in state" (947), from a raised chair at the opposite end of the space.[48]

Milton develops the action of the masque to fit this physical arrangement. Comus and his rabble, during an antimasque presented in the stage area, shout and dance in disorder beating the ground with heavy steps as they perform an unruly "round" (144). Later, the enchanter and his followers are seen on stage within or in front of Comus's stately palace. Comus's chair, to which the Lady is magically bound, stands before the palace. At the conclusion of the masque, the Lady, accompanied by her two Brothers, breaks free of the stage area and moves across an open space to the opposite chair of the noble peer. There the three virtuous children would have bowed low before the state, and then performed on "lighter toes" (962) the ordered main masque dances which contrast with the disordered antimasque movements of Comus and his crew. In accord with the usual custom of main masquers at the English court, the Lady and her two Brothers could be expected to unmask and to dance completely around the chair of state moving in patterns representing mazes and simple figures such as circles and chains. The main masque dances in *Comus* are said to be performed on a "Sun-shine holiday" (959), a statement suggesting that all possible illumination was used for the masque's finale. Often at court a chorus sang and sometimes approached the state during the dances, but at Ludlow the diminutive nature of the production allowed only for a presentation song by the Attendant Spirit. Still a banquet might have been held at Ludlow, as often was the practice at court, following the staging of a masque.

If Milton traveled to Ludlow Castle and witnessed the first performance, he actually may have looked toward the stage to see Comus and his crew moving with heavy step, noise, and disorder in the semidark wood and palace. Afterward, he may have turned to watch the light, harmonious dances of the main masquers in front of, and perhaps around, the brightly illuminated chair of the noble peer. The poet also would have seen a youthful Lady resisting Comus's temptation at the stage end of the hall. Through her reaction to temptation, she is in effect rationally choosing either to remain in the chair of Comus or to proceed to the chair of the peer. However, Milton, whether or not he was present, surely would have been conscious of the polarities of light and dark, order and disorder, and nimbleness and heaviness that relate to the evil or virtue represented in the opposing authority figures of Comus and the peer. By appropriating and transforming the character-types, structural polarities, and visual settings drawn from the masque, Milton was able to use these elements to depict in epic form the divine opposition of heaven and hell. Parallel elements in the two regions also could have been partly inspired by balanced segments in works like Dante's *Commedia* and Spenser's *The Faerie Queene;* yet in many episodes of *Paradise Lost* the influence of the masque seems pervasive.

As early as 1809 Henry Todd had noted, in his edition of Milton's poetry, the resemblance between the palace Pandemonium, described in Book I of *Paradise Lost,* and a scenic palace in William Davenant's masque *Britannia Triumphans* (1637).[49] The similarity was subsequently commented upon by Enid Welsford and Merritt Y. Hughes. Because Henry Lawes performed in Davenant's masque and in the same year wrote an introduction for the first quarto printing of *Comus,* Lawes may have had occasion to talk with Milton about the court presentation. The subject of Davenant's masque, how Britanocles enlisted the services of Fame for the benefit of Britain, would have been of interest to a poet soon to contemplate composing an epic about the English nation.

In *Britannia Triumphans* the great stage palace designed by Jones appears during the main masque spectacle:

The earth open'd and there rose up a richly adorn'd palace, seeming all Goldsmiths work, with porticoes vaulted on pillasters running far in: the pillasters were silver of rustic work, their bases and capitals of gold. In the midst was the principal entrance, and a gate; the doors' leaves of bass-relief, with jambs, and frontispiece all of gold. Above these ran an architrave, freize, and cornice of the same; the freize enricht with jewels.

This exterior view of the palace was immediately

changed into a Peristillum of two orders, Doric and Ionic, with their several ornaments seeming of white marble, the bases and capitals of gold; this, joining with the former, having so many returns, openings, and windows, might well be known for the glorious Palace of Fame.

The climactic scenic effect came when "the gate of the Palace open'd."[50]

Milton in *On the Fifth of November* had set action having theatrical overtones within the temple of the Roman pontiff. During his Italian journey he had seen Roman basilicas and baroque palaces both in reality and as depicted in paintings, frescoes, and theatrical designs. And the poet, through personal observation and study and doubtless through collaboration with Henry Lawes, had become familiar with theatrical conventions governing the representation of stage palaces, such as the one in Davenant's *Britannia Triumphans* and Circe's "sumptuous Palace" in Townshend's *Tempe Restored.*[51] In *Comus* Milton created a palace for Circe's son, one that might possibly have risen from a stage well, as Sabrina's chariot did in a later part of the masque. And however much Milton was influenced by classical and

biblical descriptions of palaces and his own memories of actual structures,[52] he would also have had masque palaces in mind when he wrote
in *Paradise Lost:*

> Anon out of the earth a Fabric huge
> Rose like an Exhalation, with the sound
> Of Dulcet Symphonies and voices sweet,
> Built like a Temple, where *Pilasters* round
> Were set, and Doric pillars overlaid
> With Golden Architrave; nor did there want
> Cornice or Frieze, with bossy Sculptures grav'n;
> The Roof was fretted Gold. (I.710–715)

Milton continues:

> ... Th' ascending pile
> Stood fixt her stately highth, and straight the doors
> Op'ning thir brazen folds discover wide
> Within her ample spaces, o'er the smooth
> And level pavement: from the arched roof
> Pendant by subtle Magic many a row
> Of Starry Lamps and blazing Cressets fed
> With *Naphtha* and *Asphaltus* yielded light
> As from a sky. (722–730)

In *Paradise Lost* and *Britannia Triumphans* the palaces rise from
the ground, are seen from without and from within, and have gates that
open. But there is a significant difference. The palace in Davenant's
masque is the seat of Britanocles and has windows to admit the light of
day. Pandemonium is the seat of Satan, who dwells in "darkness visible" (I.63), and so is lighted with naphtha and with the asphalt that
Milton associated with the Asphaltic Pool of the Dead Sea "where
Sodom flam'd" (X.562).

Like the stage world of the antimasque, Pandemonium is the site of
disordered movement, dissonant sound, and irrational speech; but all is
now magnified to heroic dimensions. The devils enter in thick swarms
and "clusters" (I.767, 771) as bees that fly to and fro in springtime
(772). Perhaps Milton was here ungraciously associating the fallen
angels with the clerical members of the Barberini family, whose bee
emblem appeared not only imprinted in books but also conspicuously
carved on the main altar pilasters of St. Peter's Basilica. In any case, the
combined murmuring of the devils creates a noise "as when hollow
Rocks retain / The sound of blust'ring winds, which all night
long / Had rous'd the Sea" (II.285–287). "Thir rising all at once was
as the sound / Of Thunder heard remote" (476–477). And the

"deaf 'ning shout" of the throng before Pandemonium is "heard far and wide" throughout the abyss of Hell (519–520). Inside the palace, Satan, a transmuted counterpart to Comus, reigns "high on a Throne of Royal State" (1). Like Comus, who debates with the Lady using "false rules prankt in reason's garb" (*Comus*, 759), Satan employs arguments that are largely the product of "proud imaginations" (*PL* II.10) rather than right reason. At the end of a debate among a council of devils, Satan wins the blasphemous adoration of followers who bow too low, even as their leader has enthroned himself too high (477–479).

At the opposite cosmic pole from Satan sits God the Father, emanating dazzling light, "high Throned above all highth" (III.58), a transformed counterpart to the noble peer in *Comus*. And in the manner of a king or nobleman on a chair of state during main masque songs and dances, God the Father is eulogized through the harmonious hymns and movements of the angels.

After writing three versions of *Comus*, four outlines of "Adam Unparadiz'd," and lines for a representation of the Fall, Milton had necessarily grown conscious of Renaissance theatrical forms; and his general debt to Renaissance theatrical genres deserves, at last, to be recognized. One of the leading themes in *Paradise Lost*, the freedom of man's mind to choose rationally between enslavement and enlightenment, derives from specific passages in *Comus* that are echoed in Book IV of the epic. And without minimizing in the slightest the influence of biblical and other works upon Milton's imagination, one can still assert that a basic structural feature of the opening and central books, the antithesis of disorderly action in Hell and harmonious action in Heaven, is to a great extent a development of the antimasque–main masque structure of *Comus*. The last two books are in part a transformed depiction of a processional masque of the world's evils planned for "Adam Unparadiz'd," a processional masque borrowed from the intermezzi of sacred representations.

There is also a definite "staged" quality to the vast design of *Paradise Lost*, which opens out upon a visionary projection of the cosmos with different realms coming magnificently into view. This grand visual panorama of Hell, Chaos, Earth, and most of Heaven draws one into its enveloping depths like a gigantic, three-dimensional Renaissance setting that leads the eye into infinity. In the far-flung reaches of Milton's universe, Hell flames below, a massive palace rises from Hell's center, and within the palace Satan is discovered on a chair of state. Above the infernal regions, beyond Hell's gate, is the cloudy maze of Chaos, a "dark / Illimitable Ocean without bound" (II.891–892).

Higher still, this "pendant world" hangs by a "golden Chain" from a heavenly region that gleams above with "Opal Tow'rs and Battlements adorn'd" (1049–1052). Angelic messengers of Heaven descend to and ascend from a garden placed upon this pendant world at the middle of creation. But in one respect Milton's visual cosmos differs from the colossal scenic hieroglyphs of all creation that appeared on Renaissance stages: God the Father, on the throne of the universe, remains present but invisible, an Infinite Ruler manifested only as a mysterious font of spiritual light.

One should realize too that Milton's spacious universe, with Eden at its core between the polarities of Satan's throne in Hell and God the Father's throne in Heaven, is to some extent an enormously elaborated reflection of the opposed seats of power and the other polarities in *Comus*. Just as the main masque action in *Paradise Lost* takes place in Eden between the thrones of Satan and God, so too in *Comus* the main masquers play their roles between the chairs of the dominating good and evil figures. The antithesis of evil and virtuous actions, associated with the two ruling figures and their chairs of state, is mirrored in *Paradise Lost* in the dances, songs, debates, and actions of the devils and angels about the thrones of Satan and God.

The scenes in Hell and Heaven, which Hughes calls dramas within the epic and which F. T. Prince regards as a special kind of sublime theatrical spectacle, can now be read with an awareness of their origins in the masque and sacred representation.[53] Satan can be clearly discerned as a counterpart to Comus; Satan's palace Pandemonium, a reflection of Comus's palace in the navel of the wood; unfallen Eve, a heroic figure suggestive of the Lady; and the Lady's temptation, a foreshadowing of the temptation of Eve. Even the wooded slopes of the mount of Eden share many characteristics with the wood in the masque. But because a parallel has never before been drawn between God the Father and a figure in *Comus*, a primary source for Milton's depiction of the Almighty has been ignored. Overlooked as well has been a clue to the depiction in the line of *The Passion* that compares God to a performer in a masque: "O what a mask was there, what a disguise!" Not until Milton wrote *Paradise Lost* did he demonstrate that God might be so represented.

Although the realms and characters in *Paradise Lost* are radically transformed from their inception in Milton's theatrical writings, Hell remains suggestive of an antimasque dominated from Satan's throne; Heaven, a main masque spectacle controlled from the throne of God; Eden, a center of main masque action involving man's Temptation and future Triumph; and the last books, a series of intermezzi on the consequences of the Fall. The opposed thrones of God and Satan, placed so far apart in the epic, emerge as a heroic, transmuted reflection of the chairs of the noble peer and Comus placed at opposite ends of the performing space in *Comus*. And God the Father, surrounded by dancing angels but free of noticeable scenic backgrounds, is like the noble peer, who, while brightly illuminated during the main masque finale, would have been far from the stage area but encircled by dancing main masquers.

III

The Vast Design Emerges

THE keen fascination of Milton with literary forms is at once evident from an examination of the slim packet of papers containing the only surviving handwritten copies of the poet's early works: the fifty watermarked pages, three of them blank, composing the manuscript in the Trinity College library at Cambridge. The scrawls, slashes, and fluid *l* and *f* curls of Milton's hand fill pages 1 through 8 and 10 through 41 with corrected copies of the entertainment *Arcades*, the song *Blest pair of Sirens*, three occasional poems, *A Mask Presented at Ludlow Castle*, and the elegy *Lycidas*, labeled in a subheading with the Italian musical term *monodie*. The last seven pages contain notes and outlines for theatrical works with scriptural and British themes. These final pages, probably written after Milton returned from Italy but before publication of the *Poems* in 1645, provide a most interesting record of Milton's progress in the disposition of a new kind of sacred, heroic, and visionary literary work.[1]

Three outlines of a sacred representation about the Fall fill the opening page (numbered 35). The initial two outlines, occupying the top half of the page in two parallel columns, are simply lists of character-types that are struck out with crosshatched lines. The third draft, penned across the full width of the lower half of the page, is entitled "Paradise Lost" and consists of listed character-types and a fragmentary plot summary divided into five acts. On the reverse side (numbered 36) of this leaf are the titles "The Deluge," "Sodom," and "Dinah" and notes in two columns enumerating nearly thirty Old Testament topoi, including one about the destruction of Jerusalem.

Four pages further into the manuscript, on an unnumbered sheet in the position of page 40, the topos of the Fall reappears, this time as an expanded summary, undifferentiated by acts, that takes up the lower half of the leaf and is entitled both "Adam Unparadiz'd" and "Adams Banishment." Filling the upper half, under the titles "Cupids funeral pile" and "Sodom Burning," is the body of a summarized representation about the evil city on the shore of the Dead Sea. The summary begins on numbered page 39 and is continued in midsentence above "Adam Unparadiz'd" on the unnumbered sheet.

It has been suggested that Milton may have penned the double-column entries—among them the two initial crossed-out drafts of the representation of the Fall and the title "Sodom"—before writing pagewide entries such as the summaries of "Paradise Lost" and "Adam Unparadiz'd."[2] Even if one accepts this speculative view, the four outlines of the Fall, which for clarity will together be called "Adam Unparadiz'd," would nevertheless have been composed in their present chronological order with intervening notes documenting Milton's interest in a representation about Sodom.

The four drafts constitute a work-in-progress by an author who left a written annotation to himself to compare the fourth version with the "former draught."[3] When the outlines of "Adam Unparadiz'd" and the plans for "Sodom Burning" are reviewed along with the Trinity College, Bridgewater, and 1637 quarto texts of *Comus*, it is obvious that Milton, almost surely before 1645 and certainly no later than the onset of his blindness about 1652, had struck upon certain epic themes that, when expanded, would underlie pivotal episodes in *Paradise Lost*: the councils of the damned and the blessed; the entry of Satan into the Garden of Eden; the ideal marriage and divine education of Adam and Eve; the First Parents' Temptation, Fall, and repentance; Adam's "discovery" of the future suffering and Redemption of mankind; and the First Parents' banishment from Eden. The outlines suggest as well how these and other episodes, conceived of as theatrical events, were later incorporated within the twelve-book epic.

The Region of the Damned

In the most detailed speculations yet printed about the chronology of composition of *Paradise Lost*, Allan H. Gilbert, concentrating upon the plans for "Adam Unparadiz'd" and neglecting *Comus* and the plans for "Sodom Burning," maintains that there is no source in Milton's theatrical writings and outlines for the Hell scenes in Books I, II, and X. Accepting arguments first advanced by Grant McColley, Gilbert argues that most of Book I (lines 1–669) was "not suggested in the plans for tragedies and probably not planned until the epic form was settled on." And he believes that passages depicting the universe of Hell (II.521–628), the infernal palace Pandemonium (I.670–798), the devils' debate in the palace (II.1–520), and Satan's return to the palace after the Fall (X.414–473, 502–583) were late additions either substituted for other materials at some final stage of composition or "inserted when the poem seemed finished."[4]

Rudimentary plans for scenes in a region of the damned—plans that Milton eventually elaborated with material about infernal realms drawn from classical, medieval, and Renaissance writings—can nevertheless be found in the summary of "Sodom Burning" that begins on page 31 and ends on the next page over the final draft of "Adam Unparadiz'd." Given the existence of this early summary and the importance of episodes in Hell to the overall action and structure of *Paradise Lost*, it appears unlikely that Milton would have left the invention and disposition of these episodes until last.

The outline of "Sodom Burning" opens with Lot meeting shepherds at Sodom's gates. The men watch the evil "Gallantry" of the city "passe by in procession with musick and song to the temple of Venus Urania or Peor." Lot is invited to participate in the temple "solemnities" but refuses. He then learns from angels that the sinful city will be destroyed.

Milton furnishes two possible endings. In one version the "King and nobles of the citty" leave the temple and "serve to set out the terror" as the "Angels doe the deed," that is, "call to ye thunders lightnings and fires" to devastate Sodom. Lot "last is describ'd parting from the citty." In a variation interwoven with this conclusion, the king and nobles remain at the "Solemnity" in the temple. Angels appear and "dispute" with these figures "of love & how it differs from lust seeking to win them in the last scene . . . when the firece thunders begin aloft." Lot makes his escape as the city is demolished by heavenly fires.[5]

In this outline, themes used earlier by Milton can be seen to blend with newly emerging ones to be further developed in the future. As in *On the Fifth of November*, evil figures march in procession to an unholy temple, and a false argument is propounded at this seat of evil. Again, evil is overcome, in this instance through the destruction of a profligate city that, according to popular tradition, sank to perdition through the "Hell's mouth" of the Dead Sea. Remembering too previous associations relating Comus and his palace to Satan and Pandemonium, one notes that the summary contains a patterned recapitulation of Comus's movement to his palace, where Comus appears before his crew and argues in favor of lust. The outline in fact incorporates elements pointing to a number of actions, settings, and characters later to be depicted in the infernal world of *Paradise Lost* (Books I, II, and X): Hell's fiery lake area, which Milton relates to the environment of the Dead Sea's Asphaltic Pool; the flight and march of Satan and his cohorts to Pandemonium; the disputes of the Archfiend and the devils within the palace; and the final punishment of the devils in a place like the one where "*Sodom* flam'd" (X.562).[6]

A Sinful Realm and Heaven Compared

Milton had only to look again at the outlines to begin drawing parallels between a region of evil and Heaven. At the conclusion of "Sodom Burning," in a partly bracketed two-line statement that starts on the unnumbered leaf and continues within a semicircle drawn on the next page, the angel, alluding to destructive heavenly fire and lightning, delivers a "short warning to all other nations to take heed on earth, as in heavn, describes Paradise. next he bids them heare the call & command of god to come & destroy a godlesse nation."

The paradise that the angel contrasts with a sinful city on earth would appear to be God's realm in eternity, for the words "on earth, as in heavn" immediately precede the reference. Even if Milton's allusion is to the earthly paradise, an association has been made that suggests parallels between this world and the next. The verbal "hinge" foreshadows opposed and complementary realms in *Paradise Lost:* the evil city near a burning lake, the earthly paradise of Eden, and the glorious region of Heaven.

Heaven, a Mountain of God, and a Perfect Hero

Did Milton in his outlines devise a scene in a divine realm within sight of God, a scene that presages the Heaven of *Paradise Lost?*

Act I of the third draft of "Adam Unparadiz'd" indeed takes place in an incorruptible holy region where God is near and can be directly addressed and where various heavenly characters are present: Moses, Justice, Mercie, Wisdom, Heavenly Love, and a chorus of angels. Moses recounts how "he assum'd his true bodie, that it corrupts not because of his with god on the mount" and then "declares the like of Enoch and Eliah, besides the purity of ye pl (ace) that certain pure winds, dues, and clouds preserve it from corruption." The next speaker, Heavenly Love, "horts to the sight of god, tells they cannot se Adam in the state of innocence by reason of *sin* thire sin" (TCM, 35).

Created objects and the bodies of prophets are thus preserved in this spiritually pure realm, but sinful man in Eden remains invisible.

Milton's vague notes imply that Act I is set either on the peak of a holy mountain like Sinai or in some other region of the heavens within view of the Almighty. In the next act, although no scene is designated, the characters Heavenly Love, Evening Starre, and a chorus seem to be in the same heavenly setting.

Nowhere in the seven pages of outlines is Christ depicted in Heaven; but in the sketch of the projected representation "Christus patiens" at the bottom of page 41, as in *The Passion*, Milton again conceives theatrically the agony and death of this perfect hero: "The Scene in ye garden beginning fro ye comming thither till Judas betraies & ye officers lead him away ye rest by message & chorus. his agony *make* may receav noble expressions." In *Paradise Lost* the Son, enthroned in Heaven on the right hand of the invisible God the Father, gives noble expression to the future Passion before a chorus of angels; both Father and Son proclaim the mercy and justice of godhood.

An Angel Descends to Eden

The opening action in Eden, described in the last draft of "Adam Unparadiz'd,"was created by an author who definitely considered the possibility that the work would be performed. Milton arranged an entry for the angel Gabriel, as had previously been done for the Attendant Spirit in *Comus*, taking into account that a descent might be staged in a hall that could be fitted with a cloud machine. Gabriel makes his first appearance "descending or entering," that is, either flying or walking, depending on staging conditions. In writing simply that Gabriel "passes by the station of ye chorus" in coming to Eden, Milton also allowed for the possibility that the angelic musicians might be "floated" in the theatrical heavens or placed firmly upon the stage at ground level.

Gabriel's hoped-for flight foreshadows, of course, the descent of the angel Raphael to prelapsarian Eden in *Paradise Lost*. In the fourth draft of "Adam Unparadiz'd," the First Parents are not present in the area where Raphael enters the Garden, so the angel "relates" to the chorus "what he knew of man as the creation of Eve with theire love, & marriage. after this Lucifer appeares." The angel's statements are a development of the third draft in which "the chorus sing the marriage song and describe Paradise" before Satan appears.

Milton is already turning his attention to the unusual theme of the First Parents' prelapsarian love and marriage.

Inigo Jones's design for the figure Fame in Ben Jonson's masque *Chloridia* (1631). Milton in *On the Fifth of November* (1626) had a few years earlier described this traditional emblematic figure as donning wings, taking hold of a trumpet, and then flying past clouds to earth.

The drawing of Charles I printed in the promonarchist pamphlet *Eikon Basilike* (1649). Milton, believing that the emblematic scene concealed the king's supposed evil nature, wrote in *Eikonoklastes* (1649) that the "conceited portraiture" was "drawn out to the full measure of a masking scene, and set there to catch fools and silly gazers."

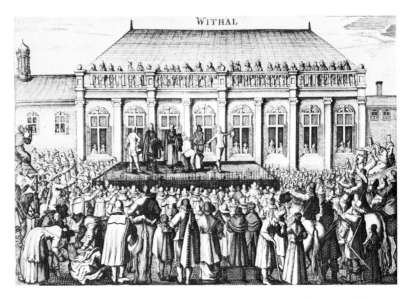

A seventeenth-century Dutch print of the execution of Charles I. The execution was specially "staged" by the parliamentarians on a platform before the Whitehall Banqueting House. The king had frequently appeared within the house, disguised as a pagan god or hero, in the lavishly presented court masques of Ben Jonson, James Shirley, and William Davenant.

Design by Jones for the mouth of a flaming inferno probably used in the antimasque Hell scene of Davenant's *Britannia Triumphans* (1637). In the main masque spectacle Charles I, surrounded by his courtiers and disguised as Britanocles, appeared from a Palace of Fame to participate in a theatrical triumph.

Alfonso Parigi's stage setting for the fifth intermezzo of the fourth act of *Le nozze degli dei favola* (1637). The enthroned Pluto and his court face a blazing inferno of satyrs and flying monsters as a heavenly chariot appears in a central sky effect.

Setting by Alfonso Parigi for the tenth intermezzo of the fourth act of *Le nozze degli dei favola*. Work continues in Vulcan's cell as the heavens open, and figures battle in the foreground.

The second intermezzo designed by Giulio Parigi for *La liberazione di Tirreno* (1617). A gargantuan satanic figure towers over monsters in an inferno.

An ideal pastoral landscape created by Jones for the main masque of Jonson's *Chloridia*. The scene stresses "delightful variety" through its depiction of streams, waterfalls, a central mount, and wooded hills.

An eighteenth-century Hell scene with limited depth and dimension in Elkanah Settle's *The Empress of Morocco* (1673). The few surviving stage
designs for English heroic operas of the Dryden period suggest that eighteenth-century stage effects were restricted in perspective and spectacle.

A bower used to frame featured masquers is placed centrally amid wooded mountainsides in this design by Jones for Davenant's *Salmacida Spolia* (1640).

Jones's design for the cloud descent of a heavenly figure

The figure Spring designed by Jones for Jonson's *Chloridia*. Milton includes a masquelike presentation of a similar figure in *Paradise Lost* (IV.226–268).

Jones's design for a goddess dressed in the manner of Iris. The figure Iris, mentioned by Milton in *Comus* (83) and in *Paradise Lost* (XI.244), appeared in Jonson's *Hymenaei* (1606).

A knight masquer created by Jones possibly for Jonson's *Hymenaei*. The figure wears a typical military masquing costume with plume, helm, shield, and sword. In *Paradise Lost* the angel Michael is depicted "Clad to meet Man" in very similar garments dipped in "Iris . . . woof" (XI.240, 244).

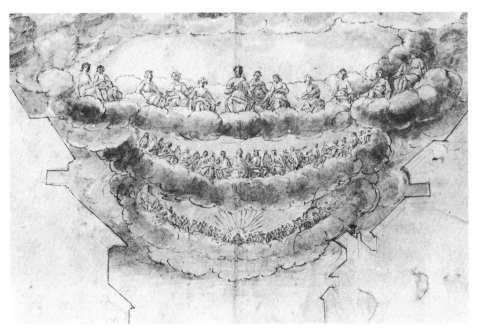

The "whole Heaven" designed by Jones for Davenant's *Salmacida Spolia*

Design by Bernardo Buontalenti for the first intermezzo, "L'armonia delle sfere," of *La pellegrina* presented in Florence in 1589

Lucifer Is Discovered

The fallen Archfiend in the third outline, appearing for the first time in Act III, wanders alone through the earthly paradise "contriving Adams ruin" (TCM, 35). In the fouth draft also, which is not divided into acts, Satan enters the Garden "after his overthrow, bemoans himself, seeks revenge on man." The Tempter's evil designs and presence in Eden elicit a sharp response: "The Chorus prepare resistance at his first approach at last after discourse of enmity on either side he departs" (TCM, 40).

Satan, approaching Eden in Book IV of *Paradise Lost*, will again "bemoan" himself in the famous soliloquy to the sun, a soliloquy that Edward Phillips identified as having been written very early as part of a "tragedy." The Archfiend in Book IV will roam through the Garden before espying Adam and Eve; and the Fiend will be driven off after having been resisted in a hostile encounter with the angel Gabriel.

The First Parents' Ideal Existence and Fall

The greatest scholarly and critical enigma posed by the outlines concerns the core actions of Adam and Eve. The First Parents in all drafts enter *after* the Fall. Missing is any plan for the enactment of their happy marriage, Temptation, and Fall. What form did these actions initially take, commentators have asked, when Milton filled in this crucial theatrical "blank space" in the work-in-progress?

McColley and Gilbert, intrigued by Edward Phillips's quotation of lines from what presumably was a lost fifth draft of this "tragedy" of the Fall, assumed that Milton ordered this last version with a classical five-act structure.[7] The poet, they surmised, turned back to the five-act form listed only in the third outline and revised his work by including within this five-act structure previously missing episodes: Satan's lament to the sun during the journey to Eden; the ideal and innocent marriage of the First Parents in the Garden; Satan's temptation of Eve; and the Fall of Eve and then Adam. But it seems to me that Samuel Johnson was more critically perspicacious when he wrote in *The Lives of the Poets* that "in the *Mask of Comus* may very plainly be discovered the dawn or twilight of *Paradise Lost*."[8]

The only lines that Phillips quoted from the lost draft, lines later declaimed by Satan in Book IV, have been observed to be a rhetorical paraphrase of a passage about the sun in *Comus*. It should now be obvious that the most immediate theatrical model for Eve's temptation was the Lady's temptation in Milton's masque, that the theme of man's rational power to stand or fall served as the "hinge" for *Comus* and

Tempe Restored in which Lady Alice Egerton played roles.[9] Even the innocent nuptial delights of the unfallen First Parents in Milton's Eden, pleasures generally foreign to the *sacra rappresentazione* and to classical epic and classical theatrical literature, will be shown to have their source in masque tradition. For in writing of the Fall as a unique sacred spectacle derived in part from the Italian *tragedie di lieto fine*, Milton was influenced as well by the genre actually mentioned in the fourth outline: the masque.

The First Parents' Anguish and Punishment

The First Parents step forth "fallen" in the third draft as "Conscience cites them to God's examination," and a "chorus bewails and tells the good Adam hath lost." The themes of loss and divine punishment ring much more forcefully in the fourth draft when

> man next & Eve having by this time bin seduc't by the serpent appeares confusedly cover'd with leaves conscience in a shape accuses him, Justice cites him to the place whither Jehova call'd for him. in the mean while the chorus entertains the stage, & his inform'd by some angel the manner of his fall Adam then & Eve returne accuse one another but especially Adam layes the blame to his wife, is stubborn in his offence.

This action will have its fulfillment in the epic when the First Parents, clothed in leaves, bitterly blame each other for their plight and suffer pangs of conscience. God's justice is visited upon them when the Son descends to the Garden and announces their punishment.

Man's Future Foretold

Personified character-types introduced at the conclusion of all four drafts suggest the themes Milton will emphasize in Books XI and XII of *Paradise Lost:* man's future ills and eventual Redemption. The figures Death, Labour, Sickness, Discontent, and Ignorance appear in the first three drafts; and the personified theological virtues Faith, Hope, and Charity are introduced at the end of each list and thus point to man's deliverance from evil. In the third draft the theological virtues speak to Adam "to Comfort him and instruct him." This action is greatly expanded in the final draft when Milton writes of Adam:

> Justice appeares reason with him convinces him   the Angel is sent to banish them out of paradise but before causes to passe before his eyes in shapes a mask of all the evils of this life & world he is humbl'd relents, dispaires. at last appeares Mercy comforts him &

brings in faith hope & charity promises the Messiah, then calls in faith, hope, & charity, instructs him he repents gives god the glory, submitts to his penalty the chorus breifly concludes.

IN LOOKING back over this amalgam of materials from sacred representation, Continental theatrical spectacle, and masque, one observes Milton, early in the composition of a work on the Fall, listing in his initial two drafts good and evil character-types, crossing them out, and then making notes in a third draft for a representation in five acts. Action will take place in Heaven or on a heavenly mountain, in the Garden of Eden, and in the world outside the Garden. Yet the poet in a fourth draft gives up the five-act structure, envisages the use of stage machines and special scenic effects, merges present with future events, but keeps action centered upon the First Parents in the Garden.

Although Arthur Barker and others have argued that a five-act structure, originating in Milton's evolving theatrical outlines, can be discerned in *Paradise Lost,* such claims seem to me an oversimplified and rigid imposition of a single classical and Elizabethan theatrical form upon works that grow from varied Renaissance theatrical genres.[10] Milton in his short fourth outline, comprising one paragraph, makes only one glancing allusion to an "act." He notes that the chorus's song of creation, performed following Gabriel's entrance, is sung "after the first act" rather than after what McColley and others have presumed to be the first two acts. Indeed, Gabriel's approach to Eden and exchanges with the chorus do appear to be, not a two-act segment in the planned work, but a single, unified introductory action. This theatrical prologue is followed by the antic representation of the consequences of the First Parents' Fall; then the fourth draft ends with a promise of a future Triumph, as the figure Mercy predicts mankind's salvation. Suggested classical conventions are evident in Milton's interspersing of action with choral song and in the poet's employment of the "unities" of time, place, and action; but in general Milton can be seen moving in the fourth draft away from a five-act structure toward a more flexible Renaissance theatrical form, one that deftly interweaves minor spectacles, patterned actions, opposed character-types, intermezzi, choral interludes, and acted-out visions of the future.

In expanding this outlined theatrical work, Milton presumably took his own advice and compared themes, characters, and actions in the third and fourth outlines. He then would have probably introduced into the lost fifth draft, as commentators have suggested, a descent by Satan to the Garden followed by scenes in Eden of the marriage,

Temptation, and Fall of the First Parents. A visionary "mask" of the future would have been included near the end of the work; and the poet's theatrical writings together with sacred representations, masques, and Continental spectacles would have strongly influenced the invention, disposition, and ornamentation of all these episodes.

Because Milton's sacred show, in the manner of the later epic, is resolved with the promise of man's eventual Redemption, the planned work, though containing immediate tragic overtones, would not have been in any Aristotelian or Elizabethan sense a formal tragedy, the term used by Phillips. The major incidents in the planned prophetical representation do not depict directly that steady ascent from low to high estate that passed as a medieval and early Renaissance definition of "comedy." In the most obvious example of this form, Dante's *Commedia*, the Florentine poet descends to the depths of Hell in the first third of the poem but then ascends Mount Purgatory and flies through the spheres to Heaven in the final two thirds. Even during Dante's physical descent into the inferno, the poet, unlike Adam and Eve, fails in small ways but in general rises intellectually as he acquires knowledge that increasingly fortifies him against sin and prepares him for spiritual conversion and beatific vision. Milton's prophetical show stresses instead, not a continuous intellectual and spiritual ascent, but a decisive personal Fall followed by terrible suffering. Yet Milton, by concluding the work with the miraculous promise of man's future spiritual victory, creates a planned representation with some affinities to masques and to court spectacles that end in triumph. Adam and Eve, of course, fall and so lose the earthly paradise, but their Fall will paradoxically lead to the Triumph of Redemption.[11]

After deciding to transform his developed sacred representation into an epic, Milton would have turned to "Sodom Burning" and to classical and Christian writings on demonic regions in depicting the epic's infernal world. Scenes in Hell would serve as an antic counterpart to scenes on earth and in Heaven, and the new work would conclude with a series of visionary intermezzi. The expanding materials at his disposal were thus leading Milton to represent not only mortal heroic characters in particular places at specific times but also immortal divine and demonic beings in eternity. The speeches and actions of these beings would necessarily reflect a divine or demonic perspective, and future readers, in imaginative empathy with such viewpoints, would be projected into the bewildering paradoxes of the infinite. An epic representation of this kind, evolved from Milton's theatrical outlines, would appear to defy the constrictions of traditional heroic conventions and structures.

Yet because Milton was composing a narrative that is poetically sung rather than a theatrical show that is directly enacted, the poet introduced an epic narrator who recounts all theatrical and other events from an illumined but human viewpoint, who gives a distinct sense of heroic individuation to settings and to mortal and immortal characters, and who places actions occurring even in Hell and Heaven within a comprehensible past, present, and future time frame.[12] As the narrator explains, "Time, though in Eternity, appli'd / To motion, measures all things durable" (V.580–581).

In structuring subject matter that Milton's epic narrator claimed was "more Heroic" than the content of Virgil's *Aeneid* and Homer's *Iliad* and *Odyssey*, the poet found it necessary to rely not only on conceptions of the theatrical epic held by Christian writers such as Pareus but also on Renaissance interpretations of those poetic principles of Aristotle thought to govern heroic and dramatic works. Renaissance theorists including Mazzoni, Tasso, and Scaliger insisted that the epic, which they said is invented primarily to elicit from readers experiences of "wonder" in heroic deeds rather than tragic pity and fear, necessarily ranged over events separated in time and place.[13] The commentators consequently agreed that Aristotle's supposed demand for a restriction in dramatic works of time, place, and action applied only to tragedies. The precept requiring action to begin in *medias res*, however, was said to hold for the epic as well as the tragic form; and the theorists anxiously urged epic poets to attempt a relative "unification" of time and place in their works by introducing into a sequential narrative accounts or visions of past and future events.

Milton, using the human viewpoint of the epic voice, imposed the unities to a large degree upon *Paradise Lost*. The narrator first sings of "present" scenes unfolding in Hell and its environs in Books I and II and then in Heaven in Book III, scenes in these different realms that nevertheless direct interest upon the present activities of the First Parents in Eden. The narrator next sings of present episodes in the Garden in Books IV through XII. On occasion the narrator's song turns in the last nine books to brief, interrelated present scenes in Hell and Heaven. But in general through the narrator's use of flashbacks and visions of the future, the main arena of events remains the Garden of Eden.

Milton realized that action in *medias res* might best be established by depicting Satan vowing immortal hatred against God and man from the seat of infernal power in Hell. The action could then be shifted to the figures opposite Satan: God the Father and Son in Heaven exhibiting infinite justice and mercy toward man.[14] The First Parents, the central figures who absorb the attention of both Satan and God, would be introduced rather late. But as Milton surely knew, authority for such a disposition of epic material was provided in the *Odyssey* with the heroic Odysseus appearing initially in Book V. Milton in the first three books, then, discloses how the powers of Hell and Heaven move to influence the destiny of man. Satan in Hell plots and then sets out to seduce man into sin; the son in Heaven volunteers to die for man and so redeem him.

Milton set the rest of the work dominantly in Eden emphasizing the Fall and episodes leading up to and following that catastrophic human mistake. The flashbacks to heavenly history before the Fall and the prophetic insights into future human events that come after it—all narrated by angels in the Garden for the spiritual enlightenment of Adam and Eve—place the battle between good and evil in Eden into the wider context of the cosmic struggle between the creative and destructive forces of the universe.

In inventing Book IX of the 1667 edition, a segment that became Book X in the 1674 version, Milton allowed the unfolding action to focus briefly upon the Father and Son in Heaven responding to man's Fall, upon Sin and Death approaching Eden as the new conquerors of man, and upon Satan and his cohorts in Hell being punished for the corruption of man. Yet, from this part of the work through the end, the center of action remains the Garden of Eden.

When Milton published the 10,550 lines of the 1667 edition, he obviously conceived the human consequences of the First Parents' sin as thematically unified by the paradox of the fortunate Fall. He consequently included in the final tenth book of the 1667 edition depictions of the First Parents' repentance of sin, Adam's prophetic discovery of the future suffering and eventual salvation of man, and the First Parents' banishment from Eden.

When Milton reorganized and enlarged his epic, he kept the divisions of the first six books essentially the same. Book VII of the 1667 edition, which contained accounts of God's creation of the universe and of Adam, was separated to form Books VII and VIII in the 1674 version. Books VIII and IX of the earlier ten-book edition thus became Books IX and X, respectively. What was originally Book X appeared divided as Books XI and XII in 1674. And in the expanded epic, a total of fifteen lines were added. Three new lines (1–3) in later Book VIII and five new lines (1–5) in later Book XII effect more suitable transitions between books. The other additions seem to be final, incidental alterations within the new twelve-book design: in Book V three new lines (636, 638–639) enlarge a two-line passage about angels to five lines; and in later Book XI three new lines (485–587) elaborate a passage on death. A single line (551) in early Book X appears expanded as two lines (551–552) in later Book XI.

In both editions of *Paradise Lost*, the patterns of harmony, opposition, and repetition evident in the form and content of *Comus* and some of the theatrical outlines were obviously augmented and intricately developed. Anne Davidson Ferry, Michael Lieb, Rosalie Colie, Burton Weber, William B. Madsen, and others have pointed out Milton's extraordinary balance of plots and subplots, typological relationships, dialectical arguments, sounds, movements, character-types, and scenes.[15] In addition, it has recently been proposed that throughout the epic Milton's verse embodies Pythagorean numerical components carefully aligned or obversely arranged with near-mechanical precision.

James Whaler and John T. Shawcross argue that the 1667 edition is superior in numerical design to the 1674 version. Whaler maintains that in the ten-book edition different kinds of patterned metrical "formations" or passages, each having its own dominant Pythagorean number, are arranged in alternating series under the controlling numbers 1–2–3–4 and 4–3–2–1. The first combination of numbers is said to suggest affirmation and perfection; the second, negation and sin. The whole ten-book work, Whaler believes, can thus be read in Pythagorean fashion in terms of multiple ascents and descents embedded within the edition's 10,550 lines, 10,550 supposedly being a perfect number. On the basis of his mathematical interpretation, Whaler thinks that Milton wished to create an epic in twelve books but that mathematical considerations prompted the poet to produce initially a ten-book work.[16]

Shawcross discerns an overall "pyramidic construction" in what he believes to be a bipartite balance in the 1667 edition. Although he considers Adam and Eve the chief protagonists in the work, he avers that Satan dominates the first half of the epic; God, the second half; and at the epic's midpoint (VI.761–762), the Son ascends to Heaven just before defeating Satan on the third day of battle. The first 5,275 lines of the 1667 version are said to be devoted to the cause of the Fall and the last 5,275 lines to the effect, the fortunate Fall. So successful are various intricate correspondences and balances in the bipartite structure said to be that, in Shawcross's view, Milton could not have been "happy with the reorganization of the second edition." Shawcross writes that Milton "must have been reasoned into reorganization: sell more books, reach more people."[17]

J. B. Watson and Galbraith Crump, on the other hand, have suggested that Milton renumbered the books for the 1674 edition to achieve a new and superior structural symmetry. Watson contends that Milton sought to highlight the struggle between creative virtue and destructive evil, a struggle allegedly reaching its climax at the center of the epic in Books VI and VII, by placing five books on either side of the supposed central action. Watson then finds symmetrical and asymmetrical relationships by contrasting Books I and II with XII; III with X; and IV with IX.[18]

Crump prefers the twelve-book to the ten-book version because, he maintains, Milton effectively changes his "emphasis from Pythagorean to Christian numerology. In place of the closed perfection of the number 10, he introduces in the number 12 ... the circular vision that opens the way to God." Crump interprets the 1674 edition as a "vast hieroglyph" constructed in a circular "reflexive pattern" that turns back upon itself. "Adopting the traditional symbol of God as a point or circle, the center and circumference of all things," Crump writes, "Milton fashioned his poem to embody that symbol in its largest structural design."[19]

These divergent mathematical and thematic readings disclose, I think, important patterns and textures in a poem replete with intricate polarities, balances, and alignments. And the readings call attention to Milton's disposition of certain Triumphs of the Son in flashbacks near the center of the epic. The mathematical-thematic speculations nevertheless remain, in my view, tenuous as precise explanations of the basic structure of *Paradise Lost*. The methodical computation of lines and the "flat," book-by-book definition of related themes tend to obscure subtle inflections in point of view, aesthetic emphasis, and character disguising. Episodes are fitted too mechanically into presumed mathematical schemes. Narrative flashbacks to divine history, because of their "numerical" position, frequently receive greater critical stress than foreground action involving the First Parents. Although such readings usefully point to the Triumphs of the Son and, by contrast, the anti-Triumphs of Satan, they sometimes distract attention from the Fall and future Triumph of man. Milton's epic universe, of course, flows from and is centered upon God, the creator and sustainer of being and the victor over the forces of evil. But Milton's epic action centers upon the First Parents in Eden as they waver between the powers of Hell and Heaven.

In any event, a comprehensive mathematical structure for *Paradise Lost* could only have been superimposed by Milton—with laborious addition, subtraction, and counting of thousands of lines—upon numerous completed and rearranged verse segments composed over a period of years. The fundamental underlying form of *Paradise Lost* obviously developed from planned sacred shows about Adam and Eve, shows gradually subsumed within classical and Renaissance epic conventions. The division of the poem into twelve books was most likely made by Milton, whether or not he was influenced by mathematical concerns, so that the work would have a traditional epic structure to match its traditional epic blank-verse form.

Obvious in the book divisions of the 1674 edition are those elements that Milton originally envisaged in theatrical terms and, conscious of the unities, later ordered in the narrative of the epic voice. Demonic action in a city of the damned (Book I) and a debate among devils and their punishment in or near a temple of that city (Books II and X) contrast with the divine debate and the rituals of praise upon a mount of God (Book III). These demonic and divine episodes direct interest toward theatrical scenes in and near Eden: Lucifer's approach to the Garden and the Fiend's movements in disguise in Eden (Books IV and V); the First Parents' prelapsarian love and marriage (Books IV and V); the angelic accounts in Eden of God's creation of man and the universe (Books VII and VIII); the First Parents' Temptation and Fall (Book IX); the visions and recitations in Eden of man's future suffering but ultimate future Triumph (Books XI and XII); and the banishment of Adam and Eve from the Garden (Book XII).

In creating a Christian epic that reflects a transformed masque of opposites in the first ten books and a transformed, visionary processional masque in the last two books, Milton both used and reordered classical epic devices and themes. In Virgil's twelve-book *Aeneid*, for example, narrated flashbacks appear in Books II and III, athletic games in Book V, prophecies in Book VI, and battles in Books IX through XII. Milton, accommodating his Christian subject and also its underlying theatrical representation, retained but rearranged Virgilian epic elements by incorporating into *Paradise Lost* athletic games in Book II, flashbacks that include a battle in Books V through VIII, and prophecies in Books XI and XII.

Employing a staggering range of classical, biblical, and secular literary sources, Milton thus forged his work using the conventions of the classical epic yet manipulating materials never before merged in "Prose or Rhyme." He pens an invocation classical in form but dedicated to a Holy Spirit whose Christian inspiration is said to reign on Mount Sinai and Mount Sion. The opening statement of theme by the epic narrator draws in content from Genesis. A heroic simile of the kind found in the *Iliad,* the *Odyssey,* and the *Aeneid* compares Satan to Leviathan of the Bible and to the Titans of pagan myth. The devils' military maneuvers in Hell are borrowed in large measure from parades in Tasso's *Jerusalem Delivered;* Satan's shield from Achilles' in the *Iliad* and from images associated with the new astronomy; and Hell itself from the underworlds of classical myths and the infernos of Dante, Tasso, and biblical tradition. The epic conventions are there—the great orations, divine transformations, councils of immortals, wars, heroic journeys— but conflated within a vast design embracing, through foreshadowed and fulfilled typological relationships, crucial events in universal Christian history. From the past "begetting" of the Son to the future Redemption and Second Coming, Milton presents his epic of the human race through a narrator who sings of the revolt of the angels, the Creation, the Fall, God's judgment of man and Satan, Cain's slaying of Abel, the Flood, the Tower of Babel, and the Exodus. This universal history, hinged upon the Fall and the promised Redemption, is acted out in that cosmos of boundless space discovered by the new astronomy, a cosmos that Milton also allows to harbor the concentric spheres of the old Ptolemaic astronomy. Yet the events are given coherence by the regulated, human narration of the epic voice.

By constructing his work from theatrical scenes disclosing antithetical extremes of action and argumentation, Milton filled *Paradise Lost* with a wealth of internal argumentation and conflict engendered by characters who "speak" both through words and through the emblematic movements and visual images of the theatrical arts. God the Father and Son present the divine Argument of godhood. Satan declaims and plays out the demonic view. Adam and Eve give expression to the argument of innocent and then fallen man, and various immortal beings further speak and act out the epic disputation between corruption and regeneration, between evil and good.

The stress Milton placed upon internal argumentation may well have confused some early readers. "There was no Argument at first intended to the Book," wrote printer Samuel Simmons in 1667 when the poet did not submit a separate prose synopsis for publication with the epic. Milton doubtless believed, and quite correctly, that the epic itself made the "great Argument." However, in his preface to the second printing of the ten-book version of *Paradise Lost* in 1668, Simmons added that the Argument, "for the satisfaction of many that have desired it, is procur'd."[20] Milton, then, had been prevailed upon to write for each book a prose summary that appeared in the second and all subsequent printings.

Such prose statements were unnecessary. The essential narrative, evaluative song of the epic voice controls the sequence and presentation of the divers arguments and enacted events, conflates these elements into the epic narrative structure, and states the great Argument of godhood from a human perspective and with a powerful compassion for the First Parents. The influence of the voice upon the tone, meaning, and form of the work can never, therefore, be expunged by removing individual passages; for *Paradise Lost* is an epic because, among other reasons, the voice sings every line of the poem. But by imagining radical excisions and changes, it is nevertheless possible to uncover the subsumed theatrical core of *Paradise Lost*.

Delete the epic narrator's invocations, commentary, and ordered interweaving of episodes; retain the name of each speaker and the dialogue; include suitable stage directions, particularly for Adam's final visions of the future; and *Paradise Lost*, unlike other major Western epics, would read rather well as an unprecedented, visionary sacred representation, a massively enlarged series of prophetical scenes having considerable inherent theatrical structure and incorporating disguisings that culminate in various antic and holy triumphs. The immediately enacted addresses and episodes and the flashbacks, future visions, and accounts within the enacted episodes themselves propel the thematically interrelated events onward and disclose didactic and symbolic meaning. Opposed events in Hell and Heaven focus upon and find their fulfillment in events in the Garden of Eden and in the promise of future events upon earth.[21] There are many dramatic encounters, but heroic melodrama is avoided, largely through the device of disguising, which gives symbolic dimension to good, evil, and corrupt character-types. As in a masque, an overall sense of drama within limited settings is dispelled as disguised and revealed character-types perform, in different parts of the universe, actions that would seem to overflow any circumscribed stage area. The action, though it has significant thematic and structural cohesion, nevertheless unfolds somewhat disparately both in the mortal world and in an eternity of boundless space; for now the human epic narrator neither introduces and intermeshes incidents nor evaluates the pronouncements and movements of immortal beings. Such was the theatrical work that Dryden vaguely perceived in *Paradise Lost* but, without an understanding of the poem's theatrical form and aesthetic workings, failed to reproduce "in little" on an imagined stage within a five-act structure.[22]

When the invocations and commentary of the epic voice and all the other narrative materials are replaced and when the verse is divided into books following the pattern of the 1674 edition, then *Paradise Lost* in genre becomes a Western epic with unusual Christian content set within a classical twelve-book form.

IV

The Anti-Triumphs of Hell

L IKE the infernal flames twisting in darkness visible,
Milton's Hell glitters with unholy paradoxes. It is a realm
of grand illusion. Because evil lurks as the dislocating reality beneath
inflated public disguises, appearances in Hell shift, alter, and contort
into surrealistic relationships. Distortions at once unmask depraved
characters and objects even as they are being rendered in supposedly
glorious trappings. In no other poem has Milton so obviously and
pointedly used a disguising to disclose inner depravity.

Outwardly, the inhabitants of Hell manifest a superficial facade of
wealth, grandeur, freedom, and reason, a facade whose overall effect
has since the Restoration beguiled many readers unable or unwilling to
perceive the grotesqueries that disfigure this lavish show. An irrevoca-
ble gulf separates the crassly pretentious external appearances of Satan
and his legions from the inner meanness of their desperate souls. And
however passionate, willful, and unyielding critics have found them to
be in their roles as anti-heroes, these figures are in their deepest natures
beings in states of never-ending dissociation and disintegration. It is the
Archfiend and his followers who make of the eternal ruin of Hell,
masked in its veil of illusion, a big, noisy kaleidoscope of vain posturing, confused philosophy, empty rhetoric, puffed-up pageantry, and
pompous architecture.

The theatrical pattern of demonic action constituting the epic plot
can now be seen as a direct development of narrative themes in Milton's masque, outlined sacred dramas, and Latin exercise *On the Fifth
of November:* a crew assembled and led forward by a commanding figure to a palace with a throne (Book I); a sharp debate among figures
before that throne (Book II); a temptation at the navel of a wood (Book

IX); and a punishment or anti-triumph of evil figures at the palace and throne.

In scenes set in Hell, gestures, external shapes, and public declamations display the excesses of the region. Movements are too high or too low, too irregular or too exquisitely mannered. Physical beings are too gigantic or too diminutive, too magnificent or too simple, too dim or too bright. Speeches are too grand or too obsequious, too vain or too despairing, too passionate or too imaginative. When balanced external proportions are evident in Hell, actions and orations express disproportion within. All the beings of Hell are riven with contradictions.

Hell contains, for example, "many a Region dolorous" (II.619) in which, the epic narrator records,

> ... Nature broods,
> Perverse, all monstrous, all prodigious things,
> Abominable, inutterable.[1]

In a gulf on the frozen continent, "the parching Air / Burns frore, the cold performs th' effect of Fire." There the damned suffer through "fierce extremes, extremes by change more fierce" (594–599).

In Book I the "Angel Forms, who lay intrans't / Thick as Autumnal Leaves" (301–302) arise in swarms from their extreme stupor and soon display extreme fury: "highly they rag'd / Against the Highest, and ... / Clash'd on thir sounding shields the din of war" (666–668). Their dissonant shouting "tore Hell's Concave" (542). And in the very act of building Pandemonium, they injure and destroy. The devils "Op'n'd into the Hill a spacious wound" (689) and "Rifl'd the bowels of thir mother Earth" (687), for perverse demonic destruction opposes God's divine creation of earth. Later, in Book II, the individual "inclination or sad choice" of each rebel angel "Leads him perplext" into bewildering activity (524–525). Those philosophizing find "no end, in wand'ring mazes lost" (561). As a penalty for their rationally confused but emotionally unrestrained complicity in evil, the devils in Book X experience the last of several physical transformations:

> They felt themselves now changing; down thir arms,
> Down fell both Spear and Shield, down they as fast,
> And the dire hiss renew'd, and the dire form
> Catcht by Contagion, like in punishment,
> As in thir crime.   (541–545)

The most striking disharmonies are reserved for Satan, whose "bulk" is said to be as huge as fabled beings "of monstrous size" (I.196–197). The Archfiend is first described ignobly "rolling in the fiery Gulf / Confounded" (52–53). But with implied contradictory movement, he "upright . . . rears" (221) and is soon "uplifted beyond hope" (II.7) enthroned in a palace more grossly gargantuan than "*Babel*, and the works of *Memphian* Kings" (I.694). Amid exaggerated outward pomp and savage splendor, the Archfiend presides over an excessively huge infernal court consisting of "A thousand Demi-Gods on golden seats" (796). Before them looms the demonic state:

> High on a Throne of Royal State, which far
> Outshone the wealth of *Ormus* and of *Ind*
> Or where the gorgeous East with richest hand
> Show'rs on her Kings *Barbaric* Pearl and Gold,
> Satan exalted sat, by merit rais'd
> To that bad eminence. (II.1–6)

After volunteering in front of the devils to be the seducer of man, the Archfiend journeys to the Gate of Hell. He there meets and scornfully addresses Sin and Death, the other members of the unholy trinal family that is the antithesis of the traditional three persons in God. Satan and his only Son, Death, raise spears against each other in an action that is the exact opposite of the unified, harmonious enthronement of the Father and Son in Heaven. Then the Fiend, traveling forward into Chaos, ascends in flight but soon "vain plumb down he drops / Ten thousand fadom deep" (933–934). Satan leaves Chaos and, approaching the sphere of the Sun, briefly disguises himself as a stripling cherub. With outward luster dimming, the Archfiend flies to earth and moves to the wall of Eden, where "At one slight bound" he "high overleap'd all bound" (IV.181). In the Garden the Fiend, transforming in appearance from angel to beast, moves and acts like a cormorant and then a toad and subsequently enters into the bodies of four-footed animals and finally into the body of a serpent.

In these scenes and in all that follow the revolt of the angels in Heaven, the fixed, consistently drawn inner soul of the Fiend does not "repent or change" (I.96) its eternal hatred for God or its eternal desire for revenge. Yet Satan, in his soul and entire being, also forever "back recoils / Upon himself" (IV.17–18) in eternal, restless change. The forever changeless and forever changing character of Satan is but one of the many paradoxes of the Fiend's nature, which perplexes discursive reason but is made aesthetically acceptable by Milton's theology and art. The consistency of the satanic portrait throughout *Paradise Lost* resides in inconsistencies that are successfully absorbed and reflected in a single monstrous personality of enormous energy, power, and will. By merging antithetical elements in the Fiend's nature, Milton in a heroic poem utilizes *discordia concors* to project a protean but coherent demonic consciousness.

The paradoxes and problems of Satan's nature are various and confounding. From the standpoint of the Aristotelian-Ramist logic that Milton espoused, Satan as metaphysical contrariety embodies no truth and has no existence. Having once vowed "To wage by force or guile eternal War" against the perfection of God (I.121), the Archfiend becomes, in Milton's syllogistic logic, a contradiction and ceases to be. The Fiend's statement "Evil be thou my good" (IV.110) is in context a declaration of nonbeing. Yet, given the poem's dominating artistic and theological values, Satan convincingly arises as an entirely malignant personality that remains both fixed and endlessly recoiling in immortal hatred. With consistent inconsistency Satan assumes a series of sometimes jarringly discordant roles that are essential to his nature as Deceiver. Within the framework of the narrative, the Archfiend degenerates internally and externally as his angelic brightness progressively dims, as he takes on outward shapes ranging from cherub to serpent, as he makes a series of corrupt irrational choices, and as he descends in pseudoheroic postures from warrior-leader to infernal king and cunning diplomat, to adventurous traveler, to lurking spy in Eden, to disguised, ingratiating tempter. But the Fiend never wavers in basic motivation and purpose: Satan seeks a victory over God by open war or by guile; the Archfiend's attack upon man is indirectly an attack upon God. The postures and roles juxtapose in Book IX when Satan rises for a few moments to a mysterious height of fallen vanity and, appearing from blazing light, announces to the devils in Hell an assumed final victory over man. Then the Fiend, like the devils, is transformed into a last hideous shape: "down he fell / A monstrous Serpent on his Belly prone" (X.513–514). The epic narrator enigmatically explains that "some say" the punishment will be repeated throughout eternity (575).

This strange seventeenth-century Hell has grown even stranger because it has been viewed so frequently through the disorienting shadows and lights of the Restoration and the eighteenth-century criticism of Dryden, Byron, Hazlitt, Coleridge, Blake, and Shelley. These men wrote against the background of middle-class English culture after the aristocratic tradition of Renaissance disguising had become archaic, and they often failed to note fully the inner and outer distortions of Hell and its denizens. Romantic and neoclassical sensibilities, though often critically incisive, were in general not adequately conscious of all the pseudoheroic qualities of a satan and a hell born from the unification of then outmoded theatrical forms with traditional biblical and epic materials. John M. Steadman rightly describes many of the earliest readers of Milton's *Paradise Lost* as puzzled: "Some of them disagreed violently on such crucial issues as the *genre* of his [Milton's] poem, its hero, and its fidelity to the rules of epic poetry. A few of them approached his work with the mingled admiration and dismay a Homeric scholar might experience on first opening Joyce's *Ulysses.*"[2]

Coleridge did point out that the Fiend's aura of grandeur coexisted with a fundamental depravity; and Shelley, in the preface to *Prometheus Unbound*, considered Milton's Satan flawed in comparison with Prometheus.[3] But it was primarily sympathetic comment about Satan by Shelley, Byron, Hazlitt, and Blake—Coleridge stressed mainly the sublime but pernicious character of the Fiend—that stimulated the long, misdirected, and by now conventional discussions of whether Milton in the words of Blake's narrator is "a true poet and of the Devil's party without knowing it."[4]

The many sophisticated insights provided by representatives of the Romantic "Satanist" school exempt these commentators from the charge that they were uncritical of the Archfiend and his realm.[5] Yet it is evident that, in rebelling against eighteenth-century middle-class culture and art, they often empathized with Satan without demonstrating sufficient cognizance of his false, theatrical masks.[6] Quite frequently the Tempter's disguise was mistaken for reality, and his uncontrolled sublime fury, disproportionate size, pretended egalitarian sympathies, and flawed rhetorical arguments were taken out of context and praised as having positive value. Because poetic contexts and Milton's verbal appeal to all the theatrical arts were ignored, the clear, structured political and aesthetic content of *Paradise Lost* was to a large degree reversed. Satan was extolled for having the qualities of an emotional, libertarian rebel, and God the Father condemned for having the traits of a vindictive tyrant.

This small but influential group among a large number of Romantics left a legacy of critical unease for nineteenth- and twentieth-century commentators. Deep disparities in the poem had been experienced and variously reported, doubts raised about the "true" aesthetic and moral values of both the work and its author. Yet, the origins of the epic's disparities in Renaissance disguising had not been adequately uncovered and examined.

Largely because modern critics, following the precedent of this group of Romantics, continue to confuse disguise for reality in *Paradise Lost*, the problem of poetic and personal dissociations troubles even recent commentary. Critics project onto the character of God the Father, the epic narrator, the author Milton, or the modern reader dislocations and deficiencies that reside primarily in evil and corrupt figures and realms within the epic.

T. S. Eliot quoted an illogical and emotional speech by Satan in an attempt to demonstrate that a "dissociated sensibility" existed, not in the Archfiend, but in Milton.[7] F. R. Leavis soon joined Eliot in arguing that Milton, because of personal limitations of sensibility, indecorously divorced rhetorical devices in verse from appropriate poetic meaning.[8] A. J. A. Waldock, J. B. Broadbent, and John Peter find alleged disparities between what the epic narrator, usually identified as Milton, says about Satan and God the Father and the way these eternal beings are depicted, between the theological content of the poem and its aesthetic representation.[9] William Empson, however, discerns no serious deficiencies in the sensibilities of either Milton or Satan. Empson argues instead that in *Paradise Lost* dissociations are to be discovered in God the Father.[10] He also claims that Milton, in poetically drawing the Supreme Being, reflected and sought unsuccessfully to overcome defects and contradictions in the God of Christianity. Stanley Fish, on the other hand, shifts the dissociations to "the reader in *Paradise Lost*." According to Fish, Milton consciously tries to tempt the reader again and again into a partial acceptance of sin and then to surprise the reader into a more refined recognition of good and evil.[11]

It must be acknowledged that *Paradise Lost*, an epic written in short passages over many years, contains numerous inconsistencies, that the epic narrator's perspective differs from the outlook of the major figures, that the representation of God as a "perfect" character is deficient, and that some modern readers may indeed be occasionally drawn toward sin and then shocked into virtue as they peruse Milton's lines. But it must also be averred that most of the basic irregularities associated with the poem are not those of Milton, the epic narrator, the reader, or the figure of God; rather, they are disparities consciously introduced by Milton into the evil characters, events, and realms of *Paradise Lost*. A balanced critical approach to the epic demands that these dissociations be clearly recognized within narrative and poetic contexts.

Had *Paradise Lost* been published during the Stuart period before the demise of the English court masque, sophisticated aristocrats, it seems to me, would have easily penetrated the emotive, rhetorical, and physical disguises of Satan and his realm while at the same time accepting the objectively stated evaluations of the epic narrator. Educated primarily in grammar, rhetoric, and logic at Latin grammar schools and at the universities, born to a centuries-old tradition of pre-Lenten and holiday disguising, observing and participating in masques, entertainments, and triumphal processions in country and city, such aristocrats would have recognized Satan as a rabble-rouser pretending to be a "leveler" but in fact acting the tyrant. They would have detected the Archfiend's well known antic ruses, his appeals to sophistic logic, his hidden but consummate ugliness, and his violations of hierarchical order and degree.

In recent years a number of commentators have realized that dissociations previously thought to be deficiencies in the epic, the narrator, the fallen reader, or Milton are consciously arranged and modulated revelations of evil characters, places, and actions. Jackson Cope, Raymond Waddington, and Thomas Kranidas, although unconcerned about theatrical sources, have pointed the way toward an appreciation of how Satan's distorted outward disguises as angel and beast unveil inner character.[12] Frank Kastor has turned to sacred representations such as Andreini's *L'Adamo* and Vondel's *Adam in Ballingschap* (1664) and *Lucifer* (1654) to argue that in characterization the Fiend is a "trimorph." Kastor has helpfully analyzed Satan as a figure compounded of "three related but distinguishable personages: a highly placed Archangel, a grisly Prince of Hell, and the deceitful, serpentine Tempter." "Usually," he writes, "the roles are unified by a single consciousness"; but Kastor pays insufficient attention to the unalterable qualities in the Fiend's paradoxical personality when he adds that "it is by no means uncommon to find the roles separated into distinctly separate characters."[13] Steadman, drawing upon archetypes of the hero in epic tradition, goes far in overcoming the difficulty by explaining the divergent "personages" as a series of "masks" obscuring a consistent character that "does not 'develop' (in the literal sense of the word)": Satan as pseudohero "wears a succession of heroic masks, shifting from one heroic formula to another as expediency dictates." In examining the "pattern of opposition between Satan and the Messiah," Steadman finds that only in the Archfiend's "mimicry of the Son of God" is the "heroic standard ... valid, but the Adversary perverts it." Steadman thus concludes that the Fiend is "a counter-image of the incarnate Word."[14]

Milton himself conceived and depicted both the pseudoheroic and the pseudogodly masks of demonic tyranny drawing upon elements in English masques and triumphs. In these works the English court acted

[63]

out in disguise the anti-heroic, heroic, and godly exemplars shadowed in the archetypes of *Paradise Lost*. Commoners became monsters; courtiers and ladies, heroes and heroines; and the king, a mirror of divine perfection. But as art critic Roy Strong has documented at length, Caroline masques, beginning with Carew's *Coelum Britannicum* (1634), contained compliments to the royal state so extravagant that the "relentless glorification" of the monarchy changed to "concrete deification." In the masques of Carew and Davenant, Strong correctly notes, "the Caroline court is not only a reflection of the virtues of Olympus, it is so marvellous and miraculous that heaven itself must be purged and model itself on this earthly court."[15] The monarch, courtiers, and ladies now play blasphemous roles.

Milton made startling use of this alteration in the nature of the theatrical compliment. Influenced by the Stuart masques of Jonson, Milton in *Comus* had praised the heroic virtue of a noble peer and placed this ruling, court-appointed aristocrat high on a theatrical chain of being under Jove. But in later prose writings after having become acutely critical of the institution of monarchy and its aristocratic supporters, he referred to the Caroline masques of Davenant in an attempt to demonstrate that homage to a tyrannical king is idolatry. Then in *Paradise Lost* he presented the devils' adoration of a tyrannical Satan on his chair of state as a comparable masquelike ritual of idolatry. Lavish pageantry employed to consolidate illegitimate political and religious power now seemed to Milton a sign of blasphemous vanity and an exercise in deceptive illusion.

"A king," writes Milton of Charles I in *The Ready and Easy Way to Establish a Free Commonwealth* (1660), "must be ador'd like a Demigod, with a dissolute and haughtie court about him, of vast expense and luxurie, masks and revels, to the debauching of our prime gentry, both male and female."[16] The monarch must "set a pompous face upon the superficial actings of the State, to pageant himself up and down in progress among the perpetual bowings and cringings of an abject people, on either side deifying and adoring him for nothing don that can deserve it." Milton therefore objects to the creations "of a late court poet," one who has been identifed as William Davenant, that present the king "like a great cypher set to no purpose before a long row of other significant figures" (p. 121).

Referring to the drawing of Charles I printed at the beginning of the promonarchist pamphlet *Eikon Basilike*, Milton lashes out in *Eikonoklastes* (1649) against "the conceited portraiture before his book, drawn out to the full measure of a masking scene, and set there to catch fools and silly gazers." What the author of the pamphlet "aims at," writes Milton alluding to the magic and the disorderly figures in masques, is a "worthles approbation of an inconstant, irrational, and Image-doting rabble; that like a credulous and hapless herd, begott'n to servility, and inchanted with these popular institutes of Tyranny, sub-scrib'd with a new device to the Kings Picture" (p. 309). Milton con-tends that the tyrant rules through deception, employing "quaint Emblems and devices begged from the old Pageantry of some Twelf-night's entertainment" (p. 68). Milton adds that the tyrant, in his role of evil masquer, is responsible for the dissonance, disorder, ugliness, and strangeness of antimasque performers: "On the Scene he thrusts out first an Antimasque of two bugbeares, *Noveltie* and *Perturbation*, that the ill looks and noise of those two, may as long as possible, drive off endeavours of a Reformation" (p. 247). Foreshadowing the hissing that Satan hears in the last infernal council scene in *Paradise Lost*, Milton writes that the English tyrant's failure to convene a full and free council, namely, parliament, has resulted in "the general voice of the people almost hissing him and his ill-acted regality off the Stage" (p. 78). In *The Ready and Easy Way to Establish a Free Commonwealth* Milton adds that virtuous rule is best exercised through a free and open council of the participants' "own electing where no single person, but only reason swaies" (p. 122).

The epic tradition also, of course, provided Milton with exemplars of evil in disguise. Having written in 1634 of the power of Circe's son Comus "to cheat the eye with blear illusion" (*Comus*, 155), Milton would have recalled from Homer's *Odyssey* how the enchantress magi-cally transfigured the appearance of Odysseus's men. He probably would have remembered the false illusions of the witch Armida in Tasso's *Jerusalem Delivered* as well as the alluring but evil visions conjured by Archimago in Spenser's *The Faerie Queene*.[17] Very pos-sibly, Milton, author of an entertainment and a masque, would have recognized the Bower of Bliss in Spenser's epic as a place of enticing, artificial surfaces that hid frightful corruption. In short, one can safely assume that the poet was acquainted with the opinion of Tasso in *Dis-corsi dell' arte poetica*, an opinion attributed to Aristotle and held by various Renaissance theorists, that evil characters in epics be depicted creating "lying wonders," fraudulent phantasms designed to impress and astound.[18] It was upon this appeal for lying wonders and for vir-tuous wonders as well that the theorists based their defense of grand, startling action in epics and amazing spectacle in masques and heroic theatrical works.

When in *Paradise Lost* this veil of lying wonders is stripped away, Hell at its core is revealed as an anti-type of Heaven, the blasphemous figural opposite of all that is virtuous and holy. Total antithesis—one-for-one opposition of characters, actions, and places—this is the artistic norm that governs Milton's rendering of the infernal and blessed regions. The transcending artistic and theological presuppositions dominating the poem require the existence of the hidden pride, envy, wrath, and other evils that in Hell coalesce as the terrible counterpart to Heaven.

Satan's first "bold words" in Hell (I.82), however extravagant in their grandiloquence and defiance, ring with a bitter undertone of injured vanity and serve as a heroic mask for a very private, interior desperation. Stung by the admitted "misery" and "ruin" (90–91) into which he and his cohorts have fallen, the Fiend cries out in a rage so overwhelming that, in this initial declaration, the inner recesses of his being are exposed:

> . . . What though the field be lost?
> All is not lost; the unconquerable Will,
> And study of revenge, immortal hate,
> And courage never to submit or yield:
> And what is else not to be overcome?   (105–109)

Unconquerable willpower, immortal hatred, revenge indulged in as a study, courage associated with unyielding and unsubmissive determination, wrath manifested in the tone of the outcry—these are among the wellsprings of satanic judgment and action. Wounded demonic pride, moreover, drives Satan to proclaim that it was his own

> . . . fixt mind
> And high disdain, from sense of injur'd merit,
> That with the mightiest rais'd me to contend.   (97–98)

Consumed by a desire for revenge, Satan, through his passion and unalterable defiance, surely fascinates by stirring buried primordial feelings. The theme of revenge, after all, is one of the fonts of Western epic and drama. But had *Paradise Lost* been available to educated aristocrats of the Elizabethan and Stuart periods, it seems to me that these readers, while doubtless being moved by Satan, would also have felt the need to distance themselves from all the repellent disfigurements and contradictions that rack and fragment this fallen angel. They would have recognized and experienced Satan as a type of antic evil, the enemy of their person, their society, and their culture. And they would have agreed with the epic narrator that the Archfiend is "vaunting aloud, but rackt with deep despair" (126).[19]

Even in his opening speech, Satan, the slave of passion, seeks to don the intellectual disguise of the egalitarian Leveller. He asks if the angel lying beside him "join'd / In equal ruin" is Beelzebub, the one who in "equal hope, / And hazard in the Glorious Enterprise, / Join'd with me once." While consciously stressing the equality of the relationship, Satan in his speech unintentionally provides contradictory evidence suggesting that a hierarchical differentiation in degree and in virtuous brightness separates the angels. According to Satan, Beelzebub "Cloth'd with transcendent brightness didst outshine / Myriads though bright." And as leader Satan claims a position higher than the other angels when he declares that he was "rais'd" to contend against God and "brought along / Innumerable force of Spirits arm'd" (86–101).

Perhaps the most interesting feature of Satan's blatant inconsistencies is that they would have appealed neither to Levellers seeking to overturn what was, in theory at least, an established hierarchy of political power nor to monarchists adhering to traditional notions of order and degree. The passions, gestures, actions, and disguises of Satan brand him as an exemplar of the very tyranny that he professes to hate, a tyranny dedicated to the irrational, self-aggrandizing exploitation of absolute authority without regard for the natural laws of God or the natural duties of living beings.

In an act of emotional projection, which is also one of concealment, the Fiend attributes the tyrannical fury and excess exhibited in his opening speech to the Almighty. Satan promises not to "repent or change" despite the punishments that the "Potent Victor in his rage / Can else inflict" (95–96). And the Fiend pledges to wage "eternal War" against the "grand Foe" who "in th' excess of joy / Sole reigning holds the Tyranny of Heav'n" (122–125).

Educated aristocrats of an earlier period, then, would have had no difficulty in accepting the epic narrator's objective definition of the Fiend's inner nature. In the opening argument, the narrator states:

> Th' infernal Serpent, hee it was, whose guile
> Stirr'd up with Envy and Revenge, deceiv'd
> The Mother of Mankind; what time his Pride
> Had cast him out from Heav'n, with all his Host
> Of Rebel Angels, by whose aid aspiring
> To set himself in Glory above his Peers,
> He trusted to have equall'd the most High.   (34–40)

After examining Satan's initial address in context, educated aristocrats would have been in a position to agree with the narrator that passion for revenge moved Satan, that pride led to his fall, and that ambition impelled him to place himself above his angelic peers and seek equality with God.

Unequivocal confirmation of Satan's tyranny comes during those scenes of prodigious distortion at Hell's capitol Pandemonium. Here indeed is an epic charade arranged to "set a pompous face upon the superficial actings of the state" and "drawn out to the full measure of a masking scene." Laboring at different tasks, a multitude of devils construct "in an hour," by means of transcending human art, a "Fabric" more grossly gargantuan than man's greatest "Monuments of Fame" (695–710), a fabric designed by the demonic architect Mulciber, whose "hand was known / In Heav'n by many a tow'red structure high" before his fall (732–733).[20] Masque historian Enid Welsford has astutely associated Mulciber with Inigo Jones, who designed the Palace of Fame in Davenant's *Britannia Triumphans* and supervised the making of its fabric by the Revels Office carpenters and painters.[21] And Christopher Hill, citing a wide body of literary and historical materials, has demonstrated that the tyranny of Satan in Hell, the allegedly despotic rule of the "great Sultan" (348) in "great *Alcairo*" (718), and that of the pope in Rome are analogous to the supposed tyranny of Charles I in England.[22]

In *Britannia Triumphans*, after an antimasque of several scenes including one of a fiery hell, it was King Charles I who, disguised as Britanocles, made his entrance from the Palace of Fame. Before the "discovery" of the king, the antimasque figure Action defends heavenly and mortal authority against charges of tyranny, which were in fact then circulating in Britain. Action complains to Imposture about "such as impute / A tyrannous intent to heavenly power, / And that their tyranny alone did point / At men." A number of "ancient impostures" who are threatening Britanocles' power enter and perform antic dances as "The whole Scene transformed into a horrid hell, the further part terminating in a flaming precipice." It is in a later main masque spectacle that music sounds, the Palace of Fame rises, the palace gates open, and Charles I as Britanocles, accompanied by his masked courtiers, appears within a "Peristilium of two orders, Doric and Ionic," that is, within a colonnaded cloister.[23] In this manner did court writer Davenant and designer Jones on Twelfth Night, 1637, deck out Charles I in, to use Milton's words, "quaint emblems and devices begged from the old pageantry of some twelfthnight's entertainment."

[68]

In the Miltonic Hell which integrates theatrical elements from "Sodom Burning," *On the Fifth of November, Comus,* and English and Continental spectacles, Satan assumes his antic, pseudoheroic role amid comparable scenic surroundings that, although now brilliantly transfigured and blended into the heroic narrative, nevertheless are developed from the well-known "fire effects" of the Renaissance theater. The Archfiend utters his defiance from that "Lake of Fire" (280), which is compared to the Asphaltic Pool; calls to the devils from a "Beach" (299) of the fiery lake; and, after reviewing the demonic troops, retires to the navel of his infernal empire near a "Hill" that "Belch'd fire and rolling smoke" (670–671). Pandemonium ascends in an area where, a later passage declares, there is "Fruitage fair to sight, like that which grew / Near that bituminous Lake where Sodom flam'd" (X.561–562).

After the devils swarm into the palace and instantaneously seem to contract into tiny creatures, their incongruous movements are compared to those of "Faery Elves" engaged in "midnight Revels" under a moon that "Wheels her pale course" (I.781–786). The devils, viewed as antic revelers, are similar to the less awesome "ancient impostures" in *Britannia Triumphans*—or, to be more nearly exact, to Comus and his crew who wheel in "fantastic round" (144) beneath a moon that, in turn, circles in a "wavering Morris dance" (116). Far within the palace the enthroned Satan and a select, cloistered council of infernal demigods sit "In close recess and secret conclave" (795), in an episode suggesting the supposedly tyrannical meetings of Roman cardinals in the Sistine Chapel. These cloistered devils debate and then pay idolatrous homage to the Archfiend in his chair of state:

> . . . Towards him they bend
> With awful reverence prone; and as a God
> Extol him equal to the highest in Heav'n.   (II.477–479)

The underlying falseness of Satan's position is exposed when the Archfiend speaks in favor of an egalitarianism that would seemingly undermine the ambitious power of tyrants:

> . . . for none sure will claim in Hell
> Precedence, none, whose portion is so small
> Of present pain, that with ambitious mind
> Will covet more.   (32–35)

The irony is jolting. Satan has just announced himself "Leader" by virtue of "merit," "free choice," and "the fixt Lawes of Heav'n" (18–21). That the Fiend merits what he may not fully recognize as his "bad eminence" is undeniable. However, the irrationality of his other claims mark them as shams. The rebel angels have not been given an opportunity to elect a leader by free choice or to grant him a "Throne / Yielded with full consent" (23–24). And the "fixt Lawes of Heav'n" to which Satan appeals are those of the supposed tyranny the Tempter has sworn to overthrow.

Again, the epic narrator objectively characterizes the deepest nature of the Fiend; it is "from despair" (6), the narrator informs readers, that Satan impossibly

> . . . aspires
> Beyond thus high, insatiate to pursue
> Vain War with Heav'n, and by success untaught
> His proud imaginations thus display'd.　　　　　　(7–10)

The varied shadings of parody implicit in Satan's many masks are well illustrated in the Deceiver's roles of manipulating diplomat-adventurer and beautiful, youthful cherub. The ironic seriousness of the first role contrasts sharply with the ironic humor of the second.

At the end of the debate of the infernal council, from which most devils are excluded, Beelzebub theatrically stands and appears to present as his own a plan to seduce man that was "first devis'd / By Satan" (379–380). The eyes of the listening devils sparkle with joy, and immediately "they vote" (389) in favor of the plan without discussion. Satan, pretending spontaneous fervor, rises and volunteers for the role of seducer in a way that prevents "all reply" (467). The council falls to the ground in adoration of the Fiend. The devils reveling outside in the main hall learn what has been decided by proclamation. The mock-seriousness of Satan and Beelzebub fails to conceal that, despite a thoughtless vote by the cloistered few, this has not been a free council. The Archfiend has neatly "programmed" the depressing political processes of Hell.

On the long journey from Hell to the earthly paradise, Satan passes through seemingly limitless celestial spaces and then, upon approaching the angel Uriel at the Orb of the Sun, puts on a rather foppish guise quite different from his previous mask of stately seriousness:

> And now a stripling Cherub he appears,
> Not of the prime, yet such as in his face
> Youth smil'd Celestial, and to every Limb
> Suitable grace diffus'd, so well he feignd;
> Under a Coronet his flowing hair
> In curls on either cheek play'd, wings he wore

> Of many a color'd plume sprinkl'd with Gold,
> His habit fit for speed succinct, and held
> Before his decent steps a Silver wand.　　　　　(III.636–644)

Satan is now manifested as an aging cherubic gallant "Not of the prime" with playful, cheek-length curls and wings "sprinkl'd with Gold," a cherub self-consciously pretending to be graceful with his silver wand and decent step. Only his garments are "fit for speed succinct." Here the narrator adopts a light tone as he unveils with glancing humor yet another disguise of the Fiend.

The ultimate unmasking of Satan takes the form of a perverse anti-Triumph in Pandemonium after the Fall of man. Satan, by seeking exaltation in Hell comparable to that given to the Son in Heaven, participates in a disguised entrance, a false discovery, and evil Triumph and revel, and a grotesque concluding banquet. The language used to describe Satan's crew during the anti-Triumph relates them to vile anti-masque-type figures: they are a "revolted Rout" (X.534), accessories to the Fiend's "bold Riot," and, finally, transformed, beastly monsters that make a dreadful "din" (521).

Satan, upon his return from Eden, moves disguised into Pandemonium's council chamber "In show Plebeian Angel militant / Of lowest order" (442–443). Secretly ascending his throne, he seeks to surprise and awe his followers with a sudden dazzling appearance:

> ... as from a Cloud his fulgent head
> And shape Star-bright appear'd, or brighter, clad
> With what permissive glory since his fall
> Was left him, or false glitter.　　　　　(449–452)

With the throng "All amaz'd / At that so sudden blaze," Satan now proclaims a Triumph. He announces that he will lead his followers "forth / Triumphant out of this infernal pit" (452–464). Other devils remain outside the hall "with expectation when to see / In Triumph issuing forth thir glorious Chief." But Satan, transformed by the power of God, emerges as a hideous dragon, and those waiting are "Catcht by Contagion, like in punishment." Even as these demons seek to participate in a triumph, they are struck down by God: "Thus was th' applause they meant, / Turn'd to exploding hiss, triumph to shame" (536–546).

No harmonious dance unites the corrupt denizens of Hell. Instead, "they roll'd in heaps" (558) to trees bearing an infernal fruit. Climbing the trees, the deceivers become the deceived. Through God's *contra-passo* justice, their demonic banquet, described with repellent-sounding words, mirrors their inner degradation:

> Deceiv'd; they fondly thinking to allay
> Thir appetite with gust, instead of Fruit
> Chew'd bitter Ashes. (564–566)

The punishment of Satan and the devils is an all-embracing anti-type of evil. Shortly before his "devolution," the Fiend, as self-proclaimed "Antagonist of Heav'n's Almighty King," had boasted to Sin and Death that his own presumably eternal creation would rival God's. In founding "Th' Infernal Empire . . . so near Heav'n's door," Satan claimed that "Triumphal with triumphal act have met" (387–390). But the final anti-Triumph of the Fiend turns his empire into an even more terrible Hell and his one conquest of man into a fleeting victory. The grand antagonist of God is bruised, and the Son is exalted. The forced anti-incarnation of the Fiend in the very serpent form he had chosen earlier—but a form that is now consonant with his deepest nature and so horribly loathesome—is the anti-type of the Son's future voluntary incarnation in the form of man.

The theme of demonic grand illusion thus ends with Satan and the devils condemned to eternal, restless change in a realm and a condition that the Fiend had thought eternally changeless. Satan and his cohorts must perpetually reenact the typological counterpart to man's single transgression: "so oft they fell / Into the same illusion, not as Man / Whom they triumph'd, once lapst" (570–573).

V

Love's Revel in Eden

WHEN evening comes to the paradisal garden and Adam and Eve are charmingly depicted retiring hand in hand to their "inmost bower,"[1] Milton concludes the scene with an epithalamium to the personified figure of Love:

> Here Love his golden shafts imploys, here lights
> His constant Lamp, and waves his purple wings,
> Reigns here and revels.   (IV.763–765)

Milton wrote of Love in the epithalamium remembering that this personified figure officiated over the final revels of court masques celebrating marriage, often leading the bride and groom to the very bedroom in which the connubial "rites" were to be performed. But the poet, who in his occasional verse early displayed an awareness of such mundane ceremonies, reacts strongly in *Paradise Lost* against the masques of corrupt man. A contrast is drawn in the epithalamium between the First Parents' enjoyment of a revel of true love in Eden and fallen man's inability to find such love in "Court Amours, / Mixt Dance, or wanton Mask, or Midnight Ball" (767–768). This contrast is instructive, for it hints at an underlying conception governing the scene that commentators have yet to discern.

Milton, it seems to me, creates major segments of the opening episode in Eden (1–775) by casting in epic mold transformed and idealized elements from a masque of Hymen, thus producing a patterned *exemplum* serving in content and form as a heroic counterpart to the supposedly wanton masquing revels of love indulged in by fallen man. The biblical, classical, and secular literary references in the prelapsarian love scene in Eden have had no lack of commentators. What has been overlooked is the manner in which Milton builds very harmonious aesthetic effects by incorporating into the scene allusions to the theatrical arts of song, dance, dialogue, and scenic spectacle. While acknowledging fully the poet's use of nontheatrical elements, one still needs to direct critical attention to those features embodied in the verse that make the episode such good "visionary theater": the memorable entrance of the First Parents; their fluid, choreographic movements hand in hand; their dialogue on love and dramatic embrace; the wanderings and frustrated reactions of a disguised Satan; the swift descent from Heaven to Eden of the angel Uriel; and finally, the First Parents' address to God the Father and retreat to a delightful evening of love.

This presentation of the First Parents' prelapsarian love and marriage is a development of a love theme that Milton introduced into all four extant outlines of "Adam Unparadiz'd." The four outlines, though depicting Adam and Eve only in a fallen state, point together with other evidence to Milton's probable inclusion of unfallen Adam and Eve in an actual prelapsarian marriage episode in the lost fifth draft.

Sacred representations such as Grotius's *Adamus Exul* and Andreini's *L'Adamo*, cited as theatrical sources for "Adam Unparadiz'd," contain no sensuous love scenes in a bower;[2] but the theatrical conventions for such scenes were firmly established in the masque. Milton depicted married love, even in his early verse, by reference to masques of Hymen. The "God that sits at marrige feast" (18), the poet had written in *An Epitaph on the Marchioness of Winchester* (1631), was present with flame and garland at the marchioness's wedding. In *L'Allegro* the poet went so far as to proclaim pageants and masques featuring Hymen as a source of poetic inspiration. Speaking of the delights of "Tow'red Cities" (117), Milton adds:

> There let *Hymen* oft appear
> In Saffron robe, with Taper clear,
> And pomp, and feast, and revelry,
> With mask, and antique Pageantry—
> Such sights as youthful Poets dream
> On Summer eves by haunted stream. (125–130)

In the next passage Milton mentions *"Jonson's* learned Sock" as another of the cities' pleasures. Here he seems to be following a chain of theatrical associations, for it is well known that when *L'Allegro* was composed, Ben Jonson was celebrated for his comedies and his masques of Hymen.

At the beginning of Jonson's masque *Hymenaei* (1606), which would have been available to Milton in either the quarto edition of 1606 or the folio edition of 1616, the stage directions record that *"Hymen (the god of marriage)"* entered *"in a saffron-coloured robe, ... in his right hand a torch of pine trees."*[3] Two years later the god strode upon the stage in the opening scene of Jonson's *Haddington Masque*, another marriage presentation available in quarto (1608) and folio (1616) editions; and on his second appearance Hymen, according to the author's marginal notes, was dressed *"as you haue him describ'd in ... Hymenaei"* (203–204).

In the prologue to *Hymenaei*, there enter onto the stage not only Hymen but also his attendants, who are accompanying a Bride and Groom. The attendants sing of the *"mysteries"* to be enacted, and the marriage god speaks of these *"Rites, so duely priz'd"* (69, 104).

The disorderly antimasque of unruly figures begins when performers, disguised as the "foure Humors, and foure Affections," leap from a scenic device described as a "Microcosme, or Globe (*figuring Man*)." Rushing forward, they draw *"all their swords"* and seek to *"disturbe the* Ceremonies," but they are soon dissuaded from their purpose by the figure Reason, who admonishes them from a seat on top of the globe (109–116).

During the main masque featuring a spectacle, the scenic heavens suddenly open to "discover" a host of glittering celestial figures. At the heavens' summit stands Jupiter *"brandishing his thunder"* (225–226); below him is Juno *"sitting in a Throne"* (215); and under her appears the rainbow goddess Iris. Eight female figures near Juno, her "noblest powers" (239), float to the stage on cloud machines and, to restore complete order, join with the eight men playing the Humors and Affections.

A main masque address and presentation take place after the noble performers pace from the stage into the hall, join hands, and form, among other choreographed devices, a *"Golden Chaine* let downe from *Heauen"* (320). In his presentation address, Reason explains exactly how the masquers should approach the king, the honored guest, who was seated in state on a raised dais in the main hall:

> ... doe front the *state*,
> With gratefull *honors*, thanke his *grace*
> That hath so glorified the place:
> And as, in *circle*, you depart
> Link'd *hand in hand*; So, *heart in heart*. (420–424)

The presentation and the concluding revel of the Bride and Groom, during which the performers traditionally unmasked, are mentioned in the stage directions: "They *pac'd once about, in their* ring, *euery payre making their honors, as they came before the state; and then dissoluing, went downe in couples, led on by* Hymen, *the* Bride, *and* Auspices *following, as to the* nuptiall bower" (431–435).

Pacing to and moving within the bedroom representing the "nuptiall bower," the masquers present the epilogue. Musicians walking behind the Bride and Groom render a song *"which was call'd* Epithalamium" (438); and after the married pair ceremoniously come to rest in their nuptial bed, the singers direct Hymen's attendants to shower the couple with flowers:

> Now, *youths,* let goe your pretty armes;
> The place within chant's other charmes.
>   Whole showers of *roses* flow;
>   And *violets* seeme to grow,
>   Strew'd in the chamber there.   (485–489)

In *Paradise Lost* the epic narrator places a verbal frame around the love scene. In the prologue to Book IV (1–31) he defines the hinge of the ensuing action: the First Parents in the earthly paradise have been warned against Satan, and now the Tempter is coming to Eden to seek their ruin. The narrator's epithalamium (750–775), in which Love is invoked and wedlock exalted, brings the episode to a close.

After the prologue Satan is revealed speaking of his evil plans, descending to Eden, and wandering through the wood and garden of the paradisal mount. The Tempter acts to some degree as would a disruptive figure in an antimasque. Like Comus, Satan speaks of reigning over man, moves through an "entwin'd" wood (174), and steals in disguise to a place from which he can spy upon human beings. And like the four Humors and four Affections, the Tempter first seeks to attack a joyous marriage by assaulting the internal faculties of that microcosm man (800–807). Satan's initial, tormented monologue, moreover, relates the fallen Archangel to an antimasque figure. When Satan cries out "O Sun, . . . how I hate thy beams / That bring to my remembrance from what state / I fell" (37–39), one is reminded that these lines, which appear also in Milton's "tragedy," were derived from a comparable passage in the 1634 and 1637 versions of *Comus*. The passage applies very directly to the evil enchanter of that masque:

> . . . he that hides a dark soul and foul thoughts
> Benighted walks under the midday Sun;
> Himself is his own dungeon.   (*Comus*, 383–385)

Derivative too in this section of *Paradise Lost* is the scenic background. As Satan approaches the forested slopes of the earthly paradise, there unfolds before his gaze

> A Silvan Scene, and as the ranks ascend
> Shade above shade, a woody Theatre
> Of stateliest view. (140–142)

This "woody Theatre" is a "wilderness" filled with "Cedar, and Pine, and Fir, and branching Palm" and "thicket overgrown, grotesque and wild" (135–139). The Fiend, stalking through the forest,

> . . . further way found none, so thick entwin'd,
> As one continu'd brake, the undergrowth
> Of shrubs and tangling bushes had perplext
> All path of Man or Beast that pass'd that way. (174–177)

The tangled wood through which Satan wanders, though apparently of a high spiritual order in nature, is comparable to the spiritually inferior but equally "tangl'd Wood" (181) in which Comus dwells.[4] The forest in the antimasque of *Comus* comprises a "leavy Labyrinth" of trees and thickets (184–185, 278). Curtains were probably hung about the stage to conceal Comus's crew, for the sorcerer instructs his followers to hide by running to "shrouds within these Brakes and Trees" (147). Moreover, the stage design for the wood ideally would have been drawn and painted to suggest, as the Lady states, "blind mazes" (181). According to the Attendant Spirit, travelers in the region have to pass

> . . . through the perplex't paths of this drear Wood,
> The nodding horror of whose shady brows
> Threats the forlorn and wand'ring Passenger. (37–39)

Although in *Paradise Lost* the mountainside setting and the antic behavior of the questing Satan resemble elements in *Comus*, a counterbalancing pattern of orderly action can be detected in the epic at the moment attention centers upon the First Parents in their summit garden. The entrance of Adam and Eve in front of the concealed Fiend, for example, is theatrically arranged to heighten suspense through the use of "natural" music, dance, choreographed movement, and suitable scenic backgrounds.

Milton knew that in court masques the main performers often danced to center stage. As tension mounted and the dances reached a climax, a featured performer, dressed to represent a pagan god or a personified idea appropriate to the theme of the work, was led forward toward the audience by another performer playing an important but somewhat less significant role.[5] Sudden and striking presentations of this kind appear in Milton's occasional verse.

The dancing figure May is so presented in the opening lines of Milton's *Song: On May Morning* (1629-30):

> Now the bright morning Star, Day's harbinger,
> Comes dancing from the East, and leads with her
> The Flow'ry *May*, who from her green lap throws
> The yellow Cowslip, and the pale Primrose.   (1-4)

In *L'Allegro* Milton elaborates upon this masque presentation technique. After an atmosphere of pleasure is conveyed through a description of the rollicking dance of Jest, Jollity, Quips, Cranks, Wiles, Nods, Becks, Wreathed Smiles, Sport, and Laughter, the narrator commands Mirth to step forward leading the most important dancer of all:

> Come, and trip it as ye go
> On the light fantastic toe,
> And in thy right hand lead with thee,
> The Mountain Nymph, sweet Liberty.   (33-36)

Then, following a passage on the delights of the early morning, the narrator introduces figures appropriate to the pastoral theme:

> ... the Plowman near at hand,
> Whistles o'er the Furrow'd Land,
> And the Milkmaid singeth blithe,
> And the Mower whets his scythe,
> And every Shepherd tells his tale
> Under the Hawthorn in the dale.   (63-68)

Writing of the First Parents' entrance in *Paradise Lost*, Milton exploits fully this theatrical means of focusing attention upon the last in a series of character-types. There, in the woody theater of Eden, idyllic music is heard when a chorus of birds bursts into song and with their "airs, vernal airs, / Breathing the smell of field and grove, attune / The trembling leaves." Next, "Universal *Pan*" is discovered in joyous celebration "Knit with the *Graces* and the *Hours* in a dance." A presentation follows, for Universal Pan in dancing forward "Led on th' Eternal Spring." At this crucial moment just before the First Parents step into the sylvan scene, interest is intensified by the narrator's insistence that man is far superior to the pagan gods and goddesses who in the past roamed wood and grove (264–283).

At last, Adam and Eve appear:

> Two of far nobler shape erect and tall,
> Godlike erect, with native Honor clad
> In naked Majesty seem'd Lords of all,
> And worthy seem'd, for in thir looks Divine
> The image of thir glorious Maker shone.   (288–292)

Like noble main masquers pacing before antimasque figures of discord, the First Parents manifest their beauty and love through choreographed action. "So pass'd they naked on" (319), writes Milton of their graceful stroll across the hidden Satan's field of vision. Milton employs repetition to emphasize their movement through the Garden: "So hand in hand they pass'd, the loveliest pair / That ever since in love's imbraces met" (321–322). One is at once reminded of how the virtuous Lady in *Comus* glided with a "different pace" and "chaste footing" (145–146) past an evil enchanter who was disguised and hidden in a wood.

Some distance from their "inmost bower," Adam and Eve pause at a green:

> Under a tuft of shade that on a green
> Stood whispering soft, by a fresh Fountain side
> They sat them down.   (325–327)

After a delicious dinner of fruit and a pleasant conversation about love, the First Parents act in accord with those most enduring and successful of theatrical cliches: they "half " embrace, exchange "kisses pure," and then find themselves "Imparadis't in one another's arms." When Eve "half imbracing" leans "On our first Father," some of her sexual allure is of a sort well known to the traditional visual arts and even to the modern cinema: "half her swelling Breast / Naked met his under the flowing Gold / Of her loose tresses hid." Yet, as even Satan realizes, it is the complete spiritual and physical union of the pair that affords them a "happier *Eden*" with "bliss on bliss" (494–508).

When Milton highlights Eve's sensual charm by writing of her "Dishevell'd" hair that "in wanton ringlets wav'd" (306), he is attempting, not to mislead readers into believing that the Mother of mankind might have the traits of a seventeenth-century "scarlet woman," but to stress that Eve enjoys the "Simplicity and spotless innocence" (318) of a pleasurable sensuality infused with human and divine love.[6] Aristocrats of the period would have recognized Eve as an ideal marriage partner who had adopted a hairstyle popular with chaste brides at wedding masques and ceremonies. Princess Elizabeth, who surely was not regarded as a scarlet woman by Henry Peacham, is said by him to have come to her wedding in 1613 with "her haire discheueled, and hanging downe ouer her shoulders."[7] The Bride in *Hymenaei*, wearing only a garland of roses on her head, appeared throughout the masque with "hayre flowing, and loose" (57). Jonson in his commentary provides an aesthetic reason for this style: when a lady's hair is "carelesly" arrayed, the resulting coiffure has "yet ... more art, then if more affected" (623–624).

Neither is there anything particularly surprising about Eve's subjection to her husband. The First Mother's quite traditional relationship to Adam is apparent even in the arrangement of her tresses; they are "wav'd / As the Vine curls her tendrils, which impli'd / Subjection" (306–308). A comparable analogy is developed in Jonson's *Hymenaei*: "a lone vine, in a naked field / Neuer extolls her branches, never beares" (826–827), says the figure Truth, who continues:

> But if, by fortune, she be married well
> To th' elme her *husband*
> . . . . .
> Her fortune, and endeuor lets her clime,
> Deare to her *loue*, and *parents* she is held.
> *Virgins*, O *virgins*, to sweet Hymen yeeld. (832–840)

The setting for the First Parents' love scene, the walled enclosure of the Garden, also has a clear masquing analogue that until now has escaped critical attention. Although in *Comus* the Gardens of Hesperus are not discovered on stage as an actual backdrop, they are, nevertheless, described by the Attendant Spirit in the epilogue as if a masque setting, with revelers in the foreground, were being visualized. Located "in the broad fields of the sky," the gardens contain a tiny chorus composed of "*Hesperus*, and his daughters three / That sing about the golden tree." Nearby stands the rainbow goddess, Iris, clothed in a "purfl'd scarf" and apparently carrying a curved, multicolored staff representing a rainbow. Her "humid bow / Waters the odorous banks that blow / Flowers of more mingled hue." In the foreground amid "crisped shades and bow'ers" which further vary the scene, revelers—some of them girls appearing bare bosomed, as did some female performers in masques—romp engagingly in a main masque dance.[8]

There in the Hesperian Gardens "Revels the spruce and jocund Spring, / The Graces and the rosy-bosom'd Hours" (979–995).

The gardens and revelers stand as an early and limited pagan model for the perfected biblical Eden of Milton's epic. Writing of the "various view" within the walled area on the summit of Mount Eden, Milton quickly identifies the garden with "*Hesperian* Fables true"; but, immediately growing more cautious and wishing to qualify the identification, he adds, "If true, here only" (247–251). Terms associated with seventeenth-century painting and scenic design are used to describe Eden as a "Lantskip" (153) that, from Adam's point of view, has a "prospect large" (144) with extensive perspectives.[9] At least some of the vegetation visible in the landscape is referred to as if rendered in divers enamels dabbed on a canvas backdrop; in Eden "Blossoms and Fruits at once of golden hue / Appear'd, with gay enamell'd colors mixt" (144–153). Yet, to transcend the constrictions of human art, Milton merges images of limited artifice with allusions to the variety and apparently unlimited profusion of prelapsarian nature (241–243).

If the gardens in *Comus* have in their midst a "golden tree," the Eden of *Paradise Lost* has "the Tree of Life, / High eminent, blooming Ambrosial Fruit / Of vegetable Gold" (218–220). The chorus in *Comus* has been replaced in the earthly paradise by a natural choir of birds; and instead of the rainbow goddess Iris, it is God in Heaven who controls the "humid Bow," which together with the "Evening Cloud" showers the earth and so rejuvenates the vegetation (151–152). But the main masque revelers of the Hesperian Gardens—the Spring, the Graces, and the Hours—are found dancing in Eden with Universal Pan (266–268).

After Adam and Eve embrace, Satan steals away into the Garden, and the scene shifts. It is sunset at the jutting pillars of stone that mark "the eastern Gate of Paradise" (542):

> Betwixt these rocky Pillars *Gabriel* sat
> Chief of th' Angelic Guards, awaiting night;
> About him exercis'd Heroic Games
> Th' unarmed Youth of Heav'n, but nigh at hand
> Celestial Armory, Shields, Helms, and Spears
> Hung high with Diamond flaming, and with Gold. (549–554)

At this juncture in *Paradise Lost*, a divine being flies to earth and, like one or more celestial masque figures after a descent from Heaven, assists other virtuous figures in controlling evil. In the main masque of

Hymenaei, of course, it was Juno's "noblest *powers*" who floated to the ground on their cloud machines. But the nearest precursor of the angel Uriel's flight to earth in *Paradise Lost* is the descent in *Comus* of the Attendant Spirit. "Swift as the Sparkle of a glancing Star," the Attendant Spirit announces, "I shoot from Heav'n" (80–81). And at the Gate of Paradise in Milton's epic, Gabriel and his angelic troop receive word of Satan's presence when "Thither came *Uriel*, gliding through the Even / On a Sunbeam, swift as a shooting Star" (555–556).

Once Uriel has delivered his message and Gabriel has promised to seek out Satan, the scene shifts back to the central Garden for the conclusion of this segment of the action. With the approach of evening, Adam and Eve move from their lush green while speaking graciously together of the vastness and beauty of God's creation. Then, much like a bride and groom holding hands and pacing the stage at the climactic moments of a masque of Hymen, the First Parents "hand in hand . . . pass'd / On to thir blissful Bower." This innermost setting with a "verdant wall," a roof of "inwoven shade," and a lavish assortment of "beateous flow'r"—a place "Chos'n by the sovran Planter, when he fram'd / All things to man's delightful use"—is an idealized, prelapsarian counterpart to the flower-strewn bowers to which couples in masques retired for a revel of love (689–697).

Statements by the epic narrator suggest how Adam and Eve participate, first, in an extraordinary "presentation" to the "divine" state and then in an innocent revel. Acting as main masquers would have upon arriving at a presentation area, Adam and Eve turn in the direction of the heavenly state:

> Thus at thir shady Lodge arriv'd, both stood,
> Both turn'd, and under op'n Sky ador'd
> The God that made both Sky, Air, Earth and Heav'n.
>
> (720–722)

The First Parents' presentation address takes the form of a prayer "said unanimous" (736).

During the final masque revel of love in a bower bedroom, aristocratic performers slipped sequined visors from their faces and so unmasked. But Adam and Eve, having no need before the Fall to adopt the disguises of sinful man, pace in unadorned innocence to their revel:

> . . . into thir inmost bower
> Handed they went; and eas'd the putting off
> These troublesome disguises which wee wear,
> Straight side by side were laid.   (738–741)

At this instant, with the First Parents lying together in their bower, the details of the poetic narrative become less concrete, the action less immediate; the scene in effect fades from the reader's direct view. The voice of the epic narrator breaks in to intone in the concluding epithalamium words echoing those sung by the musicians at the end of *Hymenaei*. Intimacy in marriage, the musicians proclaimed, "is no sin, / But chaste, and holy loue, / Which *Hymen* doth approue" (502–504). Thus the wedded pair in the masque were urged to "mutuall ioyes" (510) as "showers of *roses*" (487) rained upon them. With far greater eloquence and power, the narrator of *Paradise Lost*, in lofty poetic flight, sings of how in sinless purity the First Parents enjoy the "Rites / Mysterious of connubial Love" (742–743) and drift peacefully into slumber. Then the epic voice, growing gentler and sounding in a lower key, presents a haunting vision of perfect innocence, an innocence still free of satanic fancies and desires. Adam and Eve

> ... lull'd by Nightingales imbracing slept,
> And on thir naked limbs the flow'ry roof
> Show'r'd Roses.
>
> (771–773)

Milton fashioned the love scene in *Paradise Lost*, not by crudely introducing a court masque into an epic narrative, but by gracefully fusing masquelike sequences with a variety of literary modes and conventions. For there was in the masque an essential and inescapable quality that forcefully appealed to Milton when he sought to depict man's brief moment of ideal joy before the Fall. The ephemeral nature of these opulent "toys" corresponded to the evanescence of the Earthly Paradise; the glittering world of a supposedly perfect theatrical realm, like the perfect delights of Eden, lasted for only a fleeting span of time and then passed forever into memory. And in the masque as in Milton's epic, sadness quickly followed upon delight. Jonson himself conveyed a sense of the sadness that followed pleasure in writing of the "exquisit performance," "*pompe*," and "*splendor*" of *Hymenaei*. "Onely the enuie was," Jonson commented, "that it lasted not still, or (now it is past) cannot by imagination, much lesse description, be recouered to a part of that *spirit* it had in the gliding by" (568–579).

In Milton's epic the incomparable pleasures of Eden are irretrievably lost. Until Adam in Book XII learns of future Redemption, confusion and despair alternately overwhelm the First Parents as they contemplate that glorious state from which they fell. A somber note of longing for lost perfection thus rings through the last books of the poem. But

[83]

even before the Fall occurs, a presentiment of what will become a deep, fervent, ever-heightening remorse is heard as the epic narrator sings the final words of the epithalamium over the slumbering Adam and Eve:

> ... Sleep on,
> Blest pair; and O yet happiest if ye seek
> No happier state, and know to know no more.   (773-775)

VI

The Triumphs of Heaven

THERE are no disfiguring disguises in Heaven. In depicting a realm where false appearances are scorned but deepest realities overwhelm and cloud finite powers, Milton tried to ensure that every outward manifestation of being served as the fullest, most luminous, and most exacting mirror possible of inmost perfection. All paradise is suffused with the mystical light of invisible godhood. Each angel is radiant with an internal, undimmed glow of holiness; and the jubilant hymns, graceful dances, and circular and straight movements of the angels are intended as external revelations of their harmonious natures. Even the shining gates, battlements, and fields of paradise were invented as exterior symbols for an underlying spiritual splendor.

Milton, moreover, sought to disclose Heaven's mysteries with the utmost rational lucidity possible. God the Father is presented within his fountain of spiritual light, explaining with attempted logical precision the ways of eternal justice toward man. God the Son gives personal, reasoned expression to heavenly mercy. The angels sing and speak of divine virtue and glory. And the freely and rationally chosen actions of God the Father, God the Son, and the heavenly hosts are intended as illustrations of that heavenly wisdom, love, and glory.

The representation of perfect godhood in a perfect paradise, however, is the ultimate challenge to art; and Milton's depiction is in some respects less than satisfactory. Through the nearly omniscient vision of his prophetic narrator, the poet chose to confront the all but insuperable problem of portraying the faultless persons of God, both in regular narration and in flashbacks, as characters speaking, acting, and reacting in a variety of crucial heroic scenes. Milton could not in his theatrical epic, as Dante had in his *Paradiso*, describe in a single passage a personal and humanly limited experience of beatific vision. The persons of the Christian God had to appear immediately as characters in extended episodes, after the fashion of Olympian immortals in classical epics, but without the pagan gods' human flaws. Biblical and theological materials had to be scrupulously followed and at the same time elaborated and poetically transformed.

Milton's artistic dilemma was theoretically if not imaginatively insoluble: how to portray directly a godhood "Omnipotent, / Immutable, Immortal, Infinite";[1] a godhood in heaven of supreme perfection that could not be readily embraced by mortal poetic images, analogies, and metaphors; a godhood of infinite mystical depths, yet one embodying a rationality comprehensible to man; a godhood of different divine persons—one both God and man—in a single perfect divine being.

In recent years certain commentators have accentuated the real and suspected deficiencies of Milton's God with such persistence and force—and occasionally with malicious pleasure—that the main areas of critical dissatisfaction are by now very well known. God the Father's theological arguments are said to be, upon analysis, often contradictory; the Father's character, excessively wrathful and unforgiving.[2] Criticism of the Son has centered not so much upon his role as future Redeemer as upon his part in what has been regarded by some as a rather unimaginative mock-angelic battle. The Son appears on the third "heavenly day" of warfare to lead angels who cannot die in a fight that involves the use of swords, spears, cannons, and uprooted mountains.[3]

Criticism of this kind, I think, requires qualification. It seems to me that Milton's presentation of grand, ceremonial, masquelike triumphs in Heaven and his related employment of both concealing and revelatory light imagery do successfully convey a sense of the awesomeness, meaning, and mystery of God the Father and God the Son while, at the same time, forwarding essential narrative action. The Son's battle scene in Book VI, a scene that imitates and at times parodies the battle conventions of classical and biblical literary tradition, does display a somewhat forced absorption in the literal details of physical conflict, but other passages on the participation of Father and Son in a heavenly military triumph effectively capture godhood's mystical power and glory.

Aesthetic difficulties arise when the Father appears, not as the lofty and majestic object of heavenly ritual, but as a speaking and acting character belligerently confronting evil. When the Father in Book III, for example, delivers legalistic pronouncements in a tone of testy irritation and next makes judgments colored by unnecessary self-justification, then the anthropomorphic traits of this Divine Person become much too obvious and suggest a restrictive human martinet more than a universal divine ruler. "Whose fault? / Whose but his own? ingrate," the Father scornfully remarks of Adam's Fall, "he had of mee, / All he could have; I made him just and right, / Sufficient to have stood, though free to fall" (III.96–99).

The Father, in this passage and elsewhere, wins the great theological Argument, but as a single Divine Person he loses in majesty, grandeur, and mercy. His logical arguments about eternal justice, it seems to me, "follow" reasonably enough insofar as they are carried, provided readers accept, as many readers do not, Milton's contextually established religious assumptions and values. But as generations of students have discovered, much to their confusion and frustration, the pursuit of the Father's statements beyond delineated argumentative confines inevitably leads to divine paradoxes or contradictions of faith involving the persons of God, divine foreknowledge and man's free will, time and eternity, and the issue of man's "fortunate" Fall.[4] Moreover, commentators who think the Father's anger a character flaw tend to disregard or minimize how Milton, with symbolic and didactic emphasis, constantly discloses the sometimes wrathful Old Testament Father as one in *substantia* with the merciful New Testament Son. In considering this one God of at least two Divine Persons, aesthetic criticism must take into account the paradoxes of theological art.

The basic problem with the Father as a perfect and very active figure in the epic, commentators have rightly noted, is that he has too many roles: loving creator, analytical lawgiver, wrathful prosecutor and judge, almighty law enforcer, and awesome universal ruler. Milton's God the Father, though encompassed in dazzling light, must enact all these parts with his spiritual character revealed in the fullest and most direct manner possible. Given the difficulties of such a rendering, some measure of critical recognition needs to be accorded not only to the degree of Milton's partial failure but also to the degree of his unanticipated success.

Milton's images of light for both a visible and an invisible godhood are strikingly conceived, subtle in emotional tonalities, and rich in theological suggestiveness. "God is Light," sings the epic narrator in an invocation to Book III that echoes a passage in John 1:1:

> And never but in unapproached Light
> Dwelt from Eternity, dwelt then in thee,
> Bright effluence of bright essence increate.   (4–6)

The Almighty Father enthroned beyond height, unseen by created beings but seeing all, is first disclosed bending "down his eye" upon the universe from amid angelic hosts serving as a "starry front":[5]

> About him all the Sanctities of Heaven
> Stood thick as Stars, and from his sight receiv'd
> Beatitude past utterance.   (60–62)

So supremely awesome is this infinite and invisible Being that, even when bewilderingly "clouded" within an effusion of dazzling light, he overwhelms the spiritual vision of the greatest of the angels. The heavenly choir with "golden Harps" (365) glittering sings of the Father:

> Fountain of Light, thyself invisible
> Amidst the glorious brightness where thou sit'st
> Thron'd inaccessible, but when thou shad'st
> The full blaze of thy beams, and through a cloud
> Drawn round about thee like a radiant Shrine,
> Dark with excessive bright thy skirts appear,
> Yet dazzle Heav'n, that brightest Seraphim
> Approach not, but with both wings veil thir eyes.   (375–382)

But if to the heavenly hosts this Transcendent Presence is necessarily masked yet paradoxically revealed like a "radiant Shrine / Dark with excessive bright," the Father, the angelic choir continues, can be seen fully and without cloud by only a single Divine Person, the

> Begotten Son, Divine Similitude,
> In whose conspicuous count'nance, without cloud
> Made visible, th' Almighty Father shines,
> Whom else no Creature can behold.   (384–387)

The Son is begotten of the Father and so proceeds from the Father; the shimmering emanations and power of the Father are one with those of the Son. The Father consequently sees and addresses the Son as "thou in whom my glory I behold; / In full resplendence, Heir of all my might" (V.719–720). The angelic choir praises the Father's conference of this radiant glory upon the Son: "on thee / Impresst th' effulgence of his Glory abides, / Transfus'd on thee his ample Spirit rests" (III.387–389). And the epic narrator takes note of this total manifestation of one Divine Person in another, the luminous union of persons in one God. The Father, the narrator records,

> . . . on the Son
> Blaz'd forth unclouded Deity; he full

Resplendent all his Father manifest
Express'd.   (X.64–67)

While the father states that his glory will encompass "Mercy and Justice both" (III.132), this radiant Divine Person of one God acts upon, speaks about, and primarily embodies divine justice. The Son, as the individualized Divine Person of one God, visibly and primarily embodies grace and love. The epic narrator, then, gives expression to the Son's substantial union with the Father and to the Son's individuality:[6]

> ... the Son of God was seen
> Most glorious, in him all his Father shone
> Substantially express'd, and in his face
> Divine compassion visibly appear'd,
> Love without end, and without measure Grace.   (138–142)

Only the Son can fully see the Supreme Father. Once begotten, the Son, transfused with the total power, glory, and light of the Father, becomes visible to and is seen by the angels. Thus, the symbolic "holy Light" invoked in Book III, though open to many dimensions of meaning, is contextually defined as the "offspring of Heav'n first-born, / Or of th' Eternal Coeternal beam" (1–2). Unlike the Son, who completely sees the Father, and unlike the angels, who in Heaven see the Son, the physically blind epic narrator, uncertain of his powers, prays for a more limited but prophetic illumination that will enable him to "see" spiritually the invisible and infinite (51–55).

Although influenced largely by biblical texts and commentary in his representation of heaven, Milton nevertheless derived from main masque triumphs and processions a form that allowed him to cloud divine perfection from finite beings yet partially "unmask" before them the creative substance of godhood.

Four great Triumphs of God, each interrelated as part of a repeated divine type that is opposite the grotesque unveiling of destructive evil in Hell, suggest the central role of godhood in human and cosmic history. The most portentous of the Triumphs, the one dramatically emphasized during the first and longest direct rendering of Heaven in the epic, is proclaimed when the Son declares before a full council of angels his future triumphant Redemption of the human race. This Triumph, initially introduced in Book III, is stressed again at the end of the epic when Michael in Book XII tells Adam of man's future salvation through the Son. In Books VI and VII heavenly Triumphs of the past are narrated in Eden by the angel Raphael after Adam and Eve enjoy a day of ideal human felicity. Raphael descends from Heaven to speak with Adam about the divine chronology of universal history. The angel tells Adam of God the Father's triumphant and mysterious begetting of the Son in the presence of the heavenly hosts. Raphael speaks as well of the subsequent war in Heaven and of the Son's triumphant celebration following a victory over the forces of Satan. Finally, the angel recounts the story of the Creation and the Son's Triumph in Heaven after the crucial seven days.[7]

The Triumph of man's future Redemption gains aesthetic prominence because it is announced in the epic's immediate present by the Son in Heaven (Book III) and by Michael in Eden (Book XII). The other three Triumphs—the Father's begetting of the Son (Book V), the Son's defeat of the sinful rebel angels (Book VI), and the Son's role in creating the universe (Book VII)—are presented by the angel Raphael in flashbacks as explanations to Adam of epochs of divine history. Although Raphael's speeches eulogize the Son's power and glory and his substantial union with the Father, these background narratives are there at the approximate middle of the epic primarily for Adam's education. And their placement in the completed twelve-book epic does not seem to be governed by any mathematical calculation of the work's center line. In the finished epic this line (VI.766) indeed appears in a passage about the Son's entry into battle against the rebel angels, but the line itself does not glorify the Son: "Of smoke and bickering flame, and sparkles dire." The Son triumphs in this and other flashbacks related by Raphael, but man remains the focal point of foreground epic action.

Nowhere more than in the first, extended depiction of Heaven in Book III does the reader acquire such a condensed and sharply drawn insight into the triumphant roles of the persons of God in cosmic history. There before the angelic hosts the Father declares his "Only begotten Son" (80) to be "from my bosom and right hand" (279) and "Both God and Man, Son both of God and Man, / Anointed universal King" (316–317). The blessed angels sing of how the Son, encountering the rebellious angels,

> . . . threw down
> Th' aspiring Dominations: thou that day
> Thy Father's dreadful Thunder didst not spare,
> Nor stop thy flaming Chariot wheels, that shook
> Heav'n's everlasting Frame, while o'er the necks
> Thou drov'st of warring Angels disarray'd. (391–396)

The angels acknowledge in song that the Son, in concert with the Father, the "Heav'n of Heavens and all Powers therein ... created" (390–391). And the Father explains that the Son's death and resurrection will result "to compass all" during a future millennium in the creation of a "New Heav'n and Earth":

> The World shall burn, and from her ashes spring
> New Heav'n and Earth, wherein the just shall dwell
> And after all thir tribulations long
> See golden days, fruitful of golden deeds,
> With Joy and Love triumphing, and fair Truth.
> Then thou thy regal Sceptre shalt lay by,
> For regal Sceptre then no more shall need,
> God shall be All in All. But all ye Gods,
> Adore him, who to compass all this dies,
> Adore the Son, and honor him as mee.   (334–343)

With these words of the Father, there takes place in paradise a prefiguring of what one heavenly day in the future will be the fulfilled, ultimate Triumph of the Son. The angels in unison shout their "Hosannas" of jubilee; "Loud as from numbers without number, sweet / As from blest voices, uttering joy" (346–348). They make their obeisance to the divine state:

> ... lowly reverent
> Towards either Throne they bow, and to the ground
> With solemn adoration down they cast
> Their Crowns inwove with Amarant and Gold.   (349–352)

Acting as musicians would have during a main masque presentation, they begin to sing while ranged in formation around the state:

> Then Crown'd again thir gold'n Harps they took,
> Harps ever tun'd, that glittering by thir side
> Like Quivers hung, and with Preamble sweet
> Of charming symphony they introduce
> Thir sacred Son, and waken raptures high.   (365–369)

Their hymn of triumph on this day, one of those "solemn days ... Spent in song and dance" (V.618–619), first extolls the Father but then concludes with an exultation of the Son in his role as man's Redeemer:

> Hail Son of God, Savior of Men, thy Name
> Shall be the copious matter of my Song
> Henceforth, and never shall my Harp thy praise
> Forget, nor from thy Father's praise disjoin.   (III.412–415)

Milton had long sought to present God poetically in divine masque-like rituals as a figure mysteriously hidden yet spiritually revealed. In 1630 the poet had exclaimed in *The Passion*, "O what a Mask was there, what a disguise!" and had attempted to depict the Son as an annointed Priest-Hero whose divinity was somewhat veiled on Jerusalem's mount by the "fleshly Tabernacle" of the body. Some twenty-three years later, in a paraphrase of Psalm II (1653), Milton again wrote of Christ, the annointed Priest-Hero on Jerusalem's mount, both as fleshly man and as the begotten Son of God.

The paraphrase begins with a description of a revolt by the "Kings of th' earth" against the Lord who "shall scoff them." The Lord responds:

> ... but I, saith hee
> Anointed have my King (though ye rebel)
> on Sion my holi' hill. A firm decree
> I will declare; the Lord to me hath said,
> Thou art my Son, I have begotten thee
> This day.   (11–16)

These lines hint at themes that are poetically realized in *Paradise Lost* in the statements of the angel Raphael: the begetting of the Son in Heaven; the mocking attitude of the Father toward those in revolt; and the war between the forces of good and evil. But the begetting of the Son, unlike his Passion and death, was a triumph that could be given masquelike "corporeal form." Thus, Milton was at last able to fulfill his desire, first expressed in the 1630s, to depict the Son as a figure both clouded and unveiled.

The annointed Priest-Hero with the shimmering "starry front" of a masquer in sequined costume becomes the Priest-King of Heaven obscured in blinding light. Mount Sion, the holy hill that supports the temple and "seat" of God, serves as the earthly reflection of the mount in Heaven upon which godhood is enthroned. And in the action that opens the chronology of past history in *Paradise Lost*, an action related by Raphael, the Son is initially seen by the angelic hosts during a cosmic, masquelike discovery and holy revel.[8]

In the Miltonic heavens, where "Time, though in Eternity, appli'd / To motion, measures all things durable / by present, past, and future," the begetting of the Son occurs "on such day / As Heav'n's great Year brings forth, th' Empyreal Host / Of Angels" (V.580–584). The heavenly year is a period of celestial time that Plato in the *Timaeus* (39D) measures by the return of the stars to their first positions after a fluctuating, circular round lasting, the philosopher implies, the equivalent of thirty-six thousand earthly years. The divine convocation on "such a day" of Heaven's year is comparable to the regular earthly gatherings of nobles in January to celebrate with courtly Twelfth Night revels the "showing forth" of Christ at Epiphany. Twenty-six of the sixty-two major extant masques of the seventeenth century were in fact performed as part of the annual January festivities.[9] It will be remembered that Milton in *Eikonoklastes* (1649) mocked the English king, who often performed and unmasked in the ceremonies, for maintaining tyrannical power by using the emblems and devices "begged from the old pageantry of some Twelfthnight's entertainment."[10] In Book V of *Paradise Lost*, the poet was able to depict the "showing forth" of mankind's divine Ruler in a scene that is the obverse of an earthly unmasking and, by implication, contains typological reflections of the Epiphany.

Like earthly main masquers approaching and preparing to whirl in circular ballet formations about a chair of state, the heavenly hosts assemble before the brilliance of the Father's throne. They advance toward the throne with concern for "Hierarchies, of Orders, and Degrees"; and then they surround the supreme state "in Orbs / Of circuit inexpressible . . . Orb within Orb." Even the tiny, shimmering "spangs" and hieroglyphs that decorated the costumes of mortal masquers as speaking pictures have their divine counterparts in Heaven. The "orders bright" of angels, decorated as warriors of virtue, "in thir glittering Tissues bear imblaz'd / Holy Memorials, acts of Zeal and Love / Recorded eminent" (587–597).[11]

The enthroned Father, "By whom in bliss imbosom'd sat the Son" (597) remains, together with the Son, shrouded in holy light "as from a flaming Mount, whose top / Brightness had made invisible" (598–599); for the Old Law revealed on flaming Mount Sinai is about to be fulfilled "as from a flaming Mount" in the New.

The Voice of the Father is heard making the pronouncement that accompanies the unique revelation and presentation of the Son:

> This day I have begot whom I declare
> My only Son, and on this holy Hill
> Him have anointed. (603–605)

The only Son, the Father intones,

> . . . ye now behold
> At my right hand; your Head I him appoint;
> And by my Self have sworn to him shall bow
> All knees in Heav'n, and shall confess him Lord. (605–608)

Any angels disobeying the command to confess the anointed Son as Lord, the Father continues, will be "Cast out from God and blessed vision" (613).

The Son of God, having once been begotten and visibly beheld as the anointed Priest-King on a heavenly mount, remains visible throughout the epic casting about him his own and his Father's refulgence. But the Son when begotten is surely not created. In the manner of a main masquer with two related, contiguous identities—one arising from the world of the disguising, the other from the actual social world—the "imbosom'd" Son has been in existence veiled in the "unapproachable light" of the "Coeternal beam"; the begetting in Heaven is the revelation of the Son to the society of angels in his role as Lord.

"That day, as other solemn days," the epic narrator avers after the Son has been shown forth and exalted, the angels engaged "In song and dance about the sacred Hill" (618–619). Consequently, when the circling angels participate in comparable revels of triumph on other exceptional days, their songs can be presumed to be rendered to the accompaniment of celestial ballets.

Venetian ambassador Orazio Busino, in a description of the main masque dances and the banquet that concluded Jonson's *Pleasure Reconciled to Virtue*, provides an exemplary illustration of just how earthly revels were conducted after the presentation and unmasking. About the performance of the Prince of Wales and the other main masquers, Busino writes:

> After they had made an obeisance to his Majesty, they began to dance in very good time, preserving for a while the same pyramidical figure, and with a variety of steps. Afterwards they changed places with each other in various ways, but ever ending the jump together. When this was over, each took his lady [to begin the revels]. The king now rose from his chair, took the ambassadors along with him, and after passing through a number of chambers and galleries he reached a hall where the usual collation was spread for the performers.[12]

He adds that two of the dancers, leaping about with individualized movements, "cut capers"; the others also appear to have executed personal, "eccentric" steps while maintaining the overall ballet formation and "ending the jump together." A figure in the masque, Daedalus, offers helpful comment on the design of the prearranged dance formations:

> Then, as all actions of mankind
> are but a Laberinth, or maze,

> so let your Daunces be entwin'd,
>   yet not perplex men, unto gaze.
> But measur'd, and so numerous too,
>   as men may read each act you doo
> And when they see ye Graces meet
>   admire the wisdom of your feet.   (261–268)

The angelic revel of dancing in Heaven, which follows the divine "unmasking" of the Son, displays the same eccentric harmony that characterized earthly main masque revels. The angels perform

> Mystical dance, which yonder starry Sphere
> of Planets and of fixt in all her Wheels
> Resembles nearest, mazes intricate,
> Eccentric, intervolv'd, yet regular
> Then most, when most irregular they seem:
> And in thir motions harmony Divine
> So smooths her charming tones, that God's own ear
> Listens delighted.   (620–627)

When the heavenly hosts turn "Forthwith from dance to sweet repast" (631), the luminous angels—exercising a grace, decorum, and virtuous restraint unknown on earth—stand in intended contrast with the aristocrats, whose behavior before and after the revels was sensual and frequently raucous. On the evening of 6 January 1605 when Jonson's *The Masque of Blacknesse* was performed at the Whitehall Banqueting House, for example, a crush of shoving lords and ladies clogged entrances where attendants armed with long staffs administered hearty whacks. "The confusion in getting in was so great," observes Dudley Carleton in a letter, "that some Ladies . . . complaine of the fury of the white stafes." Once inside, some nobles suffered yet other indignities: "They were shutt up in several heapes betwixt dores, and there stayed till all was ended." In Carleton's view this squeezed, imprisoned minority did not miss very much. Upon seeing the masque, Carleton objected to the featured performers, the queen and her ladies, who were wearing most revealing costumes "too light and Curtizan-like for such great ones." Noting as well that the ladies' "Faces and Arms up to the Elbows, were painted black," he remarks caustically: *"You cannot imagine a more ugly Sight than a Troop of lean-cheek'd Moors."* Nor was he amused later in the evening when a hungry, lurching horde of guests crashed into the dining table: "The Night's work was concluded with a Banquet in the great Chamber, which was so furiously assaulted, that down went Table and Tresses before one bit was touched." There was in fact yet more to recount, for the observant Carleton implies that all was truly lost: "It were infinit to tell you what losses there were of chynes, Jewels, purces, and such like loose ware, and one woeman amongst the rest lost her honesty, for wch she was caried to the porters lodge being surprised at her business on the top of the Taras."[13]

Milton consequently asserts that holy "wedded Love" (IV.750), as distinct from base earthly lust, reigns and "revels" (765) in divine masquelike form:

> . . . not in bought smile
> Of Harlots, loveless, joyless, unindear'd,
> Casual fruition, nor in Court Amours,
> Mixt Dance, or wanton Mask, or Midnight Ball.   (765–768)

The heavenly masquelike revel in *Paradise Lost* ends when the angels harmoniously gather "all in Circles" (V.631) around tables

> . . . pil'd
> With Angels' Food, and rubied Nectar flows,
> In Pearl, in Diamond, and massy Gold,
> Fruit of delicious Vines, the growth of Heav'n.   (632–635)

They take their repose "On flow'rs"; and "In communion sweet," they "Quaff immortality and joy, secure / Of surfeit where full measure only bounds / Excess" (636–640).

When the banquet is over, the angels retire to a celestial plain that is the opposite of the baneful earthly plain viewed by Adam in Book XI. The temperate angelic hosts in a divine encampment are the inverse type for the encamped earthly People of the Plain, whom Adam will see gratifying themselves in anti-triumphs of licentiousness. The angelic throng, extending themselves "Wide over all the Plain" (647) of Heaven, erect

> Pavilions numberless, and sudden rear'd,
> Celestial Tabernacles, where they slept
> Fann'd with cool Winds, save those who in thir course
> Melodious Hymns about the sovran Throne
> Alternate all night long.   (653–657)

THE NEXT Triumph of God, according to the account of Raphael in Eden, takes place when the Son, in the role of the biblical Lord of Battles, returns in military splendor to the courts of Heaven after he has overthrown Satan and the rebel angels. The saints in Heaven praise the Son's power and glory: "each order bright / Sung Triumph, and him sung Victorious King" (VI.885–886). A passage in Psalms is thus fulfilled: "Who is the King of glory?" asks David in a holy song fierce with the righteous anger of the prophets. "The Lord, strong and mighty, / The Lord, mighty in battle," echoes the refrain (24:10).

Before his formal entry into Heaven, the Son, riding in a mystical chariot that reflects the vehicles of classical warriors as well as the chariots of biblical tradition, charges among the rebel angels "in his right hand, / Grasping ten thousand Thunders, which he sent / Before him" (835–837). Astonishing and overpowering the enemy but taking care to "check" his thunder so as not to destroy, the Son drives the accursed angels in terror down through a "spacious Gap" that opens in the "Crystal wall of Heav'n" (860–861).

The Son's subsequent pageant of victory derives its original pattern of action from the victorious triumphs of Roman generals who, riding in chariots, led their troops and captives in festive panoply through the streets of Rome to the throne of the emperor. In the presence of the emperor, the generals were exalted and crowned with wreaths. The Renaissance princes of Europe imitated the Roman triumphs by sponsoring street pageants on holy days, but with the chariots of the generals replaced by elaborate floats carrying allegorical and mythic figures. Francesco Petrarch wrote his *Triumphi* with just such Roman and Renaissance processions in mind; and Dante, also influenced by the pageants, depicted in the *Purgatorio* a divine procession that descends from Heaven to Eden and terminates with the sudden discovery of Beatrice in a triumphal chariot.

Milton's poetic imagination was similarly stirred by earthly triumphs, such as the one involving more than five hundred persons in which his collaborator on *Comus*, Henry Lawes, took part. On the evening of 3 February 1633, Lawes, dressed as a Constellation in a star-seeded sky robe, rode in a "chariot" through the streets of London as a participant in James Shirley's pageant and masque *The Triumph of Peace*. Moving after dark from Ely and Hatton Houses to the British king enthroned in the Whitehall Banqueting House, the procession with Lawes in its midst included numerous torchbearers, caparisoned horsemen, feathered and "winged" attendants, and six military chariots adorned "after the Roman fashion."[14]

The triumph was held during a period when Milton and Lawes, then probably planning or working on *Comus* to honor the Earl of Bridgewater as Lord President of Wales, would have been acutely conscious of new court triumphs honoring the British crown. Although the Earl was installed as Lord President in September 1634 when *Comus* was first performed, he had in fact been commissioned to the post by the king in June 1631. At that earlier date he may well have asked Lawes, his children's music teacher, to begin planning a triumph for performance at the installation.[15]

The long column of marchers and vehicles in Shirley's triumph wended its way through London behind a "presenter" wearing "wings on his shoulders." There followed about twenty antimasquers in allegorical costumes, fourteen trumpeters in crimson satin coats, a marshall with forty-two attendants attired in silver lace and "hats and feathers," and one hundred gentlemen "gloriously furnished," each served by two pages and a groom. Lawes came next in line, riding in the second of two chariots, each surrounded by torchbearers and drawn by four horses "richly furnished and adorned with gold and silver." At the end of the procession amid other torchbearers rolled the "four Triumphals or Magnificent Chariots" of the grand masquers with the "wheels, . . . spokes, and naves, all wrought with silver, and their several colour." Each of these chariots also was pulled by "four horses afront" caparisoned in traces and "rich cloth of silver, of several works and colours, answerable to the linings of the chariots." The grand masquers were uplifted on the cars with "a glorious canopy over their heads, all bordered with silver fringe, and beautified with plumes of feathers on the top" (260–261).

Milton, of course, used as a source for the Son's triumph references in Psalm 68:17 to the Lord's approach to a holy place "with mighty chariotry, twice ten thousand, thousands upon thousands." He was also indebted to images in Ezekiel 1:22 of the Son in a self-moving chariot that had eyes in the wheels, four winged living creatures adjacent, the "likeness of a firmament" constructed over the vehicle, the "likeness of a throne" placed under the firmament. Yet in their patterns of action and military symbolism, the divine pageants in Milton's Heaven reflect Renaissance triumphs in which adorned chariots and strange winged or glittering, star-sequined forms passed in the night and appeared gloriously before a prince or king.

In *Paradise Lost* the Triumph following the war in Heaven begins when the Son reviews the blessed hosts of warrior angels:

> Sole Victor from th' expulsion of his Foes
> *Messiah* his triumphal Chariot turn'd:
> To meet him all his Saints, who silent stood
> Eye-witnesses of his Almighty Acts. (881–884)

The Son's ascent of Heaven's hill, with the holy angels in attendance, is presented as a typological fulfillment of the Son's ascent of

Mount Sion on Palm Sunday. Led on by their divine leader, the heavenly hosts

> With Jubilee advanc'd; and as they went,
> Shaded with branching Palm, each order bright,
> Sung Triumph, and him sung Victorious King.   (885–887)

In this divine recreation of an earthly triumph, Milton also includes typological allusions to the enthronement of the Son on Mount Sion after a victory over the rebellious lords of the earth. Milton's paraphrase of Psalm 2 opens with allusions to this earthly revolt: the Gentiles, Nations, Princes, and Congregations, he writes, "Lay deep their plots together through each Land / Against the Lord and his Messiah dear." But Milton quotes the voice of the Father as saying that the Son has been anointed King on Mount Sion (Psalm II.11–13).

As the divine figural fulfillment of this event on Mount Sion, the Son on the holy hill of Heaven is received and enthroned by the Father:

> . . . he celebrated rode
> Triumphant through mid Heav'n, into the Courts
> And Temple of his mighty Father Thron'd
> On high; who into Glory him receiv'd,
> Where now he sits at the right hand of bliss.   (888–892)

FAR GRANDER in literary design and more elaborate in ritual is Raphael's account of the Son's entry into Heaven after the Creation, an entry that is a reenactment on a higher spiritual plane of the foreshadowing ascent of the Son to Heaven after the angelic battle. "Clouds / Fuming from Golden Censers" hide the mount during this more important return. Heaven rings with a rising crescendo of harmonious music from "Harp," "solemn Pipe," "Dulcimer," "all Organs at sweet sop," and instruments played "by String or Golden Wire." And a host of angelic voices, singing "Choral or Unison" in the manner of the King's Music, joyously pronounce the Son "greater now" in his return "Than from the Giant Angels" following the battle in Heaven (VII.594–605).

This great entry is narrated by Raphael with an emphasis upon the Son's rising:

> . . . Up he rode
> Follow'd with acclamation and the sound
> Symphonious of ten thousand Harps.   (557–559)

The vast, new, and glorious universe expands in perspective as the Son

> . . . up return'd
> Up to the Heav'n of Heav'ns his high abode,
> Thence to behold this new created World
> Th' addition of his Empire, how it show'd
> In prospect from his Throne, how good, how fair.　(552–556)

In the higher regions of the universe, the constellations, personified like
main masque singers, join in the celestial music. In a lower "station" of
this theatrical Heaven, the personified "Planets in thir station list'ning
stood, / While the bright Pomp ascended jubilant" (562–563).

Echoing Psalm 24 with its references to Christ's movement into
Jerusalem, the choir of Constellations continues its song in this second
and more significant reenactment of a prefiguring biblical entry:

> Open, ye everlasting Gates, they sung,
> Open, ye Heav'ns, your living doors; let in
> The great Creator from his work return'd
> Magnificent.　　　　　　　　　　　　　　(565–568)

The "blazing Portals" of Heaven swing wide as the "house" of the
Miltonic Heaven unfolds. The Son, with "glorious Train ascending"
(574),

> . . . led
> To God's Eternal house direct the way,
> A broad and ample road, whose dust is Gold
> And pavement Stars, as Stars to thee appear,
> Seen in the Galaxy, that Milky way
> Which nightly as a circling Zone thou seest
> Powder'd with Stars.　　　　　　　　　　(575–581)

Thus, the Son, in fulfillment of his previous entry into Heaven and of
his entry into Jerusalem upon earth, arrives again at the imperial throne
of the author and omnipresent cause of the Creation.[16] For the Father,
though enthroned in heavenly state,

> . . . also went
> Invisible, yet stay'd (such privilege
> Hath Omnipresence) and the work ordain'd,
> Author and end of all things.　　　　　　(588–591)

OF ALL THE Triumphs of God, it is the announcements in Books III
and XII of the Son's future Redemption that remain the pivotal holy
episodes which thematically and structurally frame the First Parents'
innocence, Fall, and repentance in Eden. The Redemption episodes

place man's fate into cosmic perspective through summations of universal Christian history.[17]

Paradise Lost is thus transformed from what might have been an epic of unadulterated human tragedy into an epic of paradoxically fortuitous human transgression and future human triumph.

Even before Adam and Eve are introduced in Book IV, God the Father in Book III speaks of their impending Fall and the Son of their salvation. "I shall rise Victorious," the Son prophesies, alluding to his role as Messiah. He then proclaims his future triumphant Ascension into Heaven and defeat of evil:

> I through ample Air in Triumph high
> Shall lead Hell Captive maugre Hell, and show
> The powers of darkness bound.   (254–256)

The reader, who learns early in the epic of the divine plan for salvation, waits throughout the later books with ever-growing anticipation for a fallen Adam and Eve to discover that they will be saved. But the postlapsarian First Parents must prepare themselves through their own free choice to receive God's redeeming grace. Consequently, the full revelation of God's grace is denied them until the very end of Book XII. Eve receives in a Heaven-sent dream a presentiment of future good. And Adam hears from Michael of the Son's future sacrificial death, resurrection, and triumphal entry into Heaven:

> . . . to Heav'n of Heav'ns he shall ascend
> With victory, triumphing through the air
> Over his foes and thine; there shall surprise
> The Serpent, Prince of air, and drag in Chains
> Through all his Realm, and there confounded leave;
> Then enter into glory, and resume
> His Seat at God's right hand, exalted high
> Above all names in Heav'n.   (451–458)

Adam rejoices, and the reader rejoices with him. And Milton's masterly aesthetic disposition of divine history culminates in a fresh and trenchant awareness of the human condition following the Fall: sorrow over sin and its consequences, hope for salvation through the Son's coming intervention.

VII

The Future Triumph of Man

THE last books of *Paradise Lost* gain harmony from their unremitting concentration upon two themes essential to the final resolution of the epic: the degree of man's corruption and suffering after the Fall and the exact typological delineation of man's eventual Triumph.

Was postlapsarian man moderately or radically corrupt? Could a divinely instituted society be reestablished upon earth? Was regeneration possible for the few or for the many? Calvinists, Lutherans, Puritans, Quakers, Millenarianists, High and Low Churchmen, Roman Catholics, and divers other religious groups warmly debated these issues; and early readers of *Paradise Lost* could be expected to have scanned the last two books urgently seeking, as Milton's Adam does, to learn about the bitter "Fruit / Of that Forbidden Tree" (I.1–2).

In the digressive intermezzi ending Renaissance *sacre rappresentazioni*, themes arising from these questions were theatrically illustrated. The First Parents would appear "fallen"; personified evils and virtues then entered in procession or in groups, acted out short didactic episodes, and sometimes talked with Adam and Eve. Little or no attempt was made to give depth of character to the personified figures; and usually no "presenter" was in evidence to mediate between the First Parents and the actors playing the virtues and vices. For example, Giambatista Andreini concludes *L'Adamo* (1613) by bringing before Adam and Eve, in a quite haphazard manner, the Seven Deadly Sins, the World, the Flesh, Hunger, Fatigue, Despair, Death, Vain Glory, a chorus of hobgoblins, and the angel Michael.[1] Serafino della Salandra similarly ends his representation *Adamo caduto* (1647) with intermezzi featuring, among others, the First Parents, Cain and Abel, Sin, Death, a chorus of devils, Mercy, and an angel.[2]

Confining elements of masque, biblical story, secular verse, sacred intermezzi, and morality play within the contours of traditional epic visions of the future, Milton gave a freshness of point of view and an originality of presentation and form to episodes that, when read in context, are suggestively symbolic but at times labored narratives. At the very least he avoided inserting pedestrian and loosely structured epochal scenes of future history like those in many *sacre rappresentazioni* and in the dream sequence of Abraham Cowley's unfinished epic *Davideis* (1656; II.460–781).

Critical reaction to the last two books of *Paradise Lost* has been mixed. Milton has recently been acclaimed, with some reservations, for the "vividness" and the "cool objective" quality of passages in Book XI that describe certain allegedly "realistic" visions. However, he has also been censured for adopting a supposedly awkward "middle" style in Book XI and much of Book XII and for committing a "structural error" by having placed a "brief outline of sacred history" in a "momentous position" at the end of the work.[3]

The emphasis of much of this criticism is, I think, misplaced. The visionary scenes in Book XI are emblematic rather than realistic; and when "read" like the moving hieroglyphs on court stages, point within the epic to past and future Triumphs and so draw together central epic themes. And while Milton relies upon Genesis and traditional hexameral materials, he interweaves scenes and events in a somewhat unorthodox and unanticipated fashion. Unexpected similarities and contrasts stimulate the reader to develop new contextual and typological associations. In addition, the poet's less formidably emotive middle style, though surely open to challenge in individual passages, has the effect of suitably tempering the emotional impact of visions in Book XI and early in Book XII showing a terrible pageant of human suffering. Milton reserves his return to a more powerful and lofty poetic flight until later in Book XII when his theme is the future Triumph of man and God.

In general, I find the style appropriate to the subject and the epic conventions of vision and prophecy introduced in an aesthetically satisfactory and thematically revealing manner. But the grand heroic tonalities of the early books are indeed missing from Milton's occasionally faltering representations of human affliction. Individuals reading those early books today grow accustomed, I think, to a monumental epic centered upon figures and episodes that are theatrically opposed, an epic derived in part from seventeenth-century theatrical forms. These readers then become less critically responsive to the "procession" of character-types and scenes in the last two books, a procession that mirrors sixteenth-century masques and shows as well as sixteenth-century "literary pageants" like those featuring the Seven Deadly Sins and Cupid in Spenser's *The Faerie Queene* (I.4.16–36; III.12.3–26). Still, Milton gives great variety and meaning to his prophetic episodes.

A distraught, questioning Adam is placed in the foreground and is made to react with intellectual and emotional instability to each historical vision or story presented by a teacher, the angel Michael. The allegorical figures and character-types rivet attention through the thematic importance of their actions. Adam sees and then distractedly asks Michael about death. The Father of mankind, rejoicing at the lusty pleasure of the envisioned People of the Plain, is rebuked by the angel. Adam plunges into depression watching a scene of battle, but soon after grows elated upon viewing the good man Noah.

The early Christian reader, familiar with the epochs of Christian history and the dispensation of the New Law, could be expected to respond to the scenes from a different religious perspective from that exhibited by this fallen but unredeemed First Parent. The reader could test his own knowledge and feelings against the anguish and vacillating moods of Adam. But it is inaccurate to say, as one critic has, that "Adam's experience is brought abrest of that of Milton's readers" when the First Parent learns that there will be a Messiah.[4] Adam is given only the promise of future Redemption. The early Christian, living after the time of Christ, would have the spiritual experience of actual Redemption. This reader would nevertheless have searched the last two books for revelations about the extent of man's depravity and about the nature of man's "election" in Christ.

The six consecutive visions of evil shown to Adam by Michael in Book XI are balanced against the angel's spoken account in Book XII of a hierarchy of episodes that climax in statements about the future Messiah. At the middle of the arc that this spiritual pendulum traces as it swings from evil to good, Milton places two principal actors: Noah at the end of Book XI and Nimrod at the opening of Book XII. Each is present, Noah unwillingly, at debased anti-Triumphs of sin that contain patterned reflections of past Triumphs of vice and virtue in Hell, Eden, and Heaven. Yet, the anti-Triumphs involving Noah and Nimrod, located at the very center of the epic's outline of future human history, also function as anti-types set against the fulfilling culmination of human development in the promised Triumph of Christ and, through Christ, the Triumph of man. A novel theatrical form is thus imposed upon classical epic conventions of vision and prophecy, a form that enriches the meaning and increases the interwoven typological significance of coming events in mankind's spiritual history.

Appearing to Adam in a fifth vision in Book XI, Noah, as one of the two dominating figures at the middle point in man's history, is seen vainly seeking to convert the lustful People of the Plain to holiness. Adam has already looked upon the people's forebears as they luxuriate in wanton marriage masques of Hymen, the antithesis of the ideal masquelike marriage sequence of the First Parents in prelapsarian Eden.

> . . . of love they treat till th' Evening Star
> Love's Harbinger appear'd; then all in heat
> They light the Nuptial Torch, and bid invoke
> *Hymen*, then first to marriage Rites invoke't;
> With Feast and Musick, all the Tents resound.[5]

The brutal wars that Adam has observed in earlier visions are said to be a "product / Of these ill-mated Marriages" (XI.683–684). Now, in the fifth vision, Adam sees these people, more dissipated than before, occupied in "luxury and riot, feast and dance, / Marrying or prostituting, as befell, / Rape or Adultery" (715–717). Noah, the lone person opposed to these perversions of married love, appears and frequents

> . . . thir Assemblies, whereso met,
> Triumphs or Festivals, and to them preach'd
> Conversion and Repentance, as to Souls
> In Prison under Judgments imminent:
> But all in vain.   (722–726)

These people, Michael explains to Adam, are "of true virtue void" (790).

At this low point in human history, with intemperate mankind indulging in what are in fact corrupt anti-Triumphs, Adam looks on as Noah builds a "Vessel of huge bulk" (729), as "Beast, and Bird and Insect small" (734) enter the vessel with Noah, and as this arc floats safely away on floodwaters that destroy the world. A despondent Adam recovers slightly when he sees Noah still alive and the waters receding, but it is clear that a sorry human epoch has come to an end at this "Noontime of Adam's experience." The presenter angel Michael hesitates:

> As one who in his journey bates at Noon
> Though bent on speed, so here th' Arch-Angel paus'd
> Betwixt the world destroy'd and world restor'd.   (XII.1–3)

This moment of relief brings an expectation of better times.

But in a most effective and surprising theatrical juxtaposition of antithetical themes and character-types, Milton introduces near the beginning of Book XII, not another figure of virtue, but rather the figure of ultimate earthly tyranny and degradation. Evil still exerts its alarming power in the world through the "mighty Hunter" of men, Nimrod, an earthly type for Satan and the reverse of the "salvationist" Noah. The epic narrator explains that Nimrod

> . . . in despite of Heav'n
> Of from Heav'n claiming second Sovranty;
> And from Rebellion shall derive his name,
> Though of Rebellion others he accuse.   (33–36)

"Marching from Eden towards the West," Nimrod and his followers imitating Satan and the devils in Hell, "find / The Plain, wherein a black bituminous gurge / Boils out from under ground, the mouth of Hell." In that infernal earthly landscape Nimrod and his crew, using bitumen and brick, "cast to build," in Michael's words, "A City and Tow'r" (40–44). They manage to erect only another grotesquely grandiose structure, the earthly type for the masquelike Pandemonium located at the navel of Hell's city. "Thus was the building left," comments Michael, "Ridiculous, and the work Confusion nam'd" (61–62).

The depraved human followers of Nimrod, however, live in a verbal chaos and so are incapable of engaging in the false debates and deceptive politics of the devils in Pandemonium. Michael tells Adam that "a hideous gabble rises loud / Among the Builders; each to other calls / Not understood" (56–58). Thus, tyranny rules on earth, Michael explains; and man

> . . . permits
> Within himself unworthy Powers to reign
> Over free Reason, God in Judgment just
> Subjects him from without to violent Lords;
> Who oft as undeservedly enthral
> His outward freedom; Tyranny must be,
> Though to the Tyrant thereby no excuse.   (90–96)

Before the passages on Noah and Nimrod are introduced into the middle of Milton's epic history of the human race, Adam in Book XI is

[106]

shown other visions or "dumb shows" by Michael. In content and ordering these visions or shows, which are based upon events described in Genesis, owe much to theatrical sources as well as to medieval and Renaissance conceptions of biblical epochs. In Book XII traditional biblical typology gives a more dominant form and meaning to narrated events.[6]

The visionary topoi in Book XI show the influence of both the four drafts of "Adam Unparadiz'd" and the theatrical outlines in the Trinity College manuscript. The death of Cain (vision one) derives from the figure Death listed in the first three drafts of "Adam Unparadiz'd"; the sick in what seems to be a lazar house (vision two), from Sickness in the same three drafts; the men in battle (vision four), from Hatred, Envie, and Warre in the third draft. The lustful People of the Plain (visions three and five) have their theatrical origins in "Cupid's funeral Pyre" or "Sodom Burning," the outline placed over that of "Adam Unparadiz'd" in the manuscript. The flood (vision six) stems from the projected representation "The Deluge" on page 36 of the outlines. In *Paradise Lost* the great inundation is depicted as God's immediate reaction to the lewd Triumphs of the People of the Plain, and so was in part disposed as a result of Milton's theatrical associations. Michael's descent from Heaven to Eden, which precedes the visions, originates with the reference in "Adam Unparadiz'd" to an angel's being sent to banish the First Parents "out of paradise but before causes to passe before his [Adam's] eyes in shapes a mask."[7]

The masquelike cloud descent of the mighty archangel Michael, described by an excited Adam and then by the epic narrator, is a visually compelling episode with dress, stately movement, light imagery, and tone of speech all divulging its inner spiritual significance. Adam, gazing into the eastern skies, is captivated by the sight of an illuminated "Cloud that draws / O're the blue Firmament a radiant white, / And slow descends, with something heav'nly fraught" (XI.205–207). As this cloud in flaming light touches down and obscures the highest hill in Eden, the First Parent grows even more excited:

> ... I descry
> From yonder blazing Cloud that veils the Hill
> One of the heav'nly Host, and by his Gait
> None of the meanest, some great Potentate
> Or of the Thrones above.   (228–232)

"Th' Arch-Angel soon drew nigh," reports the epic narrator, "Not in his shape Celestial, but as Man / Clad to meet Man" (238–240).

This angel, wearing special garments, approaches Adam in a manner suggesting the entrance of the rainbow goddess Iris in Samuel Daniel's masque *The Vision of the Twelve Goddesses* (1604). Iris, dressed in multicolored robes, "descends from the top of a Mountaine raised at the lower end of the Hall" and then crosses the hall to another masquer playing the role of Sybilla. Among the twelve goddesses who appear in succession and descend the mountain is "*Pallas* (which was the person her Majestie chose to represent) . . . attyred in a blew mantle, with silver imbrodery of all weapons and engines of war, with a helmet-dressing on her head, and presents a Launce and Target."[8]

Michael, "Clad to meet Man," wears a costume combining features of Iris's and Pallas's theatrical clothing:

> . . . over his lucid Armes
> A Military Vest of purple flow'd
> Livelier than *Melibaean*, or the grain
> Of *Sarra*, worn by Kings and Heroes old
> In time of Truce; *Iris* had dipt the woof;
> His starry Helm unbuckl'd show'd him prime
> In Manhood where Youth ended; by his side
> As in a glistering *Zodiac* hung the Sword,
> Satan's dire dread, and in his hand the Spear.   (240–248)

In the tradition of performers who bow with "low reverence" to the state, as the Genius did in Milton's entertainment *Arcades*, "*Adam* bow'd low, hee Kingly from his State / Inclin'd not" (249–250). "Ascend / This Hill," commands Michael after speaking briefly of mankind's future ills, "let *Eve* (for I have drencht her eyes) / Here sleep below while thou to foresight wak'st" (366–368). On this lofty summit, one foreshadowing the hill on which Christ the "second *Adam*" (383) will one day be tempted by Satan, this "first Adam" gazes into the future.

In the early 1640s, when Milton noted in "Adam Unparadiz'd" that the angel "causes to passe before his eyes in shapes a mask of all the evills of this life & world," the poet had only a few years before included three scenic discoveries in *Comus*. Milton clearly realized that the aim of such discoveries, as established in the practice and theory of Continental and English masque architects, was to catch spectators by surprise, to startle and delight them with a sudden "glory" through the unexpected exposure and alteration of scenery. Stage directions of the period reflect such aims. In Campion's *Somerset's Masque* "the eye first of all" is said to be "entertayned" by a seascape; "a strange prospect detain'd the eyes of the Spectators some time" in Carew's *Coelum Britannicum;* and in Jonson's *Chloridia* "the spectators . . . fed their eyes with the delights of a landscape."[9]

Every vision seen by Adam also begins with an allusion to the First Parent's "looking and seeing" or to Adam's "eye" "beholding" some new, unanticipated prospect. "Adam look'd," writes the narrator of a quickly altered vision, "and saw the face of things quite chang'd" (712). Adam's epic visions are in fact staged with an obvious awareness of masque production techniques emphasizing the discovery of scenes and character-types as a prelude to action. In viewing the opening vision, Adam first beholds a scenic background:

> His eyes he op'n'd, and beheld a field,
> Part arable and tilth, whereon were Sheaves
> New reapt, the other part sheep-walks and folds;
> I' th' midst an Altar as the Land-mark stood
> Rustic, of grassy sward. (429–433)

The next words imply that Adam has been allowed a pause, so that his eyes might be "entertained," before the major shapes or figures enter:

> . . . thither anon
> A sweaty Reaper from his Tillage brought
> First fruits, the green Ear, and the yellow Sheaf,
> Uncull'd, as came to hand; a Shepherd next
> More meek came with the Firstlings of his Flock
> Choicest and best. (433–438)

Action ensues as Adam watches the shepherd Cain and the reaper Abel place their respective offerings on the flaming altar. Cain's offering remains unconsumed, and in anger Cain slays Abel.

In the second vision, there first appears before Adam's eyes a house of sickness filled with allegorical figures of disease (478–490). Only after witnessing this scene of horror does Adam see a central figure in motion: "And over them triumphant Death his Dart / Shook, but delay'd to strike" (491–492). This theatrical technique of presenting sequentially the scene, central figures, and action is repeated in all visions except the fifth; in that one the depiction of a scenic background is neglected because the place of action, a plain, has already been described in the third vision. The aesthetic impact of the miraculous series of swiftly changing and startling speaking pictures is thus enhanced by Milton's use of seventeenth-century stagecraft.

The more abstract part of Adam's prophetic education takes place in

Book XII. Michael explains that, because of the limitations of Adam's spiritual sight, the greatest religious events of the future will necessarily be revealed in story but not in vision:

> ... I perceive
> Thy mortal sight to fail; objects divine
> Must needs impair and weary human sense;
> Henceforth what is to come I will relate,
> Thou therefore give due audience, and attend.   (8–12)

Yet in recounting Old Testament events focused on Nimrod, Abraham, Moses, and the Israelites, the angel enlivens his crisp monologues by speaking in the present tense and sometimes actually glimpsing the events described. "I see his Tents," says Michael of Abraham, "Pitcht about Secham, and the neighboring Plain" (135–136). At one point the angel asks Adam to look with ordinary, finite vision upon a river visible from the summit of Eden. "See where it flows," remarks Michael of the Nile, "disgorging at seven mouths / Into the Sea" (158–159). Telling visual details of this kind disappear from the angelic narrative when Michael speaks with controlled emotion of what "will" and "must" happen with the coming of the Messiah; for the future Passion, death, and Triumph of the Savior remain invisible to angelic as well as to mortal sight.

Despite some divergences, the most important themes and actions in Book XII stem from Milton's notations in the final outline of "Adam Unparadiz'd." According to the outline, Adam, after witnessing the "mask" of evils, remains in Eden with an angel and "relents, dispaires. at last appeares Mercy comforts him *& brings in faith hope & charity* promises the Messiah, then calls in faith hope, & charity, instructs him he repents gives god the glory, submitts to his penalty the chorus breifly concludes." The poet varied and added to this plan in the epic by having Adam continue to repent but not to despair, by referring to Faith, Hope, and Charity as immaterial virtues rather than as personified figures, and by allowing Michael verbally to instruct Adam and to promise the Messiah. Adam, in both the outline and the epic, "submitts to his penalty" and is driven with Eve from the Garden, but in *Paradise Lost* it is the epic narrator instead of the chorus who "briefly concludes."

Michael's comments are replete with typological messages pointing to man's reception of the theological virtues and the coming of Christ.[10] Michael observes that mankind has been renewed by Noah and now requires a

> ... Mediator, whose high Office now
> *Moses* in figure bears, to introduce

> One greater, of whose day he shall foretell,
> And all the Prophets in thir Age the times
> Of great *Messiah* shall sing. (240–244)

Moses through the Law received on Mount Sinai, Michael continues, shall inform

> . . . them by types
> And shadows, of that destin'd Seed to bruise
> The serpent, by what means he shall achieve
> Mankind's deliverance. (232–235)

The hierarchy of man's spiritual development, arranged through a series of foreshadowed and fulfilled covenants and types, is most fully disclosed in Michael's delineation of the main historical epochs extending from Noah to Christ:

> So Law appears imperfet, and but giv'n
> With purpose to resign them in full time
> Up to a better Cov'nant, disciplin'd
> From shadowy Types to Truth, from Flesh to Spirit,
> From imposition of strict Laws, to free
> Acceptance of large Grace, from servile fear
> To filial, works of Law to works of Faith.
> And therefore shall not *Moses*, though of God
> Highly belov'd, being but the Minister
> Of Law, his people into *Canaan* lead;
> But *Joshua* whom the Gentiles *Jesus* call,
> His Name and Office bearing, who shall quell
> The adversary Serpent, and bring back
> Through the world's wilderness long wander'd man
> Safe to eternal Paradise of rest. (300–314)

Faith, Hope, and Charity, now introduced thematically but not personified as they had been in the outlines of "Adam Unparadiz'd," will be attained by man through the advent of the Son. Michael says that the Son will be accepted by "all who shall believe / In his redemption, and that his obedience / Imputed becomes theirs by Faith" (407–409). Overcome by joy, the First Parent cries out:

> O Prophet of glad tidings, finisher
> Of utmost hope! now clear I understand
> What oft my steadiest thoughts have searcht in vain. (375–377)

Supported by faith and "utmost hope," man shall one day see the Law fulfilled, Michael states, through love of the Son:

> The Law of God exact he shall fulfil
> Both by obedience and by love, though love
> Alone fulfil the Law. (402–404)

The Son in a future epoch will redeem man, overcome death, and "ascend / With victory, triumphing through the air." The Savior will then resume "His Seat at God's right hand, exalted high / Above all names in Heav'n" (450–458). Michael then speaks of the "last things," the final epochal return of Christ that will introduce man to the bliss of an eternal paradise. The Messiah

> ... thence shall come
> When this world's dissolution shall be ripe,
> With glory, and power to judge both quick and dead,
> To Judge th' unfaithful dead, but to reward
> His faithful, and receive them into bliss,
> Whether in Heav'n or Earth, for then the Earth
> Shall all be Paradise, far happier place
> Than this of Eden, and far happier days. (458–465)

No wonder, then, that Adam—uplifted through an acceptance of the theological virtues, offered the promise of a Messiah, and, finally, instructed in the way mankind will one day enter a place "far happier . . . than . . . Eden"—exclaims with joy:

> O goodness infinite, goodness immense!
> That all this good of evil shall produce
> And evil turn to good; more wonderful
> Than that which by creation first brought forth
> Light out of darkness! (469–473)

With his imagination sweeping back to the first moment of earthly history, the Creation, Adam in a rapture of happiness looks forward to entering Paradise at the end of historical time. Adam can now leave the earthly paradise knowing that he and Eve will possess, in Michael's words, "A paradise within, . . . happier far" (578). The First Parents will live, the angel declares,

> ... though sad
> With cause for evils past, yet much more cheer'd
> With meditation on the happy end. (603–605)

There now remains only that most theatrical of events initially suggested at the end of the last draft of "Adam Unparadiz'd": the angel's banishment of the First Parents from Eden. The last poetic moments of the epic are charged with tension as Adam and Eve, in an unforgettable speaking picture, are torn by conflicting emotions of dismay, uncertainty, confusion, and hope. In a scene of vivid imagery and striking fire effects, movements of delay and haste, emblematic descents from level to level, and intense speech and gestures, the spiritual significance of the Fall is poignantly disclosed. A sad yet paradoxically hopeful spiritual dilemma is depicted as one or both First Parents descend emblematically in stages from hill to Garden to bower and then down from the cliff of Eden to the plain.

The patterned theatrical design for the scene can be readily found in the conventions of main masque "descent." Main masquers first appeared in an ideal scenic realm usually representing a temple, a garden, a mountain, a grotto, or a cloudy heaven. On foot or on machines and often accompanied by a presenter, they "paced" or glided downward and forward to the lower level of the stage. Then sometimes holding hands, if men and women were performing together, the masquers in pairs or in formation paced down steps from the raised stage into the main hall and the actual social world of their peers.

In the masque frequently cited as a source for *Comus*, Jonson's *Pleasure Reconciled to Virtue*, the main masquers descend from open Mount Atlas to the lower stage and then down from the stage to the green-carpeted dancing space in the hall proper. The presenter Daedalus "comes downe before" the masquers "On their descent from ye hill" (236–237). A "Guardian of the *Hill*," Hercules, remains behind on the raised stage (183). And a "Quire of Musique" then sings a "descent" song that directs attention to the pacing of the main masquers:

> Se how they come, and show
> that are but borne to know
>   Descend,
>   descend,
>   though pleasure lead,
>   feare not to follow:
>   they who are bread
>   within the hill
>   of skill,
>   may safely tread
>   what path they will.   (224–234)

"Who's this that leads?" asks the main masque figure Hermes. "A guide yt gives them Lawes / to all yeir motions" (242–244), replies Mercury.

The featured main masquers step forward on the level dancing space in the hall. Daedalus, remaining in his turn behind, sings of their curious speaking picture:

> ... if those silent arts were lost,
> Design, & Picture: they might boast
> from you a newer ground:
> .....
> Make haste, make haste, for this
> The Laborinth of Beautie is. (282–295)

The main masquers very possibly gaze back at Mount Atlas when the "Quire of Musique" later responds:

> An eye of looking back, were well,
> or any murmur that wold tell
> yor thought, how you were sent,
> and went. (323–326)

Although the thematic content of the scene in *Pleasure Reconciled to Virtue* is different from that in Milton's epic, the patterned theatrical action in the two works is similar. The last scene in *Paradise Lost* begins as Adam, Michael, and the angels guarding Eden all move down from a high to a middle level. Adam and Michael together "both descend the Hill" of Eden to the central Garden. Adam then hurries on alone before his guide and so further "Descended ... to the Bow'r where *Eve* / Lay sleeping ... but found her wak't" (605–608). From another hill in Eden, the angelic Cherubim "all in bright array ... descended" with "Gliding" movements and, like the chorus of angels in the last outline of "Adam Unparadiz'd," position themselves at a "fixt Station" in the Garden. A fiery emblematic device, one resembling the burning globes and firebrands that appeared floating in masque heavens, is very much in evidence; for "high in Front" of these advancing guardians, "the brandisht Sword of God ... blaz'd / Fierce as a Comet" with "torrid heat, / And vapor" (627–635).

Using the familiar dance gesture of presentation, the "hast'ning Angel" Michael grasps the "ling'ring Parents" in "either hand" and controls their motions as he quickly takes them to the lowest level of the scene. The angel "Led them direct, and down the Cliff as fast / To the subjected Plain; then disappear'd" (637–640). The now silent First Parents exhibit their remorse through further emblematic action:

> They looking back, all th' Eastern side beheld
> Of Paradise, so late thir happy seat,

Wav'd over by that flaming Brand, the Gate
With dreadful Faces throng'd and fiery Arms;
Some natural tears they dropp'd, but wip'd them soon.
(641–645)

Turning their gaze away from the mount, Adam and Eve, pacing uncertainly forward with hands clasped in mutual devotion, move in sadness but with renewed faith toward the plain:

The World was all before them, where to choose
Thir place of rest, and Providence thir guide:
They hand in hand with wand'ring steps and slow,
Through *Eden* took thir solitary way.   (646–649)

NOTES

INDEX

Notes

I. The Inward Vision

1. A description of the ceremonies and the hall appears in David Masson, *The Life of John Milton*, vol. 1, rev. ed. (New York, 1881; reprint ed., 1946), pp. 285–297 (hereafter cited as Masson). For accounts of the ceremonies see also *The Life Records of John Milton*, ed. J. Milton French, vol. 1 (New Brunswick, N.J., 1949), pp. 165–170; *Milton: Private Correspondence and Academic Exercises*, ed. Phyllis B. Tillyard and E. M. W. Tillyard (Cambridge, 1932), p. 140; William Riley Parker, *Milton: A Biography* (Oxford, 1968), 1: 43–49, 2: 739–740; and J. T. Sheppard, *"Music at Belmont" and Other Essays* (London, 1951), pp. 152–162. An analysis of selected criticism of the exercise appears in *A Variorum Commentary on the Poems of John Milton*, ed. A. S. P. Woodhouse and Douglas Bush, vol. 2, pt. 1 (New York, 1972). The leader of the vacation festivities at Cambridge was traditionally called the Father, and Milton so refers to himself in a short preliminary address to the other students: "I turn me, therefore, as Father, to my sons" (trans. from Masson, 1: 292).

2. Quotations with trans. from Masson, 1: 289–290.

3. Masson, 1: 39.

4. See these verse segments of *At a Vacation Exercise* in *John Milton: Complete Poems and Major Prose*, ed. Merritt Y. Hughes (New York, 1957), p. 30, lines 1–31. All references in this chapter to the verse of *At a Vacation Exercise*, to Milton's minor poems, to *Paradise Lost*, and to the Latin exercise *On the Fifth of November* with trans. by Hughes are from this edition.

5. In the extensive commentary on Milton's verse, serious study of his philosophical-epistemological views has been stimulated largely by critics concerned with the question of his alleged heresy in theology. Discussion has recently centered on the way that Milton used the terms *substantia* and *essentia* to denote man's rational comprehension of the fundamental nature

of being. See in particular the theological-philosophical essay by William B. Hunter, "Further Definitions: Milton's Theological Vocabulary," *Bright Essence: Studies in Milton's Theology,* with essays by Hunter, C. A. Patrides, and J. H. Adamson (Salt Lake City, 1971), pp. 15–25; and in the same volume the essay by Patrides, "Milton on the Trinity: The Use of Antecedents," pp. 3–13. Denis Saurat, in *Milton: Man and Thinker,* 2nd rev. ed. (New York, 1944), pp. 117–133, calls special attention to what he considers an unorthodox begetting of the Son in *Paradise Lost* (V.600–606). Arthur Sewell presents an account of Milton's supposedly changing theological views in *A Study of Milton's "Christian Doctrine"* (London, 1939). Points raised by Sewell and Saurat are examined by George N. Conklin in *Biblical Criticism and Heresy in Milton* (New York, 1949). Maurice Kelley claims that Milton was an Arian in theology in *This Great Argument: A Study of Milton's "De Doctrina Christiana" as a Gloss upon "Paradise Lost"* (Princeton, 1941). Exception to this position is taken by Patrides in *Milton and the Christian Tradition* (Oxford, 1966) and by Patrides, Hunter, and Adamson in the essays in *Bright Essence.* See also Kelley, "Milton's Arianism Again Considered," *Harvard Theological Review* 54 (1961): 195–205; Sister Miriam Joseph, "Orthodoxy in *Paradise Lost,*" *Laval theologique et philosphique* 8 (1952): 252–254; and Chapter 6. Father Walter Ong—in "Milton's Logical Epic and Evolving Consciousness," *Proceedings of the American Philosophical Society* 120 (1976): 295–305; and in "Logic and the Epic Muse: Reflections on Noetic Structures in Milton's Milieu," in *Achievements of the Left Hand: Essays on the Prose of John Milton,* ed. Michael Lieb and John T. Shawcross (Amherst, Mass., 1974), pp. 239–268—suggests that Milton, in creating the internal didactic content of *Paradise Lost,* displays a new and refined consciousness of classical and Renaissance logic. However, in "Logic and the Epic Muse" Ong adds pointedly, "About Milton as a logician, one thing can readily be said: he contributed nothing to the internal development of logic, directly or indirectly" (p. 295).

6. *Ivlii Caesaris Scaligeri, Uiri Clarissimi, Poetices libri septem, Apvd Antonivm Vincentium* (Lugduni, 1561), bk. 2, p. 50. Scaliger argues that words receive their form from that of created things: "Res autem ipsae finis sunt orationis, quarum verba notae sunt. Quamobrem ab ipsis rebus formam illam accipiunt, qua hoc ipsum sunt, quod sunt": "Things in themselves are the goal of diction, words serving as notations of things. Consequently, words receive from things themselves that form which makes words exactly what they are" (p. 80).

7. In *Paradise Lost* (V.485–490) Milton gives to the angel Raphael lines that define the logical or "discursive" and intuitive rational powers of mortal man. In a recent elaboration of a neoscholastic aesthetic theory whose general epistemological features share the Christian-Aristotelian outlook espoused by Milton and Italian theorists such as Scaliger, Jacques Maritain, in *Creative Intuition in Art and Poetry* (New York, 1953), p. 75n, approv-

ingly cites Raphael's statement. Maritain maintains that the intuitive and logical powers of the artist's rational mind, controlling and directing imagination, establish a degree of identification with the supposed immaterial essences of external being. According to Maritain, the artist then seeks to disclose the essences by molding the "matter" of his particular art. Unlike Milton in Elegy VI and Scaliger in *Poetics*, however, Maritain distinguishes between ethics, defined as knowledge for the sake of acting, and art, defined as knowledge for the sake of making. See also Maritain, *Art and Scholasticism*, trans. J. F. Scanlan (New York, 1930); and *The Situation in Poetry*, trans. Marshall Suther (New York, 1955).

In *A History of Literary Criticism in the Italian Renaissance*, vol. 2 (Chicago, 1961), Bernard Weinberg accurately observes that in Scaliger's theory "words . . . are the 'material' of poetry and they are used to express the 'form,' of things" (p. 744). Writing further of Scaliger, Weinberg adds: "Here again, we touch upon one of the characteristic features of his system, upon one of its original assumptions. We have already seen that the fundamental dichotomy of the work is 'res: verba' and that, of these elements, it is 'res' that is more important; words are merely a reflection of things. We now know further that the 'res' of poetry is indistinguishable from the 'res' of reality. As a result, Scaliger's treatment of 'Idea' (Book III) is a kind of composite of all human sciences: it combines a psychology, an ethics, a politics, a metaphysics. We discover in it what man is, and then we know what man in poetry should be. In his own words, concluding the discussion of 'Idea': 'These things, which are thus constituted by nature, must be discovered in the bosom of nature and, plucked out therefrom, must be exposed before the eyes of men' " (p. 746).

It should be noted by way of contrast that another famous Renaissance tract on poetry, George Puttenham's *The Arte of English Poesie* (1520?, 1601?), ed. Gladys Willcock and Alice Walker (Cambridge, 1936), avoids epistemological formulations and stresses the role of logic or discourse in the rhetorical process. Puttenham does not raise the issue of how reason and imagination might unveil the forms of reality.

8. Rhetorical techniques employed to create poetically a garment of sensuous imagery have been examined by Rosemond Tuve in *Elizabethan and Metaphysical Imagery* (Chicago, 1947), *Images and Themes in Five Poems by Milton* (Cambridge, Mass., 1957), and *Essays by Rosemond Tuve: Spenser, Herbert, Milton* (Princeton, 1970). See also Ruth Wallerstein, *Studies in Seventeenth-Century Poetic* (Madison, 1950); John M. Steadman, *Milton's Epic Characters: Image and Idol* (Chapel Hill, 1959), *Milton and the Renaissance Hero* (Oxford, 1967), and *The Lamb and the Elephant: Ideal Imitation and the Context of Renaissance Allegory* (San Marino, Calif., 1974); Helen Darbishire, "Milton's Poetic Language," *Essays and Studies* 10 (1957): 31–52; Christopher Ricks, *Milton's Grand Style* (Oxford, 1963); and Ernest S. Sprott, *Milton's Art of Prosody* (Oxford, 1963). The influence upon Milton of the Italian rhetorical tradition has been explored by

Steadman in *Epic and Tragic Structure in "Paradise Lost"* (Chicago and London, 1976); by F. T. Prince in *The Italian Element in Milton's Verse* (Oxford, 1954); and by Joseph Mazzeo in *Renaissance and Seventeenth-Century Studies* (New York, 1964). The authoritative account in English of the general Italian rhetorical background is Weinberg's two-volume *History of Literary Criticism.*

Illuminating examinations of the rhetoric taught in seventeenth-century Latin grammar schools can be found in Donald Clark, *John Milton at St. Paul's School: A Study of Ancient Rhetoric in English Renaissance Education* (New York, 1948); and T. W. Baldwin, *Shakespeare's Small Latine and Lesse Greeke*, 2. vols. (Carbondale, Ill., 1944). See also J. B. Broadbent, "Milton's Rhetoric," *Modern Philology* 56 (1959): 224–242; Darbishire, "Milton's Prosody in the Poems of the Trinity College Manuscript," *PMLA* 54 (1939): 153–183; William B. Hunter, "The Sources of Milton's Prosody," *Philological Quarterly* 28 (1949): 125–144; George A. Kellog, "'Bridges': Milton's Prosody and Renaissance Metrical Theory," *PMLA* 68 (1953): 268–285; and Rosalie L. Colie, *Paradoxia Epidemica: The Renaissance Tradition of Paradox* (Princeton, 1966).

9. For studies emphasizing divers modern critical perspectives rather than traditional rhetoric, see in particular the new critical analysis of Cleanth Brooks and John Edward Hardy in *The Poems of Mr. John Milton* (New York, 1951); Donald F. Bouchard's comments on structure in *Milton: A Structural Reading* (Montreal, 1974); Stanley Fish's observations on the reader's experience in *Surprised by Sin: The Reader in "Paradise Lost"* (New York, 1967); Northrop Frye's application of special literary types to *Paradise Lost* and *Paradise Regained* in *The Return of Eden: Five Essays on Milton's Epics* (Toronto, 1965); and Anne Davidson Ferry's investigation of the persona of the narrator in *Milton's Epic Voice: The Narrator in "Paradise Lost"* (Cambridge, Mass., 1963). See as well the contemporary readings of Arnold Stein in *Answerable Style: Essays on "Paradise Lost"* (Minneapolis, 1963) and *Heroic Knowledge: An Interpretation of "Paradise Regained" and "Samson Agonistes"* (Minneapolis, 1957); Jackson Cope in *The Metaphoric Structure of "Paradise Lost"* (Baltimore, 1962); and Isabel MacCaffrey in *"Paradise Lost" as Myth* (Cambridge, Mass., 1959).

10. *A Fuller Institution of the Art of Logic arranged after the method of Peter Ramus* in *The Works of John Milton*, ed. Frank Allen Patterson, vol. 11, (New York, 1935), bk. 1, chap. 7, p. 63. For a recent analysis of Milton's views concerning man's knowledge of natural things, see Lee A. Jacobus, *Sudden Apprehension: Aspects of Knowledge in "Paradise Lost"* (The Hague and Paris, 1976), pp. 45–88.

11. Hunter discusses Milton's conception of the individuation of being in "Further Definitions," pp. 15–25.

12. Both Tuve and Ferry, though approaching Milton's verse from quite different critical perspectives, rightly caution against too restricted a

reading of even seemingly conventional allegorical passages. In *Images and Themes* Tuve observes: "We see one variety after another of the delicately differentiated ways which the Middle Ages and Renaissance found to profit by the fact that reading allegorically provides multiple and extreme extensions of meaning. Historical and moral allegory are but the best-known two of these ways; Milton uses both, and others. We can if we wish find the familiar four-fold meanings; and though we shall be wise if we ape the Middle Ages in their unrigorous and sporadic application of theme, I have used the scheme where I have thought a distinction could thus be usefully made or caught." She adds, however, that in Milton's poetry "we see figures in action in which writers and readers of the age itself would never have attempted to distinguish a 'symbolical' from an 'allegorical' working" (p. 12). In *Essays by Rosemond Tuve* she discusses the symbolic quality of Milton's poetry: "We do not take in his special form of common figure just by staring at it. This is because great images *symbolize;* they do not just 'stand for' some idea which we carry around with us by nature, and hence always know enough to appreciate fully, wherever we meet it" (p. 259).

In *Milton's Epic Voice* Ferry has perceptively observed that often in *Paradise Lost*, "by supporting both abstract and concrete meanings, the diction supports at once the particular historical reference of the story and its universal and inward meanings. Fact and meaning cannot be separated as they are in allegory. Each expresses the other in the unity of divine truth, so that the two references of a single work become the two terms of a metaphor by which their meanings are identified." She concludes that the diction of many lines by Milton "therefore prevents them from being read as Spenser in many passages (especially ones which begin his episodes) tells us that *The Faerie Queene* must be read" (p. 93). Ferry's modern usage of the term "metaphor," however, somewhat oversimplifies and alters what for Milton would have been both a rhetorical and a metaphysical relationship, a presentation through words of an Argument and a grasping through words of the complexly unified predicaments, adjuncts, essences, and substances of external being.

An analysis of the various kinds of medieval and Renaissance allegory can be found in John G. Demaray, *The Invention of Dante's "Commedia"* (New Haven and London, 1974), pp. 93–115. For a discussion of the symbolic nature of the hieroglyphs or emblems frequently used by Milton, see Rosemary Freeman, *English Emblem Books* (London, 1948); and Allardyce Nicoll, "Court Hieroglyphicks," *Stuart Masques and the Renaissance Stage* (New York, 1938), pp. 154–191.

13. Other possible sources—including Giambattista Marino's *Strage de gli innocenti*, Phineas Fletcher's *Locustae, vel Pietas Jesuitica*, and the anonymous author of the Latin poem *Pareus*—are mentioned in *The Poetical Works of John Milton*, ed. Henry J. Todd, 2nd ed., vol. 7 (London, 1809), pp. 310–312. See the discussion of Milton's possible debts to Fletcher and others in *A Variorum Commentary on the Poems of John Milton*, ed.

Douglas Bush, J. E. Shaw, and Bartlett Giamatti, vol. 1 (New York, 1970), pp. 167–200. Macon Cheek has shown how Milton's depiction of an aerial flight, a view of Rome, and the celestial messenger Fame suggests passages from Virgil's *Aeneid*. See Cheek's "Milton's *In Quintum Novembris:* An Epic Foreshadowing," *Studies in Philology* 54 (1957): 172–184.

14. Quotation with trans. from Masson, 1: 224–225.

15. The quotation is from Elegy VII, dated 1628 and addressed to Alexander Gill (see Masson, 1: 189). The incident recounted is attributed by Masson to the first or second of May of that year.

16. Masson, 1: 190. See also *Of Reformation* in *Works of John Milton,* ed. Patterson, vol. 3. (New York, 1931), pt. 1. In this tract Milton plainly discloses his conception of the state as a living and single body politic: "Alas Sir! a Commonwelth ought to be but as one huge Christian personage, one mighty growth, and stature of an honest man, as big, and compact in vertue as in body; for looke what the grounds, and causes are of single happines to one man, the same yee shall find them to a whole state, as *Aristotle* both in his ethicks, and politiks, from the principles of reason layes down" (p. 38).

II. Inconstant Theatrical Designs

1. Quoted from *John Milton's Complete Poetical Works Reproduced in Photographic Facsimile,* ed. Harris Francis Fletcher, vol. 3 (Urbana, Ill., 1945), p. 69 (hereafter cited as Fletcher).

2. A factual and well-documented account of crucial dates and circumstances related to Dryden's and Milton's publications in the 1660s and 1670s appears in Fletcher, 3: 9–13. See Dryden's comment on the time of composition in *The Works of John Dryden,* ed. with notes Walter Scott, vol. 5 (London, 1808), p. 105.

3. *The Early Lives of Milton,* ed. Helen Darbishire (London, 1932), p. 7.

4. From *The Monitor,* vol. 1, no. 17, first reprinted in Raymond D. Havens, "Mr. Dryden Meets Mr. Milton," *Weekly Review* 1 (14 June 1919): 110. The statement is also reprinted in Darbishire, *Early Lives,* p. 335; and in George Thron-Drury, "Some Notes on Dryden," *Review of English Studies* 1 (1925): 79–83. Morris Freedman offers detailed comment about the meeting in "Dryden's 'Memorable Visit' to Milton," *Huntington Library Quarterly* 18 (1955): 99–108. Although David Masson, in *The Life of John Milton,* vol. 6 (New York, 1880; reprint ed., 1946), p. 708 (hereafter cited as Masson), states that the meeting "must have been in the winter of 1673–74," this conjecture is based upon only the few facts already cited and upon the date of registry of *The State of Innocence.* Exactly when the visit took place is unknown.

5. *The Tempest or The Enchanted Island: A Comedy at the Duke of York's Theatre* (London, printed by J. Macock, 1676). The special effects

mentioned are described in the stage directions on pp. 1–5, 14, 26, 37, 78, and 80. For information on dating, including the actual appearance of the printed version in 1677, and Samuel Pepys's comments about its production at the Duke of York's Theatre, see *The London Stage, 1660–1800: A Calendar of Plays, Entertainments, and Afterpieces,* ed. William Van Lennep, intro. Emmett L. Avery and Arthur H. Scoutes (Carbondale, Ill., 1965), pp. 123ff. Details about the collaboration of Dryden and Davenant are discussed in Charles E. Ward, *The Life of John Dryden* (Chapel Hill, 1961), pp. 48–53; and in *The Works of John Dryden,* ed. H. T. Swedenberg, Jr., Vinton Dearing, and Earl Miner, vol. 10 (Berkeley and Los Angeles, 1970), pp. 319–343.

6. *The State of Innocence and the Fall of Man, an Opera Written in Heroique Verse and Dedicated to Her Royal Highness the Dutchess* (London, printed by T. N. for Henry Herringman, 1677). A full account of the printing of the second edition of *Paradise Lost,* as well as a photographic facsimile of the text, appears in Fletcher, vol. 3. Masson, 6: 708–710, argues on slender circumstantial evidence that printer Samuel Simmons, fearful of losing money as the result of a competing work by Dryden on the Fall, probably urged Milton to prepare a revised edition of *Paradise Lost.* Masson assumes that Marvell had seen a manuscript copy of Dryden's "tagged" lines before writing verses to introduce the second edition. Masson's speculations could well be correct, for Simmons did exert influence upon the poet. Simmons had earlier prevailed upon Milton to add an "Argument" to the second printing of the first edition. Evidence suggests that Simmons halted or delayed his in-progress printing of Caryl on Job to set in type and publish the second edition of *Paradise Lost* (see Fletcher, 3: 9). The handwritten fair copy of Book I, produced by an amanuensis and used for the licensing of the epic—the only handwritten segment of *Paradise Lost* still in existence—is now at the Pierpont Morgan Library, New York, where I have examined it. This fair copy was held by the Tonson family from 1683 until the early 1900s, when it was brought to the United States.

7. In the prologue to *The Empress of Morocco: A Tragedy. with Sculptures. As it is Acted at the Dukes Theatre* (London, 1673), Elkanah Settle referred to the demise of the masque in addressing aristocrats, who had now become known as gallants:

> *Your best belov'd diversion is not here,*
> *All you're now like to have is a dull Play.*
> *The* Wells *have stoln the Vizar Masks away.*
> *Now punk in penitential* Drink *begins,*
> *To purge the surfeit of her London Sins.*   (Unnumbered page)

Allardyce Nicoll includes excellent accounts of the merging of genres and the development of the new "heroic" plays in *A History of English Drama, 1660–1900,* vol. 1 (Cambridge, 1952), pp. 26–42. See also Nicoll, *Dryden as Adapter of Shakespeare* (London, 1922); Gerald Eades Bentley,

The Jacobean and Caroline Stage, vol. 6 (Oxford, 1968), pp. 260–310; Edward J. Dent, *Foundations of English Opera* (New York, 1965); and Leslie Hotson, *The Commonwealth and Restoration Stage* (Cambridge, 1928). Dryden's heroic dramas are examined in Anne T. Barbeau, *The Intellectual Design of John Dryden's Heroic Plays* (New York and London, 1970); Arthur C. Kirsch, *Dryden's Heroic Drama* (Princeton, 1965); and B. J. Pendlebury, *Dryden's Heroic Plays: A Study of Origins* (New York, 1923). The details of English and Continental theatrical spectacles are included in *The Renaissance Stage: Documents of Serlio, Sabbatti, and Furttenbach*, trans. Allardyce Nicoll, John H. McDowell, and George R. Kernodle, ed. Bernard Hewitt (Coral Gables, Fla., 1958); John Nichols, *The Progresses and Public Processions of Queen Elizabeth*, 3 vols. (London, 1823), and *Progresses, Processions, and Magnificent Festivities of King James the First*, 4 vols. (London, 1828); Enid Welsford, *The Court Masque* (Cambridge, 1927); Margaret M. MacGowan, *L'art du ballet de cour en France, 1581–1643* (Paris, 1963); Marie-Françoise Christout, *Le ballet de cour de Louis XIV, 1643–1672* (Paris, 1967); Jean Jacquot, *Les fêtes de la Renaissance* (Paris, 1956); Alessandro Cervellati, *Storia delle maschere* (Bologna, 1954); Leon Chancerel and Robert Barthes, *Le masque* (Paris, 1945); Roy Strong, *Splendor at Court: Renaissance Spectacle and the Theatre of Power* (Boston, 1973); and David Bergeron, *English Civic Pageantry, 1558–1642* (Columbia, S.C., 1971).

8. The extravagantly staged production of the masque *Salmacida Spolia*, presented in the Queen's Dancing House on 21 January 1639/40, has been reconstructed by C. V. Wedgwood in "The Last Masque," *Truth and Opinion: Historical Essays* (London, 1960), pp. 139–156. When Davenant was next able to collaborate on a new production, after a period during which the theaters had been closed, he was forced by social changes to abandon the masque form and to entitle his new work *The Siege of Rhodes: Made a Representation by the Art of Perspective in Scenes, And the Story sung in Recitative Musick. At the back part of Rutland-House in the upper end of Aldergate-Street* (London, printed by J. M. for Henry Herringman, 1656). Davenant complained in the preface about the limited stage space, fifteen feet deep and eleven feet high, in this makeshift theater (p. A 2); but he nevertheless managed to introduce "framed" masquelike scenic perspectives while at the same time replacing aristocratic masque dances mainly with musical interludes. He then wrote *The Cruelty of the Spaniards in Peru* (1658) and *The History of Sir Francis Drake* (1659)—produced under more auspicious theater conditions at the Cockpit Theatre in Drury Lane— before mounting the second part of *The Siege of Rhodes* on 29 June 1661 at the Duke of York's Theatre in Dorset Garden. A quarto version of the complete work, printed for Henry Herringman, then appeared under the title *The Siege of Rhodes, the first and second part. As they were lately represented at the Duke of York Theatre* (London, 1663).

Aside from his adaptation of *The Tempest* with Dryden, Davenant's most well known Shakespearean adaptation probably was *Macbeth a Tragedy. With all the Alterations, Amendments, Additions, and New Songs. As it's now Acted at the Dukes Theatre* (London, P. Chetwin, 1674). The relatively limited stage effects in this production included flying and vanishing witches (pp. 3, 44–49), lightning flashes accompanied with thunder (p. 1), a ghost that rose and descended through a stage trap (p. 40), and a cauldron and a cave that appeared and then sank from view (pp. 48–49).

Historical evidence suggests that Milton would have been very aware of the activities of William Davenant. Printer Jacob Tonson, the elder, in a letter he composed when the Bentley edition of *Paradise Lost* was published, claimed that Milton has assisted in obtaining Davenant's release from imprisonment in the Tower and had also been the tutor of one of Davenant's sons. Tonson wrote, probably to his nephew: "I was intimately acquainted when young with one Mr William Davenant 2d Son to Sr William ye Poet ... This Mr Davenant told me that Mr Milton helped him in his study of ye lattin & Greeke Authors, to whom he used to goe in order to his Learning—. That when his father was in the tower he was very much assisted by Mr Milton in gaining his liberty, & if I am not very much mistaken he at the same time told me his father in return upon ye restoration was very helpful to Milton, & Milton was very acknowledging for it uppon that score offered his willingness in doeing any thing that should be grateful to Sr William—It was a little after Milton's death that he told me this" (*The Manuscript of Milton's "Paradise Lost," Book I,* ed. Helen Darbishire [Oxford, 1931], p. xiv).

9. See studies of this transformation in W. J. Lawrence, *The Elizabethan Playhouse and Other Studies,* 2nd ser. (Stratford-on-Avon, 1913), pp. 125ff.; Nicoll, *History of English Drama,* 1: 8–47; Lee J. Martin, "From Forestage to Proscenium: A Study of Restoration Staging Techniques," *Theatre Survey* 4 (1963): 3–28; and Bentley, *Jacobean and Caroline Stage,* 6: 265–320. Stylized musical and scenic effects within a proscenium arch characterized most productions in the 1660s and 1670s; and as Nicoll points out in *History of English Drama,* vol. 1, scenic representations of "Eliziums, Heavens, and Hells, occur fairly frequently, and fire scenes are common" (p. 40). French performers appearing in London in 1661 with special stage machines apparently inspired British scenic inventiveness. See *The Description of the Great Machines, of the Descent of Orpheus into Hell, Presented by the French Commedians at the Cock-pit in Drury Lane* (London, 1661). Masquelike effects, once inserted into stylized operatic productions, continued to exert influence. Settle, for example, introduced an onstage Hell into Act IV, scene iii, of *The Empress of Morocco,* a scene that he loosely labeled "The Mask" (1673 edition, p. 46). And Pierre Perrin's *Ariadne, or The Marriage of Bacchus, An Opera ... acted by the Royall Academy of Musick* (London, printed by Theo. Newcombe, 1674), contained a "discovery" of

three nymphs in a floating "Great Shel" (p. B 1) that seems an imitation of the shell designed by Inigo Jones for the entrances of main masquers in Ben Jonson's *The Masque of Blacknesse* (1608).

Although Dryden never demonstrated an aesthetic comprehension of the Stuart masque form, he introduced an onstage dance of masquelike figures in "The Rape of Persephone" sequence of *The Rival Ladies* (1664), and his last published work was a stylized theatrical spectacle entitled *The Secular Masque* (1700).

10. Quoted from *The Later Renaissance in England: Nondramatic Verse and Prose, 1600–1660*, ed. Herschel Baker (Boston, 1975), p. 782.

11. Baker, *Later Renaissance*, p. 785.

12. Quoted from Pendlebury, *Dryden's Heroic Plays*, p. 2.

13. See *Works of Dryden*, ed. Scott, 5:115. The statement as originally printed appears on p. p.c. of the 1677 edition published by T. N. for Henry Herringman. All future references to *The State of Innocence* are to the Scott edition.

14. See Anne Davidson Ferry, *Milton and the Miltonic Dryden* (Cambridge, Mass., 1968), p. 226n. Ferry finds *The State of Innocence* to be "an offensive vulgarization of *Paradise Lost*" in which Milton's immense epic is reduced to a "scenario" and "everything rich and grand and strange is made coarse and mean and familiar" (p. 21). Bernard Harris, however, offers a partial critical defense of the work in "That Soft Seducer, Love: Dryden's *The State of Innocence and the Fall of Man*," in *Approaches to "Paradise Lost": The York Tercentenary Lectures*, ed. C. A. Patrides (Toronto, 1968), pp. 119–136.

15. See Ferry, *Milton and the Miltonic Dryden*, p. 226n.

16. *Works of Dryden*, ed. Scott, 5: 91.

17. This speculative view was first advanced by W. J. Lawrence in "Dryden's Abortive Opera," *Times* (*London*) *Literary Supplement* 6 August 1931, p. 606; and it has recently been presented by Fletcher, 3: 12–13.

18. *John Milton: Complete Poems and Major Prose*, ed. Merritt Y. Hughes (New York, 1957), p. 669n (hereafter cited as Hughes).

19. Pareus, *A Commentary upon divine Revelation of the Apostle and Evangelist John*, trans. Elias Arnold (Amsterdam, 1644), pp. 20, 26.

20. John Smith, *Select Discourses* (London, 1660), p. 222.

21. Fletcher, vol. 2 (Urbana, Ill., 1945), pp. 28–29.

22. Hughes, pp. 668–669, 550.

23. See Marjorie Hope Nicolson, "Milton's Hell and the Phlegraean Fields," *University of Toronto Quarterly* 7 (1938): 500–513; Roland Mushat Frye, *Milton's Imagery and the Visual Arts* (Princeton, 1978), pp. 23ff., 134–135; Rebecca W. Smith, "The Source of Milton's Pandemonium," *Modern Philology* 29 (1931): 187–198; Masson, vol. 1, rev. ed. (New York, 1881; reprint ed., 1946), pp. 768ff.; Jeffry B. Spencer, *Heroic Nature* (Evanston, Ill., 1973), pp. 111ff.; John Arthos, *Milton and the Italian Cities*

(London, 1968); Wylie Sypher, *Four Stages of Renaissance Style* (Garden City, N.Y., 1955); Roy Daniell, *Milton, Mannerism, and the Baroque* (Toronto, 1963); and Hannah Disinger Demaray, "Milton's 'Perfect' Paradise and the Landscapes of Italy," *Milton Quarterly* 8 (1974): 33–41.

24. The letter and related details appear in Masson, 1: 633–651; and in William Riley Parker, *Milton: A Biography*, vol. 1 (Oxford, 1968), pp. 177–178.

25. The view that Milton saw *Chi soffre speri* in the first months of 1639, upon his return to Rome from Naples, has been argued by Alessandro Ademollo in *I teatri di Roma nel decimosettimo secolo* (Rome, 1888), pp. 25–34; by Gretchen L. Finney in "Chorus in *Samson Agonistes*," *PMLA* 58 (1943): 658–659, and in a revision of this article that appears in her *Musical Backgrounds for English Literature, 1580–1650* (New Brunswick, N.J., 1962), pp. 228–230; and by John S. Smart in "Milton in Rome," *Modern Language Review* 8 (1913): 91. The case for this argument rests upon several points: (*a*) the known dates of Milton's presence in Rome and the known performances at the Casa Barberini; (*b*) the poet's references in his letter to a magnificent musical performance given by Cardinal Francesco Barberini and to being met at the door by this cardinal; and (*c*) the documents showing that two of the Barberini cardinals, Francesco and Antonio, did greet guests for the showing of *Chi soffre speri* at a time when Milton would have been in the city. Arthos, however, in *Milton and the Italian Cities*, pp. 53–55, quotes from the letter and then points out that Milton saw a performance that had been staged only a few days after the poet met Vatican librarian Lucas Holstein. Milton in fact wrote to Holstein that "in consequence of the mention you made of me to the most excellent Cardinal Francesco Barberini, that, when he, a few days later, gave that public musical entertainment with truly Roman magnificence, he himself, waiting at the doors, and seeking me out in so great a crowd, nay, almost laying hold of me by the hand, admitted me within in a truly most honourable manner." Arthos assumes that Milton would have met Holstein, not during the poet's second visit to Rome in 1639, when *Chi soffre speri* was performed, but during the poet's initial visit in 1638, when the work had not yet been mounted and thus could not have been viewed. In reaching this conclusion, Arthos speculates that Milton would have wished to see Holstein as soon as possible upon arriving in Rome and that the librarian would have been immediately available. Such opinions are extremely problematical. Exactly when Milton met Holstein is unknown, but the meeting could easily have taken place during the second visit. Thus, on the basis of the evidence available, it seems likely to me that Milton did see the single theatrical work of magnificence known to have been presented at the Casa Barberini during the periods when he was in the Eternal City: the musical spectacle *Chi soffre speri*.

The Vatican library holds manuscript copies of the musical work. See *Enciclopedia della spettacolo*, ed. Silvio D'Amico and Sandro D'Amico, vol. 2 (Rome, 1954), pp. 374–375, for production details. An outline of the plot appears in Hugo Goldschmidt's *Studien zur Geschichte der italienischen Oper im 17. Jahrhundret,* vol. 1 (Leipzig, 1901), pp. 90–92.

On his way to Rome Milton stayed in 1638 in Florence. It is worth noting that before and during the general time of his visit to Florence both indoor and outdoor triumphs had been recorded in *Descrizione delle feste fatte in Firenze per le reali nozze de serenissimi sposi Ferdinando II* (Florence, by Zanobi Pignoni, 1638) and in *Esequvie della maesta cesarea dell imperadore Ferdinando II* (Florence, 1638).

26. See Arthos, *Milton and the Italian Cities,* pp. 76–77; and Ademollo, *I teatri di Roma,* pp. 23ff.

27. Hughes, p. 829.

28. *La maschera trionfante nel givdicio di paride* (Florence, 1644).

29. *Il fvoco trionfante racconto traslatione della miracolo imagini della la Madona del fvoco* (Forli, 1637). Illustrations showing the chariots of Saint Elmo and Moses are opposite pp. 46 and 56.

30. See Allardyce Nicoll, *The Development of the Theatre: A Study of Theatrical Art from the Beginnings to the Present Day,* 5th ed. (New York, 1966), pp. 79–92; Vincenzo Golzio, *Il palazzo Barberini a la sua galleria di pittura* (Rome, n.d.); David Silvagni, *La corte e la società Romana nei secoli Romana nei secoli XVIII e XIX,* vol. 2 (Rome, 1884), pp. 126ff.; and Romain Rolland, *Histoire de l'opera en Europe avant Lully et Scarlatti* (Paris, 1895).

31. *Le nozze degli dei favola: rappresentata in musica* (Florence, by Amadore Mazzi and Lorenzo Landi, 1637), pp. 96–98 with illustration recto p. 96.

32. *Il giudizio di paride,* printed as *Commedia rappresentata nelle nozze del Sermo, principe di Toscana* (Florence, 1608). For the stage directions describing Jones's designs for Hell and for the House of Fame in Jonson's *The Masque of Queenes,* see *Ben Jonson,* ed. C. H. Herford, Percy Simpson, and Evelyn Simpson, vol. 7 (Oxford, 1941), pp. 282–283, 301–302. No drawing of the Hell scene is extant, but the design for the House of Fame appears as plate 4 in *Designs by Inigo Jones for Masques and Plays at Court,* intro. with notes Percy Simpson and C. F. Bell (New York, 1966). Jones's designs for a Horrid Hell and a Palace of Fame, created for Davenant's *Britannia Triumphans* (1638), appear in Allardyce Nicoll, *Stuart Masques and the Renaissance Stage* (New York, 1938), pp. 115, 116; and a reproduced illustration of the palace also appears in *Designs by Inigo Jones,* plate 36. For a description of the Hell and palace in Davenant's masque, see *The Dramatic Works of Sir William Davenant,* intro. with notes James Maidment and W. H. Logan, vol. 2 (Edinburgh and London, 1872), pp. 273, 283–286. See also Rinuccini's ballet in *Compendio delle sontvose feste fatte l'anno M.DC.VIII. nella città di Mantova, per le reali nozze del serenissimo principe D. Francesco Gonzago, con la serenissima infante Margherita di Savoia* (Mantua, 1608).

33. The Hell of *La liberazione di Tirreno* is shown mislabeled in Nicoll, *Stuart Masques*, p. 104. See also *Le nozze degli dei favola*, recto p. 84.

34. M. T. Herrick discusses Italian theatrical theory in *Tragicomedy: Its Origin and Development in Italy, France, and England*, Illinois Studies in Language and Literature, vol. 39 (Urbana, Ill., 1955); and in *Italian Tragedy in the Renaissance* (Urbana, Ill., 1956), pp. 46ff. Arthos, in *Milton and the Italian Cities*, pp. 134–180, examines Italian conceptions of tragedy. Among the Italian musical spectacles having a "fortunate" Christian outcome are Cardinal Giulio Rospigliosi's *L'erminia sul Giodano, Sant' Alessio*, and *Santa Teodora*. Watson Kirkconnell has provided a useful collection of *sacre rappresentazioni* on the Fall in *The Celestial Cycle* (Toronto, 1952).

35. The relevant documents of the academy are printed in *The Life Records of John Milton*, ed. J. M. French, vol. 1 (New Brunswick, N.J., 1948), p. 409, and vol. 5 (New Brunswick, N.J., 1958), p. 385. See *Tragedie de Girolamo Bartolommei* (Rome, 1632), sigs. a7v, b9r-b14v. A revised version was published as *Tragedie di Girolamo Bartolommei, già smeducci. Ricorrette, ed accresciute* (Rome, 1655).

36. See the Latin text, from the first edition (1601) in the British Museum, printed opposite an English translation in Kirkconnell, *Celestial Cycle*, pp. 96–220.

37. *L'Adamo* (Milan, 1613). For a selective trans. see Kirkconnell, *Celestial Cycle*, pp. 227–267. John Arthos discusses the work and its staging in "Milton, Andreini, and Galileo," in *Approaches to "Paradise Lost,"* ed. Patrides, pp. 168–175. Andreini's preface reflects, in general, a view of tragedy that was also held by Francesco Robortello, who argued in *Il librum Aristotelis de arte poetica explicationes* (Forence, 1508) that tragic imitation consists of both the writing of poetry and of its histrionic performance. Robortello observed that "the principal end of tragedy is to imitate the nature of souls and the characters of men through written words" (p. 58); and he added that the histrionic performance of the work, with spectacle and stage apparatus, also becomes an end of tragedy and contains all other elements within itself (p. 57). For the trans. rendered above and an analysis of this view, see Bernard Weinberg, *A History of Literary Criticism in the Italian Renaissance*, vol. 1 (Chicago, 1961), pp. 388–399.

38. The "Argument" and action of *Paradise Lost*—centering on the Fall, repentance, and future Redemption of the First Parents and including scenes in disparate realms of the cosmos—reveal the power of a divine mercy that contravenes pagan fatalism. Although the epic narrator turns his "Notes to Tragic" (IX.6) to describe man's transgression, a compassionate Christian vision gives the narrator's song a special pathos that prevents it from becoming tragic in a classical, fatalistic sense. Adam and Eve are not the flawed heroes or gods of classical tradition. They are innocent until their Fall. They do not rage helplessly against an inexorable fate; they have the power to change their destiny through submission to God. Thus, the narrator's theme

is lost innocence; and the remorse of that theme is immediately captured when the narrator, speaking of his tragic notes, insists that his is a "Sad task" (IX.13).

As Arthos has pointed out, sad but eventually fortuitous actions are at the core of many Italian Christian tragedies and many superficially pagan works, such as Monteverdi's *Orfeo* (1607). It should be added that this fortuitous Christian outlook is also evident in "pagan" disguisings such as Milton's *Comus* and Jonson's masques as well as in a planned "Christian" work such as "Adam Unparadiz'd."

39. See Fletcher, 2: 16, 26. All references to the outlines of "Adam Unparadiz'd" are to this edition.

40. See John G. Demaray, "Milton's *Comus:* The Sequel to a Masque of Circe," *Huntington Library Quarterly* 29 (1966): 245–254. Theatrical and masque allusions in Milton's early poetry have been examined in John G. Demaray, *Milton and the Masque Tradition: The Early Poems, "Arcades," and "Comus"* (Cambridge, Mass., and Oxford, 1968), pp. 31–58.

41. *Aurelian Townshend's Poems and Masks*, ed. E. K. Chambers (Oxford, 1912), p. 85.

42. Hughes, pp. 1034–1035. Phillips's biography of Milton, entitled *The Life of Milton*, is included in its entirety in the Hughes edition.

43. Hughes, pp. 1034–1035.

44. Allan H. Gilbert, *On the Composition of "Paradise Lost": A Study in the Ordering and Insertion of Material* (Chapel Hill, 1947), pp. 16–17.

45. Hughes, p. 173.

46. Kirkconnell, *Celestial Cycle*, p. xxiii.

47. See *Ben Jonson*, ed. Herford, Simpson, and Simpson, 7: 82. All quotations from and line references to Jonson's masques are from this edition.

48. See John G. Demaray, *Milton and the Masque Tradition*, pp. 97–121. For information on the arrangement of masquing halls and the staging of masques, see also Nicoll, *Stuart Masques*, pp. 36ff.; Willa McClung Evans, *Henry Lawes: Musician and Friend of Poets* (New York, 1951), pp. 101–105; Rosemond Tuve, *Images and Themes in Five Poems by Milton* (Cambridge, Mass., 1957), pp. 112–161; E. K. Chambers, *The Elizabethan Stage*, vol. 1 (Oxford, 1923), pp. 149–212; and Lily B. Campbell, *Scenes and Machines on the English Stage during the Renaissance* (Cambridge, 1923).

49. *The Poetical Works of John Milton*, ed. Henry J. Todd, 2nd ed., vol. 2 (London, 1809), p. 360n.

50. *Works of Davenant*, intro. Maidment and Logan, 2: 283–285.

51. *Townshend's Poems and Masks*, ed. Chambers, p. 86; see also John G. Demaray, "Milton's *Comus*," pp. 246–247, 253–254.

52. Rebecca W. Smith, in "Source of Milton's Pandemonium," suggests that the palace in Hell is modeled after St. Peter's Basilica in Rome. A general resemblance between Pandemonium and baroque architectural struc-

tures is insisted upon by Daniell in *Milton, Mannerism, and the Baroque,* pp. 94, 97; and by Sypher in *Stages of Renaissance Style,* pp. 210–211. But Frye, in *Milton's Imagery,* pp. 134–135, argues that Pandemonium is intended as an architectural monstrosity and is not essentially similar to St. Peter's or other baroque buildings.

53. Hughes, p. 173; F. T. Prince, "Milton and the Theatrical Sublime," in *Approaches to "Paradise Lost,"* ed. Patrides, pp. 53–63.

III. The Vast Design Emerges

1. *John Milton's Complete Poetical Works Reproduced in Photographic Facsimile,* ed. Harris Francis Fletcher, vol. 2 (Urbana, Ill., 1945), pp. 12–29 (hereafter cited as Fletcher). All references to Milton's writings in this chapter are to this edition. See also *Facsimile of the Manuscript of Milton's Minor Poems Preserved in the Library of Trinity College Cambridge,* ed. William Aldis Wright (Cambridge, 1899). Wright offers background material and editorial comment that appear only partially summarized in the excellent edition by Fletcher.

2. Fletcher makes the suggestion in 2: 14.

3. Fletcher, 2: 26.

4. Allan H. Gilbert, *On the Composition of "Paradise Lost": A Study in the Ordering and Insertion of Material* (Chapel Hill, 1947), pp. 145–155. Grant McColley, in *"Paradise Lost": An Account of its Growth and Major Origins* (Chicago, 1940)—hereafter cited as *Growth and Origins*—and in "Milton's Lost Tragedy," *Philological Quarterly* 18 (1939): 78–83, similarly overlooks "Sodom Burning" as a source for the Hell scenes in the epic. In *Growth and Origins* he writes: "In addition to having omitted themes found in Book III and other sections of the epic foreshadowed in the third draft, *Adam Unparadised* said nothing suggestive either of Books I–II or of the untraditional and unsuccessful first temptation of Eve" (p. 290). McColley stresses this point later when he adds that "neither *Adam Unparadised* nor the three preceding drafts included any suggestion of Books I and II." He maintains that "there stands available . . . some trustworthy evidence, all of which suggests that the order of publication was not the order of composition. A major part of this evidence comes from *Adam Unparadised* and the abandoned tragedy seemingly entitled 'Paradise Lost'" (p. 310).

5. Fletcher, 2: 26–27.

6. Milton, having theatrically associated the Asphaltic Pool area with a place of evil, may well have developed further associations about the Dead Sea region from a large body of geographic and literary materials. Torquato Tasso, in Book VII of *Gerusalemme liberata,* placed the castle of illusion of the evil witch Armida on an island in the Dead Sea. As C. P. Brand observes in *Torquato Tasso: A Study of the Poet and His Contribution* (Cambridge, 1965), p. 237, Spenser appears to have been influenced by references to the Dead Sea in Tasso's epic when he created the Idle Lake in Book II of *The*

Faerie Queene. In Ortelius's *Theatrum de Orbus*, a cartographical work mentioned in Milton's *Animadversions upon the Remonstrant's Defence against Smectymnuus*, devils were illustrated dancing gleefully on and near the flaming Asphaltic Pool. And George Sandys, in *A Relation of a Journey*, a travel book apparently known to Milton, wrote of the Dead Sea fruit and the sites of the Asphaltic Pool and Sodom. For information on Milton's allusions to the Dead Sea area, see Robert Cawley, *Milton and the Literature of Travel* (Princeton, 1951), pp. 106–118.

7. Gilbert, in *Composition of "Paradise Lost,"* without referring to the impact of Pareus's commentary and of Christian theatrical forms upon Milton, implausibly asserts that the lost fifth draft of the "drama probably would have been more classical than Jonson's *Catiline*" (p. 23). McColley, referring to the extant fourth draft, writes in *Growth and Origins* that "*Adam Unparadised* had no act divisions, but following the corrected precedent established by Peck in 1740, these may be supplied from the third draft" (p. 286). McColley puts into the fourth draft his "corrections," separating a unified outline that has no listed divisions into five acts. James Holly Hanford and James G. Taaffe call attention to this imposed, hypothetical structure by similarly inserting a five-act form into their transcript of the fourth draft printed in *A Milton Handbook*, 5th ed. (Englewood Cliffs, N.J., 1970), pp. 152–153.

McColley discusses what he believes to be the classical form of the lost fifth draft in "Milton's Lost Tragedy." In *Growth and Origins*, through broad and imprecise generalization, he incorrectly implies that the fourth draft, without act divisions, is more classical in structure than the third draft, with its five divisions: "The three initial drafts . . . suggest the Italian *sacre rappresentazione*, a type of drama which set forth biblical themes and episodes by means of allegory. Combined with the influence of this form was that of classical tragedy." McColley then adds that "draft IV likewise followed the classical form, but abandoned largely the allegorical characters of the *sacre rappresentazione*" (pp. 290–291).

Because Edward Phillips used the wide-ranging seventeenth-century term "tragedy" to describe the missing fifth draft of "Adam Unparadiz'd," numerous critics, beginning with the neoclassical commentators of the eighteenth century, have incorrectly assumed that the poet was influenced almost exclusively by classical theatrical conceptions when he gave structure to this draft. This view is in need of reassessment. See in particular the comments by John Dryden in *The Original and Progress of Satire: Selections from Dryden*, ed. G. E. Hadow (Oxford, 1908); and by Joseph Addison in the 9 February 1712 edition of *The Spectator*, ed. G. Gregory Smith, vol. 2 (London, 1951), p. 385.

8. *The Works of Samuel Johnson*, ed. F. P. Walesby, vol. 7 (Oxford, 1825), p. 121.

9. See John G. Demaray, "Milton's *Comus*: The Sequel to a Masque of Circe," *Huntington Library Quarterly* 29 (1966): 245–254; and *Aurelian*

Townshend's Poems and Masks, ed. E. K. Chambers (Oxford, 1912), pp. 85ff.

10. Arthur E. Barker contends that a five-act division can be found in the ten-book epic in "Structural Pattern in *Paradise Lost,*" *Philological Quarterly* 28 (1949): 16–30. See also Jeffrey P. Ford, *"Paradise Lost* and the Five-Act Epic" (Ph.D. diss., Columbia University, 1966); and, for a comparison of structural elements in the epic and Shakespeare's *Macbeth,* McColley, *Growth and Origins,* pp. 249–250. John T. Shawcross effectively takes issue with the five-act structural reading in "The Balanced Structure of *Paradise Lose,*" *Studies in Philology* 62 (1965): 711–712.

11. Having been influenced by the Italian *tragedie di lieto fine,* Milton was able to impart a special quality to the First Parents' Fall that is alien to classical tragedy: a degree of nostalgia over the loss of Eden and innocence. The note of nostalgia is heard when the First Parents lie together in the bower, when Eve returns to Adam after her Fall, and when the First Parents look back upon the earthly paradise after their banishment. A nostalgic tone is evident even in the invocation to Book IX, when the narrator, soon after saying that he must change his "Notes to Tragic" (6), sings with pathos of his "Sad task" and of this "world of woe" (11–13).

12. See Anne Davidson Ferry, "Point of View and Comment," *Milton's Epic Voice: The Narrator in "Paradise Lost"* (Cambridge, Mass., 1963), pp. 44–66.

13. See *Le prose diverse di Torquato Tasso,* ed. Cesare Guasti, vol. 2 (Florence, 1875), pp. 14ff.; Giacopo Mazzoni, "Discorso di Giacopo Mazzoni," in *Difensa della "Commedia" del divino poeta Dante,* ed. Mario Rossi (Citta di Castello, 1898), pp. 95–96; and *Ivlii Caesaris Scaligeri, Uiri Clarissimi, Poetices libri septem, Apvd Antonivm Vincentium* (Lugduni, 1561), bk. 2. Milton's application of the concept of epic "wonder" to *Paradise Lost* is examined by John M. Steadman in *Epic and Tragic Structure in "Paradise Lost"* (Chicago and London, 1976), pp. 105–119. Steadman has investigated classical heroic structures and conventions in *Paradise Lost* in *Milton's Epic Characters: Image and Idol* (Chapel Hill, 1959) and in *Milton and the Renaissance Hero* (Oxford, 1967). The classical views of epic structure and content have been related to Milton's epic in detail by Davis Harding, *The Club of Hercules: Studies in the Classical Background of "Paradise Lost"* (Urbana, Ill., 1962); and in a more general way by C. M. Bowra, *From Virgil to Milton* (London, 1943). Francis C. Blessington, in *"Paradise Lost" and the Classical Epic* (Boston and London, 1979), has closely compared Milton's work with the *Iliad,* the *Odyssey,* and the *Aeneid.*

14. The dialectical character of *Paradise Lost* has been explored by Michael Lieb in *The Dialectics of Creation: Patterns of Birth and Regeneration in "Paradise Lost"* (Amherst, Mass., 1970); and by Dennis Burden in *The Logical Epic: A Study of the Argument of "Paradise Lost"* (Cambridge, Mass., 1967).

15. See Ferry, "Vision as Structure," *Milton's Epic Voice*, pp. 147–178; Lieb, *Dialectics of Creation*; Rosalie L. Colie, *Paradoxia Epidemica: The Renaissance Tradition of Paradox* (Princeton, 1966); Burton Weber, *The Construction of "Paradise Lost"* (Carbondale, Ill., London, and Amsterdam, 1972); William G. Madsen, *From Shadowy Types to Truth: Studies in Milton's Symbolism* (New Haven and London, 1968); and Albert R. Carillo, "Noon–Midnight and the Temporal Structure of *Paradise Lost*," *English Literary History* 29 (1962): 372–395.

16. James Whaler, *Counterpoint and Symbol* (Copenhagen, 1956). An analysis of 10,550 as a perfect number, a number that proves "true" in ten different ways, appears in Gunnar Qvarstrom, *Dikten och den Nya Vetenskapen. Det Astronautiska Motivet* (Lund, 1961). See also Qvarstrom's elaboration of numerological theory in *The Enchanted Palace: Some Structural Aspects of "Paradise Lost"* (Stockholm, 1967); and Maren-Sofie Røstvig's numerological interpretation in *The Hidden Sense: Milton and the Neoplatonic Method of Numerical Composition* (Oslo, 1963).

17. Shawcross, "Balanced Structure," pp. 696–718. Shawcross comments on Adam and Eve as the chief protagonists of the epic in "The Style and Genre of *Paradise Lost*," in *New Essays on "Paradise Lost*," ed. Thomas Kranidas (Berkeley and Los Angeles, 1969), pp. 18–21.

18. J. B. Watson, "Divine Providence and the Structure of *Paradise Lost*," *Essays in Criticism* 14 (1964): 148–155.

19. Galbraith Crump, *The Mystical Design of "Paradise Lost"* (Lewisburg, Pa., and London, 1975), pp. 18, 71, 81.

20. Fletcher, 2: 178–179.

21. Examinations of the theatrical qualities of *Paradise Lost* are frequently obscured by the restrictive terms used by commentators: "drama," "Elizabethan drama," "classical drama," "comedy," "tragedy," and "epic." The Renaissance disguising and triumph, however, escape such unqualified terminology. The triumph features performers who begin in high estate and who ultimately achieve an anticipated victory. In production and symbolism the triumph extends beyond any restraining stage to encompass the social world of the audience; and through the device of disguising and unmasking, it gives some depth to character-types by means of largely nondramatic ritual. Thus, the triumph, strictly considered, is not tragedy, comedy, drama, or melodrama, though the argument can be made on the basis of Renaissance theory that it is a special theatrical mode opposite to tragedy.

Using what I believe is restrictive terminology, Helen Gardner, John Arthos, and John T. Shawcross present different opinions on the nature of the actual or possible "drama" in *Paradise Lost*. Gardner, in *A Reading of "Paradise Lost"* (Oxford, 1965), maintains that Milton's work on the Fall has a "dramatic concentration unprecedented in epic" (p. 35) and that the work is "essentially a dramatic action expanded (pp. 32–33). Arthos, in "Milton, Andreini, and Galileo," in *Approaches to "Paradise Lost": The York Tercentenary Lectures*, ed. C. A. Patrides (London, 1968), takes exception to Gardner's interpretation and contends that the "very stuff of *Paradise Lost* is the representation of two different realms of being" which Arthos identifies, without mentioning Hell, as "the disparate realms of Heaven and Earth" (p. 168). He adds that "the substantial differences in the nature of the various realms as in the differences in God's nature and deed and in men's, made it impossible for him [Milton] to keep to the idea of classical drama as the form he required" (p. 169). Although he suggests that "Milton was strongly drawn to composing for performance" and that on occasion the poet presented scenes "as conceivably to be staged," Arthos nevertheless concludes that "the obviously controlling conception of the poem is in the presentation of a narrative and an argument" (p. 165).

Shawcross, when he writes of the alleged drama, demonstrates his awareness of the baroque background of *Paradise Lost* and to some degree draws together conflicting critical opinion. In "Style and Genre" he notes that the work "is neither drama nor epic in an unrelenting classic definition. As Roy Daniell has argued in *Milton, Mannerism, and the Baroque* (Toronto, 1963), it is an example of the baroque by virtue, here, of its placement between the manneristic and the neoclassic (or late baroque), despite some tendency toward the latter. By casting his work in epic form, while deriving it from drama and retaining dramatic sections, Milton acquired greater scope for the inexplicable and obtained answerable style" (p. 25).

22. The expansive scenes and action of *Paradise Lost* have had an influence upon modern cinematic conceptions. Marie Seton, in *Sergei M. Eisenstein: A Biography* (New York, 1960), writes: "When work on the shooting script of *Alexander Nevsky* began, Eisenstein recalled Milton's *Paradise Lost*. Thus Milton's imagery of the Battle in Heaven became the Battle on Ice in *Alexander Nevsky*" (p. 380). The possible relationship between the epic and the motion picture is examined by Concetta Carestia Greenfield in "S. M. Eisenstein's *Alexander Nevsky* and John Milton's *Paradise Lost:* A Structural Comparison," *Milton Quarterly* 9 (1975): 93–98. John Collier has recently published a theatrical adaptation of the epic, *Milton's "Paradise Lost": Screenplay for Cinema of the Mind* (New York, 1973). In a rather impressionistic essay on the whole of Milton's epic, F. T. Prince, in "Milton and the Theatrical Sublime," in *Approaches to "Paradise Lost,"* ed. Patrides, stresses "Milton's use of organized and enacted spectacle, his demonstration of the meaning of a dramatic moment; which leaves us with the impression of having witnessed a consciously complete *performance,* on the part of both the poet and his poem" (p. 55). Prince calls particular attention to the spectacle of certain council scenes (pp. 54–57). Speaking of the theatricality of the completed epic, he writes: "One cannot call it simply literary drama: it is a poem in dramatic form, not written for the stage, but for the inward eye" (p. 54).

A lavish theatrical adaptation of *Paradise Lost* made its world premier on 29 November 1978 on the stage of the Lyric Opera of Chicago. Subtitled *A Sacred Representation* by composer Krzysztof Penderecki and librettist Christopher Fry, the work contains parts for a number of choruses, the poet Milton, a Voice of God, Adam, Eve, Satan, and various other figures, including a group of angels.

IV. The Anti-Triumphs of Hell

1. *John Milton: Complete Poems and Major Prose*, ed. Merritt Y. Hughes (New York, 1957), p. 247, lines 624–626. All references to Milton's verse in this chapter are to the Hughes edition.

2. John M. Steadman, "The Idea of Satan as the Hero of *Paradise Lost*," *Proceedings of the American Philosophical Society* 120 (1976): 256. See Steadman's survey of Restoration and Romantic criticism on pp. 254–260. John T. Shawcross has edited Restoration criticism in *Milton: The Critical Heritage* (New York, 1970)—hereafter cited as *Critical Heritage*. Romantic criticism has been edited by Joseph Wittreich in *The Romantics on Milton* (Cleveland and London, 1970).

3. Roberta Florence Brinkley, *Coleridge on the Seventeenth Century*, intro. Louis I. Bredvold (Durham, N.C., and London, 1955), has reprinted Coleridge's lecture on Milton given at the Crown and Anchor on 4 March 1819. Brinkley notes that "Milton has carefully marked in his Satan the intense selfishness, the alcohol of egotism, which would rather reign in hell than serve in heaven. To place this lust of self in opposition to denial of self or duty, and to show what exertions it would make, and what pains endure to accomplish its end, is Milton's particular object in the character of Satan. But around this character he has thrown a singularity of daring, a grandeur of sufferance and a ruined splendor, which constitute the very height of poetic sublimity" (p. 578). See also *Shelley's "Prometheus Unbound": The Text and the Drafts*, ed. L. J. Zillman (New Haven and London, 1968). Shelley writes that "Prometheus is, in my judgement, a more poetical character than Satan because, in addition to courage and majesty, and firm and patient opposition to omnipotent force, he is susceptible of being described as exempt from the taints of envy, revenge, and a desire for personal aggrandisement, which, in the Hero of *Paradise Lost*, interfere with interest" (pp. 35–36).

4. Shelley, in his *Defense of Poetry* (1821), observes that "Milton's Devil as a moral being is as far superior to his God, as One who perseveres in some purpose which he has conceived to be excellent in spite of adversity and torture, is to One who in the cold security of undoubted triumph inflicts the most horrible revenge upon his enemy, not from any mistaken notion of inducing him to repent of a perseverance in enmity, but with the alleged design of exasperating him to deserve new torments" (*The Complete Works of Percy Bysshe Shelley*, ed. Roger Ingpen and Walter E. Peck, vol. 7 [London and New York, 1930], p. 129). Shelley also notes that "nothing can exceed the energy and magnificence of the character of Satan as expressed in 'Paradise Lost.' It is a mistake to suppose that he could ever have been intended

for the popular personfication of evil" (p. 129). And in *On the Devil, and Devils* (1819), Shelley, after first writing opinions on Milton's Satan, which also appear in the *Defense of Poetry*, adds that it is "certain that Milton gives the Devil all imaginable advantage; and the arguments with which he exposes the injustice and impotent weakness of his adversary are such as had they been printed, distinct from the shelter of any dramatic order, would have been answered by the most conclusive of syllogisms—persecution" (p. 91).

Byron, in a letter to Francis Hodgson dated 12 May 1821, pronounces Satan the hero of the epic: "I must also ask you, is *Achilles* a *good* character? or is Aeneas anything but a successful runaway? It is for Turnus men feel and not for the Trojan. Who is the hero of *Paradise Lost?* Why Satan—and Macbeth, and Richard, and Othello, Pierre, and Lothario, and Zanga?" (*The Works of Lord Byron*, ed. Ernest Hartley Coleridge and Rowland E. Prothero, vol. 5 [London and New York, 1901], p. 284).

Hazlitt, in *On Rochefoucoult's Maxims*, tersely but directly states that "Satan is the hero of *Paradise Lost*" (*The Complete Works of William Hazlitt*, ed. P. P. Howe, vol. 20 [London and Toronto, 1934], p. 37). In Lecture III, *On Shakespeare and Milton*, Hazlitt writes: "Satan is the most heroic subject that ever was chosen for a poem; and the execution is as perfect as the design is lofty ... His thoughts burn like a hell within him; but the power of thought holds domination in his mind over every other consideration ... Whenever the figure of Satan is introduced, whether he walks, or flies, 'rising aloft incumbent on the dusky air' (I, 226), it is illustrated with the most striking and appropriate images: so that we see always before us, gigantic, irregular, portentous, uneasy and disturbed—but dazzling in its faded splendour, the clouded ruins of a god. The deformity of Satan is only in the depravity of his will; he has no bodily deformity to excite our loathing or disgust" (5: 63–65).

In *The Marriage of Heaven and Hell* Blake's narrator speaks the now famous lines: "The reason Milton wrote in fetters when he wrote of Angels & God, and at liberty when of Devils & Hell, is because he was a true poet and of the Devil's party without knowing it" (*The Complete Writings of William Blake*, ed. Geoffrey Keynes [Oxford, 1966], p. 50).

It should be noted that John Dryden had remarked earlier that Milton would have had a better "plea" as an epic poet "if the Devil had not been his hero, instead of Adam; if the giant had not foiled the knight" (*"Of Dramatic Posey" and Other Critical Essays*, ed. George Watson, vol. 2 [London and New York, 1962], p. 233).

5. For comments on eighteenth-century criticism of Milton's Satan and Hell, see *Milton: A Collection of Critical Essays*, ed. Louis L. Martz (Englewood Cliffs, N.J., 1966), pp. 6–9; Shawcross, *Critical Heritage*, pp. 14–32; Douglas Bush, *"Paradise Lost" in Our Time: Some Comments* (Ithaca, N.Y., and London, 1945); Wittreich, *Romantics on Milton*, pp. 3–24; Arthur E. Barker, "'... And on His Crest Sat Horror': Eighteenth-Century

Interpretations of Milton's Sublimity and His Satan," *University of Toronto Quarterly* 11 (1942): 421–236; and *Milton Criticism: Selections from Four Centuries,* ed. James Thorpe (New York, 1969).

6. Shelley, for example, reveals the influence that his reformist views of religion and politics had on his criticism in the preface to *Prometheus Unbound:* "We owe to the great writers of the golden age of our literature, to that fervid awakening of the public mind which shook to dust the oldest and most oppressive form of the Christian religion. We owe Milton to the progress and development of the same spirit: the sacred Milton was, let it ever be remembered, a republican, and a bold inquirer into morals and religion. The great writers of our own age are, we have reason to suppose, the companions and forerunners of some unimagined change in our social condition or the opinions which cement it" (*Shelley's "Prometheus Unbound,"* ed. Zillman, pp. 39–40).

7. T. S. Eliot, "Milton I," *Of Poetry and Poets* (London, 1957), pp. 141–145. Eliot, in the same volume, somewhat qualifies his comments about Milton's alleged separation of "sound from sense" in "Milton II," pp. 146–161. Further comments by Eliot on Milton's supposed "dissociated sensibility" appear in "The Metaphysical Poets," *Selected Essays* (New York, 1950), p. 247.

8. F. R. Leavis, "Milton's Verse" in *Reevaluation: Tradition and Development in English Poetry* (London, 1936), pp. 42–67.

9. See A. J. A. Waldock, *"Paradise Lost" and Its Critics* (Cambridge, 1947), pp. 15–24, 143–147; J. B. Broadbent, *Some Graver Subject: An Essay on "Paradise Lost"* (London, 1960), pp. 287–298; John Peter, *A Critique of "Paradise Lost"* (New York, 1960), pp. 160–166. See also Lawrence Hyman, *The Quarrel Within: Art and Morality in Milton's Poetry* (Port Washington, N.Y., 1972), pp. 34–74.

10. William Empson, *Milton's God,* rev. ed. (London, 1965), pp. 36–146.

11. Stanley E. Fish, *Surprised by Sin: The Reader in "Paradise Lost"* (New York, 1967), pp. 1–22.

12. Jackson Cope, "Satan's Disguises: *Paradise Lost* and *Paradise Regained,"* *Modern Language Notes* 73 (1958): 9–11; Raymond Waddington, "Appearance and Reality in Satan's Disguises," *Texas Studies in Language and Literature* 4 (1962): 390–398; and Thomas Kranidas, "Satan's First Disguise," *English Literary History* 2 (1964): 13–15.

13. Frank Kastor, *Milton and the Literary Satan* (Amsterdam, 1974), p. 15.

14. Steadman, "Idea of Satan as Hero," p. 289.

15. Roy Strong, *Splendor at Court: Renaissance Spectacle and the Theatre of Power* (Boston, 1973), pp. 246–247.

16. *The Works of John Milton,* ed. Frank Allen Patterson, vol. 6 (New York, 1932), p. 247. All quotations in this chapter from *The Ready and Easy Way* are from this volume. All references to *Eikonoklastes* are from

Works of John Milton, ed. Patterson, vol. 5 (New York, 1932), pp. 61–352.

17. Spenser's pageant of the Seven Deadly Sins (I.4.16–36) and the Masque of Cupid (III.12.3–26) would have provided Milton with poetic examples of contrasting theatrical spectacles, but of the processional kind popular in the sixteenth-century English court before Ben Jonson developed the antimasque and main masque form.

18. See "Discorsi dell' arte poetica ed in particolare sopra il poema eroico," *Le prose diverse di Torquato Tasso*, ed. Cesare Guasti, vol. 1 (Florence, 1875), pp. 3–64; and *Riposta del S. Torq. Tasso, al discorso del Sig. Oratio Lombardelli* (Ferrara, printed by Vittorio Baldini, 1586), pp. 14–19. Tasso's theories and those of other critics on "wonders" in epics are related to *Paradise Lost* by John M. Steadman in *Epic and Tragic Structure in "Paradise Lost"* (Chicago and London, 1976), pp. 105–119.

19. Fish, in *Surprised by Sin*, observes that the epic narrator's "phrase 'vaunting aloud' . . . troubles, since it seems to deny even the academic admiration one might have for Satan's art as apart from his morality and to suggest that such admiration can never really be detached from the possibility of involvement (if only passive) in that morality." In other words, the narrator with the phrase "vaunting aloud" seems to deny academic admiration to Satan as a verbal artist, and the narrator in so doing allegedly suggests that artistic judgment can never really be detached from moral involvement. "The sneer in 'vaunting,'" Fish continues, "is aimed equally at the performance and anyone who lingers to appreciate it" (p. 10).

It seems to me, however, that in lines 84–124 Satan speaks with an element of vain posturing and boastfulness, that the words "vaunting aloud" represent a reasonably perceptive and accurate description of the tone and content of the Fiend's speech, and that any expressed academic admiration by the narrator for Satan's dissembling verbal art would at this point be inappropriate and indecorous. The narrator is unfairly characterized, I think, when he is said to "sneer" both at Satan and at any reader who admires the Fiend's rhetoric in an academic fashion. Moreover, I cannot agree with Fish's conclusion, which is based on this example, that "the immediate experience of the poetry will not be qualified by the perspective of the poem's doctrinal assumptions" (p. 10).

By neglecting to mention the furious tone of the Fiend's speech with its telling references to "immortal hate," "rage," "high disdain," "unconquerable Will," and "revenge," Fish provides a surprisingly good press for Satan and favorably quotes some of Waldock's understated evaluations: "The speech is a powerful one, moving smoothly from the *exclamatio* of 'But O how fall'n' (84) to the regret and apparent logic of 'till then who knew / The force of those dire Arms' (93–94), the determination of 'courage never to submit or yield' (108) and the grand defiance of 'Irreconcilable to our grand Foe, / Who now triumphs, and in th' excess of joy / Sole reigning holds the Tyranny of Heav'n' (122–124). This is our first view of Satan and the impression given, reinforced by a succession of speeches in Book I, is described by Waldock: 'fortitude in adversity, enormous endurance, a certain splendid recklessness, remarkable powers of rising to an occasion, extraordinary qualities of leadership (shown not least in his salutary taunts)'" (p. 4).

It is interesting to observe by contrast that Joseph Addison, in *The Spectator*, no. 279, 19 January 1712, believed that Satan's opening actions and others that follow would be likely to strike terror into the eighteenth-century "Reader's Imagination." Addison shows himself alert to the poem as a speaking picture that conveys meaning through motion, sound, posture, and scenic imagery as well as through the declarations of individual figures: "The Thoughts in the first Speech and Description of *Satan*, who is one of the principal Actors, in this Poem, are wonderfully proper to give us a full Idea of him. His Pride, Envy and Revenge, Obstinacy, Despair and Impenitence, are all of them very artfully interwoven. In short, his first Speech is a Complication of all those Passions which discover themselves separately in several other of his Speeches in the Poem. The whole Part of this great Enemy of Mankind is filled with such Incidents as are very apt to raise and terrify the Reader's Imagination. Of this Nature, in the Book now before us, is his being the first that awakens out of the general Trance, with his Posture on the burning Lake, his rising from it, and the Description of his Shield and Spear . . . To which we may add," Addison further remarks, "his Call to the fallen Angels that lay plunged and stupified in the Sea of Fire" (*Critical Heritage*, ed. Shawcross, p. 170).

20. After comparing Satan's palace in Hell to various Western architectural structures, Roland Mushat Frye, in *Milton's Imagery and the Visual Arts* (Princeton, 1978), astutely concludes that "Pandaemonium is actually a promiscuous architectural monstrosity, a bastard compound of Doric order and classical architrave and frieze with a Gothic arched roof, and surrounded by wide porches after the fashion of the loggias of the Uffizi courtyard in Florence or the covered walkways of the Ducal Palace in Venice. The joining of architectural elements in Pandaemonium is so promiscuous that the building cannot even be convincingly described as Baroque, though that effort has of course been made." He adds that the similarities Pandemonium shares with St. Peter's Basilica "—the hanging lamps, and the inner rooms—were shared with innumerable other structures throughout Europe" and that it would not "be difficult to find other buildings with such capacious rooms that people walking into them appeared to be dwarfed, as for example in the Hall of the Five Hundred in the Palazzo Vecchio in Florence" (pp. 134-135).

21. Enid Welsford, *The Court Masque* (Cambridge, 1927), p. 312.

22. Christopher Hill, *Milton and the English Revolution* (New York, 1977), pp. 166-167, 371ff. See also Malcolm Ross, *Milton and Royalism: A Study of the Conflict of Symbol and Idea in the Poems* (Ithaca, N.Y., 1943).

23. *The Dramatic Works of Sir William Davenant*, intro. with

notes James Maidment and W. H. Logan, vol. 2 (Edinburgh and London, 1872), pp. 234, 273, 284.

V. Love's Revel in Eden

1. *John Milton: Complete Poems and Major Prose*, ed. Merritt Y. Hughes (New York, 1957), p. 295, line 738. This edition is the source for quotations in this chapter from Milton's occasional verse and from *Paradise Lost*.

2. Patterned analogues for the First Parents' love and marriage scene are difficult to find in literary tradition and art. John R. Knott, Jr., in *Milton's Pastoral Vision* (Chicago and London, 1971), pp. 46ff., uncovers little evidence of similar detailed rural scenes in literary works; and Sister Mary Irma Corcoran, in *Milton's "Paradise Lost" with Reference to the Hexameral Background* (Washington, D.C., 1945), pp. 46ff., notes that such detailed scenes are generally lacking in hexameral materials. Roland Mushat Frye, in *Milton's Imagery and the Visual Arts* (Princeton, 1978), has "been unable to find many art works which correspond to Milton's descriptions of the prelapsarian lovemaking of Adam and Eve." In particular, Frye remarks that "there can be no doubt that Milton's repeated descriptions of Adam and Eve walking hand in hand represented a striking innovation, for which there was only the slightest precedence and reinforcement." Just three art works are then cited: Cranach's *Paradise* of 1530, the frontispiece of the English Matthew Bible of 1537; and an engraving by Saenredam after Bloemart. "The evidence developed here," Frye concludes, ". . . shows the extent of Milton's originality" (pp. 281–285).

3. *Ben Jonson*, ed. C. H. Herford, Percy Simpson, and Evelyn Simpson, vol. 7 (Oxford, 1941), pp. 210–211, lines 48–52. The quotations of Jonson's masques in this chapter are from this edition.

4. Looking beyond *Comus*, "Adam Unparadiz'd," and divers Renaissance masques to another work of central concern to Milton, one notes that Spenser's *The Faerie Queene* also would have afforded a source for visual scenes and character-types. In Milton's Eden the "woody Theatre" (IV.141) suggests the forested theater of Belphoebe in Spenser's epic (III.5.39), and in some ways the figure Amoret in Book III may well reflect the Lady of Milton's masque. See *The Works of Edmund Spenser: A Variorum Edition*, ed. Edwin Greenlaw, Charles Grosvenor Osgood, and Frederick Morgan Padelford, vol. 3 (Baltimore, 1934), pp. 75–109.

5. In Jonson's masque *Chloridia*, a work performed in 1630 and published in quarto in 1631, Zephyrus leads the Spring forward and introduces her (44–49) in a manner reminiscent of the presentation of May in Milton's *Song: On May Morning*, a sonnet apparently written in 1629 or 1630.

6. After quoting a single phrase by Joseph Hall on the image of sin-

ful woman, Stanley E. Fish, in *Surprised by Sin: The Reader in "Paradise Lost"* (New York, 1967), insists that readers of the epic would be surprised because the depiction of Eve in the love scene represents "Milton's deliberate evocation of the preacher's scarlet woman" (p. 102). Fish notes only that the scarlet woman is described by Hall as having a "loose lock erring wantonly over her shoulders" (p. 92). Readers of *Paradise Lost* are then said to be "vulnerable to . . . shock" upon discovering that Eve's hair is "Dishevell'd" (p. 101). Certain words in the love scene, such as "wanton," "loose," and "error," are said to "trouble" readers (p. 100); and the word "Subjection," used by Milton to suggest Eve's relationship to Adam, is found to come as something of a surprise because introduced in conjunction with the words "wanton," "Dishevell'd," and "wav'd," which are said to "seem to imply invitation" (p. 102). According to Fish, Eve before the Fall is in fact innocent; but he says that Milton first misleads readers into delighting in the First Mother as a scarlet woman and then shocks them into an objective recognition of Eve's unblemished virtue.

Fish's interpretation, it seems to me, inappropriately relates Eve to Hall's casual comment and disregards traditional Elizabethan marriage topoi. The interpretation thus fails to establish Milton's intent, and it is marred by an overreaction to Milton's allusions to "disorderly order." In Book IV of *Paradise Lost*, Milton's references to slight irregularities—marginal errors, disorders, and loose and wanton elements—save Eve and Eden from a mechanistic existence and in fact are necessary to the total harmony and perfection of being. For examinations of positive Elizabethan attitudes toward disorderly order and variety, see H. V. S. Ogden, "The Principles of Variety and Contrast in Seventeenth-Century Aesthetics, and Milton's Poetry," *Journal of the History of Ideas* 10 (1949): 159–182; Hannah Disinger Demaray, "The Literary Gardens of Andrew Marvell and John Milton," in *Gardens and Culture: Eight Studies in History and Aesthetics*, ed. Hannah Disinger Demaray (Beirut, 1969); and Knott, *Milton's Pastoral Vision*, pp. 43–48. After comparing Milton's prelapsarian Eve with her visual representation in Renaissance artworks, Frye, in *Milton's Imagery*, maintains that the poet wished "to create an image of Perfect Woman." Frye states that "when Milton described how Eve's hair 'in wanton ringlets waved / As the vine curls her tendrils, which implied / Subjection,' he was evoking the familiar vine symbolism . . . but he was doing so in a way which had long been established in the artistic tradition" (p. 274).

7. Quoted in *Ben Jonson*, ed. Herford, Simpson, and Simpson, vol. 10 (Oxford, 1950), p. 470. The statement by Peacham was printed in William Gifford, *Nuptiall Hymnes* (1613), H2. In Spenser's *Epithalamion* marriage ceremonies are depicted as part of a masque. Referring to the bride, the narrator says: "Bid her awake; for Hymen is awake, / And long since ready forth his maske to moue." The bride in Spenser's poem also wears her hair loose and flowing (*The Works of Edmund Spenser: A Variorum Edition*, ed. Edwin Greenlaw, Charles Grosvenor Osgood, Frederick Morgan

Padelford, and Ray Heffner, vol. 7 [Baltimore, 1947], p. 241, lines 25–26; p. 245, lines 154–158).

8. See *Festival Designs by Inigo Jones*, intro. Roy Strong, foreword Thomas S. Wragg (n.p., 1967), particularly the "topless" costumes for the female character-types in Jonson's *Chloridia*. Both the Spring and Zephyrus are shown in such costumes in fig. 56; the garments of the Spring alone are illustrated in fig. 49.

9. A comparison of scenery in Milton's Eden with seventeenth-century painting and landscape design is presented by Hannah Disinger Demaray, "Milton's 'Perfect' Paradise and the Landscapes of Italy," *Milton Quarterly* 8 (1974): 33–41, and "Literary Gardens of Marvell and Milton," pp. 138–142; Jeffry B. Spencer, *Heroic Nature* (Evanston, Ill., 1973), pp. 111–117; Knott, *Milton's Pastoral Vision*, pp. 49–51; and Roland Mushat Frye, "Milton's *Paradise Lost* and the Visual Arts, *Proceedings of the American Philosophical Society* 120 (1976): 233–244.

VI. The Triumphs of Heaven

1. *John Milton: Complete Poems and Major Prose*, ed. Merritt Y. Hughes (New York, 1957), p. 267, lines 372–373 (hereafter cited as Hughes). All quotations of Milton's verse and prose in this chapter are from this edition.

2. Polemical assertion has blended with both theological and literary criticism in the more forceful attacks upon Milton's God in recent years. A. J. A. Waldock, in *"Paradise Lost" and Its Critics* (Cambridge, 1947), has been among the most uncompromising critics of Milton's Supreme Being, asserting that a "curious ill-luck . . . seems to dog the portraiture: nothing, apparently, *can* go right with it" (p. 104). After comparing Milton's God with Dante's (pp. 97–118), Waldock states: "The truth of course is obvious—there is little need to insist on it again—that it does not come very naturally to Milton to suggest a loving God. Let him try and the tone will presently seem to change despite him, and soon we are back in the groove of divine egoism" (p. 103). A detailed and scholarly comparison of *Paradise Lost* and Dante's *Commedia* has since been published by Irene Samuel, *Dante and Milton: The "Commedia" and "Paradise Lost"* (Ithaca, 1966).

William Empson, in *Milton's God*, rev. ed. (London, 1965), has responded sharply and negatively to several general critical defenses of Milton's Supreme Being, particularly so to C. S. Lewis, *A Preface to "Paradise Lost"* (London, 1942), which contains arguments from Christian apologetics. Empson uses a false analogy to illustrate his central critical view: "A parent who 'forsaw' that the children would fall and then insisted upon exposing them to the temptation in view would be considered neurotic, if nothing worse; and this is what we must ascribe to Milton's God" (p. 116). Discussing his approach, Empson announces first that he thinks "the traditional God of Christianity very wicked, and have done since I was at school, where nearly all my little playmates did the same" (p. 10). On the assumption that the Christian God of *Paradise Lost* must also be "very wicked," Empson defines an outlook on the epic that "does at least make Milton himself appear in a better light. He is struggling to make his God appear less wicked" (p. 11).

Comments about Milton's God that are somewhat more moderate but still highly critical appear in J. B. Broadbent, *Some Graver Subject: An Essay on "Paradise Lost"* (London, 1960), pp. 144–161; and in John Peter, *A Critique of "Paradise Lost"* (New York, 1960), pp. 9–30. God in the epic is criticized as a character in Douglas Bush's *"Paradise Lost" in Our Time* (Toronto, 1941) and *English Literature in the Earlier Seventeenth Century: 1600–1660* (Oxford, 1952), pp. 381–382; Marjorie Hope Nicolson's *John Milton: A Reader's Guide to His Poetry* (New York, 1963), pp. 223–228 (hereafter cited as *Reader's Guide*); Helen Gardner's *A Reading of "Paradise Lost"* (Oxford, 1965), pp. 55–57; Dennis Burden's *The Logical Epic: A Study of the Argument of "Paradise Lost"* (Cambridge, Mass., 1967); and John S. Diekhoff's *Milton's "Paradise Lost": A Commentary on the Argument* (New York and London, 1946). In these works, however, and in most publications of the 1970s, direct statements on contextual meaning and structural problems have replaced polemical assertions and appeals in favor of or against Christian belief.

3. Charles Leslie, in *The History of Sin and Heresy* (1698), long ago exposed a moralistic zeal by taking exception to Milton's treatment of the battle in Heaven: "The gravity and seriousness with which this subject ought to be treated, has not been regarded in the adventrous flight of Poets, who have dress'd Angels in Armour, and put Swords and Guns into their Hands, to form romantick Battels in the Plains of Heaven, a scene of licentious fancy; but the Truth has been greatly hurt thereby, and degraded at last even into a Play, which was design'd to have been acted upon the Stage" (*Milton: The Critical Heritage*, ed. John T. Shawcross [New York, 1970], p. 117). Samuel Johnson became disturbed in 1779 when he found that Milton "perplexed his poetry with his philosophy. His infernal and celestial powers are sometimes pure spirit, and sometimes animated body" (*The Lives of the Poets: Cowley to Prior* [Garden City, N.Y., 1968], p. 138). Expanding this point, Waldock has recently remarked in *"Paradise Lost" and Its Critics* that Milton "will not allow us to forget for a moment, either that the warfare *is* Homeric, grossly material in its equipment and results, or that the fighters who are waging it have 'bodies' that are not material in the same sense at all, bodies that are quite incongruous with the arms and armour and all the conditions of war. The result, of course, is to keep the difficulties ever present to us in their acutest form" (p. 111).

The angel Raphael, it should be pointed out, in recounting the warfare by likening spiritual to corporeal forms in fact contrasts the crude materiality of the rebel angels with the more spiritual natures of the good angels. In Book VI the evil angels tear the earth to discover base elements for weapons just as they disembowel the earth for building materials in Book II. There is thematic consistency in Milton's use of seventeenth-century conceptions of materialism, but it seems to me that the poet does overemphasize what are now archaic notions of matter.

For critical readings of the war in Heaven, see Arnold Stein, "Milton's War in Heaven: An Extended Metaphor," *English Literary History* 18 (1951): 201–220; Stella Revard, "Milton's Critique of Heroic Warfare in *Paradise Lost* V and VI," *Studies in English Literature* 7 (1967): 119–139; Peter, *Critique of "Paradise Lost,"* pp. 63–85; and Gardner, *Reading of "Paradise Lost,"* pp. 55–57. Milton's "materialism" is examined by Robert West, *Milton and the Angels* (Athens, Ga., 1955), pp. 117–161; Kester Svendsen, *Milton and Science* (Cambridge, Mass., 1956); and Walter Clyde Curry, *Milton's Ontology, Cosmogony, and Physics* (Lexington, Ky., 1957).

4. Rosalie L. Colie offers an illuminating account of Milton's divine paradoxes, as they relate to the God of *Paradise Lost,* in *Paradoxia Epidemica: The Renaissance Tradition of Paradox* (Princeton, 1966), pp. 169–189; and in "Time and Eternity: Paradox and Structure in *Paradise Lost,*" *Journal of the Warburg and Courtauld Institutes* 23 (1960): 127–138. Instead of pressing God's arguments to the point of contradiction, Colie views them in the Renaissance tradition of theological paradox and shows their importance to the structure and narrative of the epic. In her book she notes that "where matters of doctrine were not irrevocably laid down but were 'indifferent,' Milton was free to vary or to veil, even to invent; he was free to expand or explain as he chose ... In this respect, his efforts to reconcile poetically the paradoxes involved in the concepts of eternity and time, of foreknowledge and freewill, affected the structure and technique of his poem. Form and material both called for epic" (p. 183).

For further discussions of Milton's God and theology, see C. A. Patrides, *Milton and the Christian Tradition* (Oxford, 1966); B. Rajan, *"Paradise Lost" and the Seventeenth Century Reader,* 2nd rev. ed. (London, 1962); Arthur Sewell, *A Study of Milton's "Christian Doctrine"* (London, 1939); Maurice Kelley, *This Great Argument: A Study of Milton's "De Doctrina Christiana" as a Gloss upon "Paradise Lost"* (Princeton, 1941); Michael Fixler, *Milton and the Kingdoms of God* (London, 1964); George N. Conklin, *Biblical Criticism and Heresy in Milton* (New York, 1949); and *Bright Essence: Studies in Milton's Theology,* with essays by William B. Hunter, C. A. Patrides, and J. H. Adamson (Salt Lake City, 1971), a work that contains a useful bibliography of relevant theological materials.

5. Nicolson, in *Reader's Guide,* discusses an alleged "contradiction" in the depiction of Milton's God: "Milton's God denies Milton's own premises, since, in spite of the fact that we are told that we cannot see Him, Milton gives us no alternative to visualizing Him, as He 'bent down His eye' to view His works, particularly to chart the course of Satan's voyage. Not only must we see Him, but we must listen to those long speeches, which show a startling attitude to newly created Man" (p. 225).

Hughes, p. 182, and Colie, in *Paradoxia Epidemica*, p. 177n, have indicated, however, that Milton merely reflects in *Paradise Lost* the traditional medieval and Renaissance view that the Father sees with his own eye and with the eyes of seven angels. It seems to me that Milton's use of this single image, particularly when read in the context of the poet's light imagery, surely does not suggest a visualization of God the Father.

6. In disclosing the relationship of Father and Son, the light imagery gives visual expression to the crucial distinction, discussed in Chapter 1, that Milton draws between substance and essence in the *Art of Logic* (I.7.59). As mentioned earlier, Milton observes that "things which differ in number also differ in essence" but does not attribute numerical individuation to substance. The shared refulgence of the Father and the Son suggest their oneness in *substantia;* the unique and individuating visibility of the Son, however, suggests his differentiation in essence from the Father. The light imagery also serves to delineate the subordination of the Son to a Father who has exalted and so begotten this Divine Person of the "Eternal Coeternal beam." See William B. Hunter, "Further Definitions: Milton's Theological Vocabulary," and C. A. Patrides, "Milton on the Trinity: The Use of Antecedents"; both essays appear in *Bright Essence.*

7. Concentrating upon events at or near the middle of the poem as determined by a count of lines, recent numerological and theological critics have emphasized the aesthetic and structural significance of the Son's past Triumphs narrated in flashbacks at the expense of the directly narrated account of the Son's triumphant future Redemption of man. John T. Shawcross, in "The Balanced Structure of *Paradise Lost,*" *Studies in Philology* 62 (1965): 696–718, sees the Son's ascent at the "center" of the 1667 edition (VI.716–762) as the apex of the poem's "pyramidic construction" and as the turning point in the battle between Satan and God. Shawcross remarks that up to this point the "rising action is created by the development of the seeming success of Satan," and that "from the middle point of the Son's victory . . . there is a fairly constant falling off " of action (pp. 704–705). However, Galbraith Crump, in *The Mystical Design of "Paradise Lost"* (Lewisburg, Pa., and London, 1975), finds that the "new center" in the 1674 edition (VI.766) supplies a superior numerological and thematic middle for an epic that, Crump argues, has a circular design. "Broadly considered," Crump writes, "the reorganization allowed certain aspects of the poem's circular construction to be more clearly articulated. Whereas the exact linear middle of the poem remained virtually unchanged, the redivision into twelve books emphasized the midpoint of the poem's overall structure by matching the six books of the first half of the poem with the six in the second half " (p. 74).

William B. Hunter, in "The War in Heaven: The Exaltation of the Son," *Bright Essence,* pp. 115–130, both refers to the "middle" position of the Son's past Triumphs and stresses what he believes to be their extreme thematic importance to the epic: "As Milton begins his great story with the begetting of the Son in Book 5 and its immediate consequence, the War in

Heaven, the reader must recognize that he is simultaneously narrating there three events from three very different points in time: first, the surface narrative of the fall of the angels, which took place before the foundation of the world; second, the defeat of Satan and his fellow devils described in the book of Revelation, which will take place at the end of time; and third and most important, the exaltation of the Son of God, which took place concomitantly with his resurrection as the incarnate God-man. All three of these events, from the beginning, middle, and end of time, are to be viewed as being simultaneously and metaphorically present in the one narrative framework" (p. 123). Although time in eternity is said by Milton to be measured by motion (*PL* V.580–582), Hunter argues that events in Heaven should also be considered paradoxically as happening simultaneously.

While recognizing the changing but generally central position of certain incidents in the epic as established by a count of the lines, and while acknowledging too the wealth of actual and implied typological relationships within the poem, I believe that criticism tending to make the Son's ascent to Heaven (VI.761–762) or some other past Triumph the *aesthetic* and *thematic* apex, center, or climax of the epic—as distinguished from an important narrative event with structural implications and rich typological meaning—improperly shifts the focus of the work from the dominating themes of man's Fall and Redemption, themes that the epic narrator proclaims in the opening invocation and then poetically portrays:

> Of Man's First Disobedience, and the Fruit
> Of that Forbidden Tree, whose mortal taste
> Brought Death into the World, and all our woe,
> With loss of *Eden*, till one greater Man
> Restore us, and regain the blissful Seat,
> Sing Heav'nly Muse. (I.1–6)

Although *Paradise Lost* as an epic contains actions in disparate realms, the themes of man's disobedience and restoration, developed from the outlines of "Adam Unparadiz'd," are presented directly with the greatest thematic and aesthetic force in books other than VI and VII. Throughout the epic Eden remains the focal point for narrative events, including those in Heaven and Hell.

See also the earlier article by Hunter "Milton on the Exaltation of the Son," *English Literary History* 36 (1969): 215–231; John T. Shawcross, "The Son in His Ascendance: A Reading of *Paradise Lost*," *Modern Language Quarterly* 27 (1966): 388–401; and Revard, "Milton's Critique of Heroic Warfare."

8. Denis Saurat, in *Milton: Man and Thinker*, 2nd rev. ed. (New York, 1944), pp. 117–133, held that the Son was actually "created" by the Father at this point in divine history. Herbert Grierson, however, pointed out in *Milton and Wordsworth* (New York, 1937), p. 99, that Milton in his *Christian Doctrine* had written that "the Father [is] said in Scripture to

have begotten the Son in a double sense, the one literal, with reference to the production of the Son, the other metaphorical, with reference to his exaltation." Accordingly, Grierson outlined what has now become a generally accepted position: that the begetting of the Son in Book V is a metaphorical exaltation and not a unique creation. Milton's paraphrase of Psalm 2, with its allusions to the Son's begetting, would then also refer to a metaphorical exaltation. Following the precedent set by Grierson, a number of other commentators have examined the passage of the begetting in *Paradise Lost* V in the context of early theological thought and have concluded that the Son, who in the epic apparently exists before the begetting, is indeed being exalted. The theatrical context of the passage in Book V provides further support for the view that the Son is being exalted and not created. See in particular Sewell, *Study of "Christian Doctrine,"* pp. 89–106; Kelley, *This Great Argument,* pp. 100ff.; Lewis, *Preface to "Paradise Lost,"* pp. 81–91; Edmund Creeth, "The 'Begetting' and the Exaltation of the Son," *Modern Language Notes* 72 (1961): 696–700; and Hunter, "War in Heaven."

Kelley has contended in several studies that *Paradise Lost* and *Christian Doctrine* are essentially Arian in theology: *This Great Argument;* "Milton's Arianism Again Considered," *Harvard Theological Review* 54 (1961): 195–205; and "Milton and the Trinity," *Huntington Library Quarterly* 33 (1970): 315–320. The case against Milton's Arianism in *Paradise Lost* and *Christian Doctrine* has been argued by Patrides in *Milton and the Christian Tradition;* in his essays in *Bright Essence;* and, more recently, in "Milton and the Arian Controversy," *Proceedings of the American Philosophical Society* 120 (1976): 245–252. Hunter and Adamson, in their essays in *Bright Essence,* have joined Patrides in maintaining that in *Paradise Lost* Milton is a "subordinationist" who believes in different persons in one God. James H. Sims has sought to define the points at issue between the Arian and the anti-Arian commentators in *"Paradise Lost:* Arian Document or Christian Poem?" *Études Anglaises* 20 (1967): 337–347.

9. See the presentation dates of the major masques as compiled by Allardyce Nicoll, *Stuart Masques and the Renaissance Stage* (New York, 1938), pp. 215–217. The Stuart and Caroline masques were, of course, primarily ritualistic rather than dramatic. In general, character-types, like figures in fairy tales, were unchanging "good" or "bad" figures. Action usually turned upon "magic" or upon the *deus ex machina* intervention of pagan gods or virtuous allegorical figures. The climax came during the presentation, main masque dances, and unmasking, all of which were aimed at complimenting a king or aristocrat seated in state. The ceremonial pagan disguising was in this fashion shown to conceal an underlying Christian world ruled by a seated king or aristocrat.

Thomas Stroup, in *Religious Rite and Ceremony in Milton's Poetry* (Lexington, Ky., 1968), illustrates how central events in the Hell and Heaven of *Paradise Lost* have about them the quality of Christian liturgical ritual rather than Elizabethan or classical drama. Stroup points out the liturgical overtones of the First Parents' rites in Eden, and he shows how the *Book of Common Prayer* influenced divers passages of Milton's epic.

10. Hughes, p. 784.

11. Ben Jonson frequently explains in his stage directions the meaning of designs on the masquers' clothing, and in *The Masque of Blacknesse* he mentions the fans carried by Tritons, "in one of which were inscribed their mixt Names, in the other a mute Hieroglyphick, expressing their mixed qualities" (*Ben Jonson*, ed. C. H. Herford, Percy Simpson, and Evelyn Simpson, vol. 7 [Oxford, 1941], p. 177, lines 268–269). Excellent studies of Jonson's masques as vast hieroglyphs presenting philosophical and spiritual meanings have been produced by D. J. Gordon in "The Imagery of Ben Jonson's *The Masque of Blacknesse* and the *Masque of Beautie*," *Journal of the Warburg and Courtauld Institutes* 6 (1943): 101–121; and in "*Hymenaei*: Ben Jonson's Masque of Union," *Journal of the Warburg and Courtauld Institutes* 8 (1945): 107–145. See also the seventeenth-century essay by Francis Bacon "Of Masques and Triumphs," *Essays, "Advancement of Learning," "New Atlantis," and Other Pieces*, ed. Richard Foster Jones (New York, 1937), p. 111, in which the author speaks of the "oes" and "spangs" sewn in designs on masquers' costumes.

12. *Ben Jonson*, ed. Herford, Simpson, and Simpson, vol. 10 (Oxford, 1950), p. 583; trans. in Enid Welsford, *The Court Masque* (Cambridge, 1927), pp. 448–449.

13. *Ben Jonson*, ed. Herford, Simpson, and Simpson, 10: 448–449.

14. The procession and costumes are described in the stage directions in *The Dramatic Works and Poems of James Shirley*, ed. with notes William Gifford and Alexander Dyce, vol. 6 (London, 1833), pp. 257–261.

15. The background and details are given in John G. Demaray, *Milton and the Masque Tradition: The Early Poems, "Arcades," and "Comus"* (Cambridge, Mass., and Oxford, 1968), pp. 83–85.

16. Stroup, in *Religious Rite and Ceremony*, pp. 35–36, notes that Psalm 24 was read at the beginning of the rite of church consecration, and he maintains that the Son has participated in both the creation and the consecration of the world.

17. Milton's view of universal Christian history has been summarized by C. A. Patrides, *The Grand Design of God: The Literary Form of the Christian View of History* (London and Toronto, 1972), pp. 84–90.

VII. The Future Triumph of Man

1. See the fourth act of the Andreini work, trans. Watson Kirkconnell, in Kirkconnell's *The Celestial Cycle* (Toronto, 1952), pp. 261–267. The original publication is *L'Adamo* (Milan, 1613); a second printing for "Maria de Medici" appeared in Milan in 1617.

2. See the fourth and fifth acts of *Adamo caduto*, trans. Kirkconnell, in *Celestial Cycle*, pp. 345–349. The original work was published as *Adamo caduto, tragedia sacre* (Cosenza, 1647). See also in *Celestial Cycle* the fourth

and fifth acts of Joost van den Vondel's *Adam in Ballingschap* pp. 459–479 (first published under that title in Amsterdam, 1664); and the fifth act of Hugo Grotius's *Adamus Exul*, pp. 189–220. A British Museum copy of Grotius's work is available as *Adamus Exul. Tragoedia* (1601). Although Kirkconnell does not list masques or grand-scale Italian religious spectacles by Parigi, Cappola, Rospigliosi, or others as analogues for scenes in *Paradise Lost*, he does include an excellent descriptive catalogue of early poems, prose works, and literary sacred representations written on the Fall of man. See Frank Kastor's *Milton and the Literary Satan* (Amsterdam, 1974), pp. 105–110, for a bibliography of important English and Continental sacred representations; but again masques and Italian theatrical spectacles are not included. Renaissance sacred representations about Adam and Eve were derived largely from medieval mystery plays rather than from the baroque theatrical tradition. See *The York Cycle of Mystery Plays*, ed. J. S. Purvis (London, 1957); *The Chester Cycle of Mystery Plays*, ed. Maurice Hussey (London, 1957); and *The Non-Cycle Mystery Plays*, ed. Osborn Waterhouse, 2nd ser., vol. 104 (London, 1909). In Book XI of *Paradise Lost* the theatrical "discoveries" and quick changes in scenic background were developed from theatrical materials other than those cited by Kirkconnell and Kastor.

3. J. B. Broadbent, in *Some Graver Subject: An Essay on "Paradise Lost"* (London, 1960), pp. 271–286, takes sharp exception to Milton's heroic style at the end of Book XII while expressing qualified approval of the less ornate style and the supposedly realistic presentation of scenic visions in Book XI. Quoting from a speech by Adam (XI.323–325) about the altars that the First Parent wishes to erect to God, Broadbent remarks: "The efficiency of the writing here (and in much of *Paradise Regained*)—its combining vividness with cool objective reflection in historical perspective—was new to English at the time, and was not surpassed in verse perhaps until *Four Quartets*: beside it, Augustan verse is too mannered, rapid, versy, and the varieties of 16th-century reflective blank verse, however much they owe to Milton, much more introspective, and flaccid" (p. 272). Writing of Adam's vision of the Flood in Book XI, Broadbent notes with approval that "even the description of potentially 'sublime' material is realistic. At the Flood, curt, mundane words put us in the place of a drowning man—'Ceeling . . . Rain . . . beaked prow . . . tilting . . . whelp'd and stabl'd . . . one small bottom'" (p. 273). Broadbent summarizes his critical view of the last two books in this way: "We must distinguish . . . between the 'vision' of Old Testament legend up to the Tower of Babel at the beginning of Book XII and the subsequent relation by Michael of the history of Israel and the Church. The latter fails; the former, though disappointing as a vision, has its own merits. It is far and away the most competent handling of the material with which world-histories traditionally begin and hexameral epics ended" (p. 271).

C. S. Lewis, in *A Preface to "Paradise Lost"* (London, 1942), calls special attention to the supposed defects of the last two books of the epic: "It suffers from a grave structural flaw . . . He [Milton] makes his last two books into a brief outline of sacred history from the Fall to the Last Day. Such an untransmuted lump of futurity, coming in a position so momentous for the structural effect of the whole work, is inartistic. And what makes it worse is that the actual writing in this passage is curiously bad. There are fine moments, and a great recovery at the very end. But again and again, as we read his account of Abraham or of the Exodus or of the Passion, we find ourselves saying, as Johnson said of the ballad, 'the story cannot possibly be told in a manner that shall make less impression on the mind'" (p. 125). Louis L. Martz, in *The Paradise Within: Studies in Vaughan, Traherne, and Milton* (New Haven and London, 1964), pp. 103–167, also maintains that the last books, despite their thematic importance, are deficient in poetic quality. See also the mixed views of the last books in John Peter, *A Critique of "Paradise Lost"* (New York, 1960), pp. 138–158; and in Joseph H. Summers, "The Final Vision," in *Milton: A Collection of Critical Essays*, ed. Martz (Englewood Cliffs, N.J., 1966), pp. 183–206, reprinted from Summers's *The Muse's Method: An Introduction to Paradise Lost* (Cambridge, Mass., and London, 1962).

The thematic integrity of the last two books, in which the motifs that Milton develops throughout the epic are brought into focus and clarified, has been firmly established, I think, by a number of recent studies. See Barbara K. Lewalski, "Structure and the Symbolism of Vision in Michael's Prophecy, *Paradise Lost*, Books XI–XII," *Philological Quarterly* 42 (1963): 25–35; Sister Mary Christopher Pecheux, "Abraham, Adam, and the Theme of Exile in *Paradise Lost*," *PMLA* 80 (1965): 365–371; B. Rajan, *The Lofty Rhyme* (Coral Gables, Fla., 1970), pp. 79–99; Dennis Burden, *The Logical Epic: A Study of the Argument of "Paradise Lost"* (Cambridge, Mass., 1967), pp. 178–201; John T. Shawcross, "*Paradise Lost* and the Theme of Exodus," in *Milton Studies*, ed. James D. Simmonds, vol. 2 (Pittsburgh, 1970), pp. 3–26; F. T. Prince, "On the Last Two Books of *Paradise Lost*," *Essays and Studies* 11 (1958): 38–52; and William B. Hunter, "Prophetic Dreams and Visions in *Paradise Lost*," *Modern Language Quarterly* 9 (1948): 277–285. The crucial significance of Adam's discovery in Book XII of future salvation has been pointed out by Arthur O. Lovejoy, "Milton and the Paradox of the Fortunate Fall," *English Literary History* 4 (1937): 161–179, reprinted in Lovejoy's *Essays in the History of Ideas* (Baltimore, 1948), pp. 277–295.

4. Rosalie L. Colie, *Paradoxia Epidemica: The Renaissance Tradition of Paradox* (Princeton, 1966), p. 179.

5. *John Milton: Complete Poems and Major Prose*, ed. Merritt Y. Hughes (New York, 1957), p. 466, lines 588–592. All references to *Paradise Lost* in this chapter are from this edition.

6. George Wesley Whiting, in "The Pattern of Time and Eternity," *Milton and This Pendant World* (Austin, 1958), pp. 169–200, claims that

the last two books of *Paradise Lost* are organized chronologically in accord with the following six epochs of Christian history as expounded by Saint Augustine and other church fathers: (*a*) from Adam to Noah and the Flood, (*b*) from Noah and the Flood to Abraham, (*c*) from Abraham to David, (*d*) from David to the Babylonian Captivity, (*e*) from the Babylonian Captivity to Christ's Nativity, and (*f*) from Christ's Nativity to the end of the world. This interpretation seems somewhat forced. These particular six epochs are by no means markedly differentiated from other related epochs and periods in Milton's chronology. Rather, the poet seems to have been blending materials and character-types originally drawn from theatrical materials—materials he later expanded considerably throughout the epic—with traditional epochal and typological interpretations of history. The result, especially in Book XI and in early parts of Book XII, is a blurring by Milton of the generally accepted divisions of Christian history to accommodate contextually interwoven epic themes. References to the traditional epochs, as understood by the church fathers, can nevertheless be found in the text.

For delineations of the six ages of man and relevant commentary, see St. Augustine, *Of the Citie of God*, trans. J. H. (London, 1620), p. 859; Isidore of Seville, *Patrologiae Cursus Completus*, vol. 82 (Paris, 1850), pp. 223–228; and Eusebius of Caesaria, *The Ancient Ecclesiastical Histories of the First Six Hundred Years after Christ*, trans. Meredith Hanmer, 4th ed. (London, 1636). For a recent and comprehensive study of early epochal and typological commentary, see Father Henri de Lubac, *Exégèse mediévale, les quatre sens de l'Écriture*, 4 vols. (Paris, 1959–1964); see also the discussion of typology in John G. Demaray, *The Invention of Dante's "Commedia"* (New Haven and London, 1974), pp. 93–115.

The merging of epic materials with Christian historical beliefs has been examined by Michael Cavanagh, "A Meeting of Epic and History: Books XI and XII of *Paradise Lost*," *English Literary History* 38 (1971): 206–222. An analysis of the last books as drama rather than masquelike spectacle appears in A. Sasek, "The Drama of *Paradise Lost*: Books XI and XII," in *Studies in English Renaissance Literature*, ed. Waldo F. McNeir (Baton Rouge, 1962). C. A. Patrides has examined Milton's view of history in relation to a voluminous body of Christian historical writings in his excellent *The Grand Design of God: The Literary Form of the Christian View of History* (London and Toronto, 1972), pp. 84–90. The influence of prophetical biblical literature on Milton's conception of the future of man has been discussed by E. L. Tuveson in *Millennium and Utopia* (Berkeley and Los Angeles, 1949); and by Michael Fixler in "The Apocalypse within *Paradise Lost*," in *New Essays on "Paradise Lost*," ed. Thomas Kranidas (Berkeley and Los Angeles, 1969), pp. 131–178. Although mainly concerned in his chapter with a tentative structural analysis of the epic, Fixler, in *Milton and the Kingdoms of God* (London, 1964), pp. 13–45, does carefully document Milton's changing views on man's future. See also H. R. MacCallum, "Milton and Sacred History," in *Essays in English Literature from the Renais-*

sance to the Victorian Age Presented to A. S. P. Woodhouse, ed. Millar Mac-Lure and F. A. Watt (Toronto, 1964), pp. 149–168; James H. Sims, *The Bible in Milton's Epics* (Gainesville, Fla., 1962); Pecheux, "Abraham, Adam, and the Theme of Exile in *Paradise Lost*"; Patrides, *Grand Design*, pp. 84–90; and Shawcross, "*Paradise Lost* and the Theme of Exodus."

7. *John Milton's Complete Poetical Works Reproduced in Photographic Facsimile*, ed. Harris Francis Fletcher, vol. 2 (Urbana, Ill., 1945), pp. 26–27.

8. *The Vision of the Twelve Goddesses*, ed. with notes Ernest Law (London, 1880), p. 59.

9. *The Works of Thomas Campion*, ed. with notes Walter R. Davis (Garden City, N.Y., 1967), p. 269; *The Poems and Masques of Thomas Carew*, ed. Joseph Woodfall Ebsworth (London, 1893), p. 132; *Ben Jonson*, ed. C. H. Herford, Percy Simpson, and Evelyn Simpson, vol. 7 (Oxford, 1941), p. 750, lines 28–29. See also the discussion on the designers' attempts to create "wonder" through discoveries in Allardyce Nicoll, *Stuart Masques and the Renaissance Stage* (New York, 1938), pp. 39–42.

10. See the typological analysis of the last books in relation to the epic as a whole in William G. Madsen's *From Shadowy Types to Truth: Studies in Milton's Symbolism* (New Haven and London, 1968).

Index